"It is your choice," White Messenger said, his eyes not wavering from hers. "You may serve Medicine Woman or become one with Msipessi."

Mary drew herself up to her full height. "If it is my choice," she said in a clear voice that carried through the hall, "then I wish to return to my people. Set me free so that I might be reunited with my family."

His eyes flashed in conflicting emotions as he weighed his words.

"Tell them what I said," she urged.

When White Messenger spoke, it was not to Mary but to Eagle Feathers. His head was high and noble, his words melodious in the quieted room. He waved toward Medicine Woman.

Msipessi's face grew dark. He turned and made his way through the crowd, where he disappeared from view. Medicine Woman nodded approvingly.

Mary turned to White Messenger. "What did you tell them?"

"I told them you chose to serve Medicine Woman."

"How could you do that?"

"You had but two choices: become Msipessi's squaw or serve Medicine Woman. Had I told them you wanted to return to the white man, you would have been killed."

The room was silent.

"You are now Songbird," he said. "You now serve Medicine Woman."

A young squaw firmly pulled at Mary's arm. As she approached Medicine Woman, a refrain began in her head: I am a slave. I am a slave.

She stopped as she reached the door of the community building and turned to face White Messenger. She stood tall and felt her square jaw jut forward. "Songbirds," she said in a clear, strong voice, "are free."

Songbirds

are

Free

To Phyllis

may history
come alive!

p. m. teuee

Songbirds are Free

by p.m.terrell

Published by Drake Valley Press
USA

ISBN 978-0-9728186-5-0 (Trade soft cover)

Cover art by Bonnie Watson

Printed in the United States of America

10 9 8 7 6 5 4 3 2 1

Author's web site: www.pmterrell.com

OTHER BOOKS BY
p.m.terrell

RICOCHET

THE CHINA CONSPIRACY

KICKBACK

**TAKE THE MYSTERY OUT OF
PROMOTING YOUR BOOK**

ACKNOWLEDGEMENTS

Special thanks to the following people and organizations who provided research, assistance, or editorial support:

Cheatham Historical Society

Debie Cox of the Metro Nashville Archives

Pamela June Kimmell

Karen Luffred

Mansker's Station

Joi McIntyre

John William Neelley, Sr.

Georgia Richardson

Mike Slate, publisher, *Nashville Historical Newsletter*

JoAnn Weakley of Historic Collinsville, Tennessee

and Don Terrell, the love of my life

DEDICATION

Dedicated to my father, John William Neelley, Sr., the inspiration behind my writing and my lead researcher, without whom this book would not have been possible;

And to my mother, Hazel Lois Harper Neelley ("Jo"), 1926-2007, the strongest woman I ever knew.

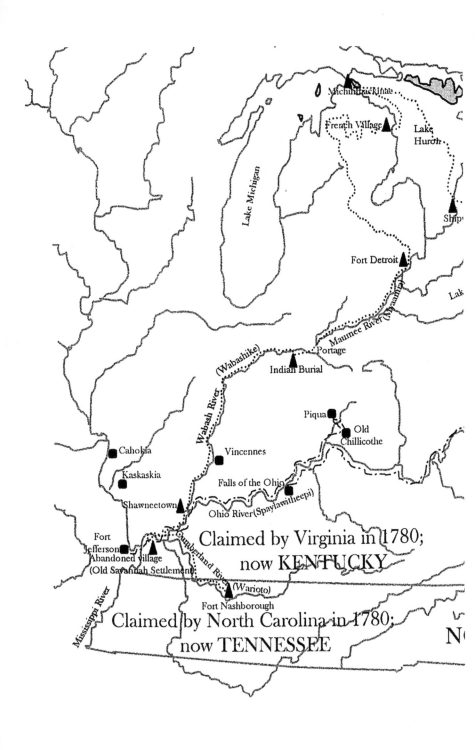

Michilimackinac

French Village

Lake Huron

Lake Michigan

Ship

Fort Detroit

Maumee River (Myaamia)

Portage

Wabash River (Wabashike)

Indian Burial

Lak

Piqua

Old Chillicothe

Cahokia

Vincennes

Kaskaskia

Falls of the Ohio

Shawneetown

Ohio River (Spaylaswitheepi)

Fort Jefferson

Cumberland River

Claimed by Virginia in 1780; now KENTUCKY

Abandoned village (Old Savannah Setlement)

(Warioto)

Fort Nashborough

Mississippi River

Claimed by North Carolina in 1780; now TENNESSEE

N

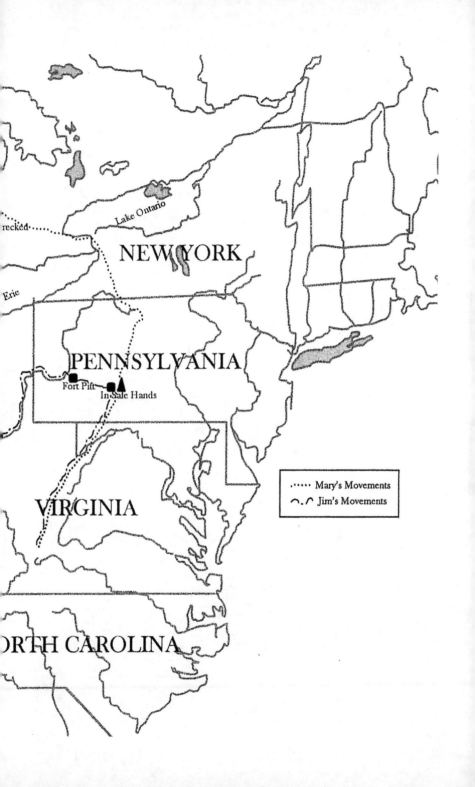

Foreword

This is a work of historical fiction. It is based on true events surrounding the capture and captivity of Mary Neely. It is set against the backdrop of the Revolutionary War and historically accurate battles and events as they unfolded. Though it was necessary to use imagination to fill in details and provide dialogue, I attempted at all times to remain faithful to the memory of a courageous young woman named Mary Neely.

Prologue

Their decision would leave two men dead. And yet she knew they had neither arrived at the decision hastily nor lightly; they had given it ample thought and more than enough debate. And ultimately, it would be a decision borne of desperation.

It had been a summer of Indian raids, of marauding and scalping, murders and captures. The settlers had become increasingly cautious, many of them retreating to nearby Mansker's Station or Fort Nashborough to seek safety inside the fortified walls.

But as the summer wore on, their food dwindled. They'd cut down the forest around the two forts to prevent Indians from mounting sneak attacks; and now the lack of forestation meant they had to travel further from the safety of the forts for their own meat and food.

And so it was, on this hot day in early August, that a group of men left Mansker's Station on a hunting expedition along the Cumberland River. William Neely was to accompany them as far as Neely's Salt Lick, where he would use the opportunity to obtain badly needed salt from the spring there. And in a decision she would see in her mind's eye too many times to count, Mary decided to go with them, to help at the salt lick and to assist the hunters. They were desperate for meat and salt; that much was true. And perhaps she had a sense of security she realized now she shouldn't have felt. But as she looked back on that fateful day, she could not have known the hunters would become the hunted…

1

Neely's Bend, The Americas, 1780

Mary Neely was a mere slip of a girl; folks liked to say they could read the Book of Psalms clear through her. Her shoulder-length hair was as fine as cornsilk and changed colors with the seasons: in winter it was light brown with streaks of copper when the light hit just right; the copper would then turn to gold in the summer, as if the sun had kissed it. Now she pushed a strand of it off her forehead with the back of her hand, exposing beads of perspiration across her brow.

In the small clearing in front of her was a large iron cauldron suspended over a fire by four sturdy wood poles. It was filled almost to the brim with water that had just begun to simmer, which meant she would be standing over it the better part of the day, stirring it and stoking the fire until all that was left was salt residue.

She was a mix of Irish, Scottish, and English, which resulted in fair skin, sea green eyes and a rugged spirit despite her slight stature.

With one hand on the stirring stick, she used her other hand to grasp the end of her apron and wipe her face. It was an unusually hot August day, the air so thick even the flies didn't have the energy to move. It was even more scorching standing over the large black cauldron near the banks of the Cumberland River.

The bend in the river was known as Neely's Bend. Situated close by was Neely's Salt Lick, which consisted of a spring surrounded by rocks over which sulfur water would flow year round. The odor took some getting used to, as it smelled of rotten eggs, particularly when Mary was boiling the water as she was doing now.

Mary was the fourth of ten children. She'd be nineteen years old in less than three weeks; her oldest sister, Jean, was six years her senior and the youngest, Jane, was not yet four years old. But it was her brother Sam with whom she was closest.

Most of her sisters and brothers were at the homestead now, working to harvest a garden that had been woefully neglected because of the Indian threat. Elizabeth, who was three years older, had just become engaged to Jacob Spears and Mary knew she'd be talking up a storm about her anticipated change in status.

Part of the reason Mary wasn't with them was because she'd taken a liking to Jacob's brother, George. And George was right on the other side of those woods yonder, along with men from Mansker's Station, taking advantage of the animals' propensity for visiting the salt lick. They hoped to bring back enough meat to feed their families for several months.

The sound of footsteps on brittle twigs reached her ears and she turned to peer through the woods as Sam and George made their way into the clearing. George tipped his hat in greeting.

Mary glanced at him with a mischievous smile. His father was of German descent and George had inherited his thick, sandy hair and gray-green eyes. He was taller than most and had wide, sturdy shoulders and beefy hands. She knew she affected him. It was widely rumored they would marry someday and with two older siblings married already and a third betrothed, she would soon be expected to follow suit.

Sam dropped some dead rabbits near Mary's feet. "Hunting's good today," he said with a grin.

Mary tore her eyes away from George. "You need me to skin them?"

"Yep. We're leaving them for you and Pa. We're about to take them deer" —he nodded his head toward two bucks they'd shot this morning—"and head back to Mansker's Station."

"Leaving already?"

"We've got work to do, woman," Sam said with a sideways glance, a grin breaking out on his handsome face.

George led two pack horses to the deer, and Mary watched as they slung the carcasses over the horses' broad backs, the two muscular young men lifting the heavy deer as if they weighed no more than a sack of potatoes.

"Everybody's leaving except you and Pa," Sam said, growing somber. "The others from Mansker's are trying to talk him into letting you come back with us. I sure don't like the thought of you staying here."

"We'll be fine," she said. "I'll finish up this salt making and we'll be headed home first thing in the morning."

He didn't answer but his brow furrowed and he appeared to be chewing the inside of his lip.

"Where's Pa now?"

"Down by the river," he said as he mounted his horse.

Mary had a vision of her father toiling away, his shirt sleeves rolled up to his elbows, his black hair shining in the sunlight, his sharp green eyes scanning the horizon for meat befitting the Neely table. He was only forty-two years old, still a man in his prime.

George tossed the reins of one of the pack horses to Sam. They watched as the horses started along the old trail, their tails swishing in the still air.

George remained still, the reins to his own horse and the other pack horse still in his hands. They appeared to hold a great deal of interest to him.

"George," Mary said by way of parting.

He stood with a fixed smile on his face, his eyes glancing up beneath a stray lock of hair to find Mary's face, and then quickly dropping to peer at the reins again.

"What is it, George?"

"I was wondering," he began, his voice barely audible.

"Wondering what?"

"I was—I was wondering if you'd—if you'd go with me to Saturday's dance."

"Why of course," Mary said coquettishly. "I was figuring all along on going with you."

A broad smile graced his face from ear to ear before he visibly subdued it. Mary held back a smile of her own as she watched the color rise in his cheeks.

"I'll be leaving on Sunday to go back to Virginia."

She lowered her eyes and kept them focused on the boiling water, hoping he would not see the disappointment she felt welling up inside her. She swallowed. "You planning on coming back this way any time soon?"

Out of the corner of her eye, she watched him shrug. "My pa doesn't want to part with his tobacco farm in Virginia…" he started, his voice trailing off. "But I aim to come back, soon as I can."

She stirred the water in silence.

"Won't you go to Mansker's Station with us?" he asked as a group of men entered the clearing.

She glanced up as one of the men shook his head. "William won't leave," he said as they approached.

"Then I'm staying, too," she said, squaring her shoulders. "We'll be back tomorrow."

George hesitated until the men had passed through the clearing, leading horses burdened with game. "Bye, Mary."

"Bye, George."

"I'll be seeing you then on Saturday."

"I'm counting on it."

"Yes, ma'am. Me, too."

She thought he would trip over his own feet as he rushed to mount his horse and catch up with the others.

Mary turned back to the water. Humming, she reached to the pile of kindling beside the fire and tossed more under the pot. It wouldn't do to have the fire go out while she stood there chatting.

Her mind wandered to this Saturday's dance. There would be at least forty in attendance—maybe even more. She'd have to pull out her fine cotton dress, the one with the blue pattern on it. She'd borrow Elizabeth's hair pins and pull her hair into a top knot, and she'd probably even use some of Ma's flower water to make her smell especially nice. As she day-dreamed about the evening, the settlers in attendance, and the music provided by Daniel Norman and his fiddle, she broke into song. The hours crept by as the afternoon began to wane. Mary loved to sing and she listened to her own voice wafting through the summer air as she sang the hymns she'd memorized from the one church hymnal that everybody shared.

Musket fire pierced the air, sending a flock of birds above the trees, their panic-stricken wings beating the air in their hasty retreat.

Simultaneously, she heard the Indians, their distinctive cacuminal cry at once harmonious and terrifying, the sound growing in escalating intensity.

Mary felt the adrenaline course through her veins as she dropped the stirring stick and raced to the edge of the clearing, where she grabbed the musket they always kept loaded and primed.

She stopped abruptly at the edge of the woods. The Indian warriors seemed to be everywhere at once, their faces obscured behind grotesque red and black paint, their bodies clad only in breechcloths.

Her eyes fell on a lone Indian at the edge of the water, kneeling over Pa's still body. She leveled the musket and aimed.

The air was filled with the dust from hurried feet, momentarily blinding her. As the dust settled, she spotted Pa lying on the bank in a pool of blood that flowed to the river.

In the next second, she fired, the smoke blast momentarily blocking out her target. Then the air was filled with a deafening war cry. As she turned, she glimpsed another warrior as he rushed her, his arm raised high with his club held tight. She grabbed the musket by the barrel and swung it with all her might into his torso. As blood erupted from him, she was struck from behind by yet another Indian.

The world blurred around her as she tumbled backward. She was surrounded by warriors, their faces otherworldly in their red and black paint. She fought with all her strength, kicking and screaming, pummeling those who came near, while they continued to encircle her.

Her last memory was a lone war club sailing through the air, the perpetrator's face devoid of expression, catching the side of her head and slinging her downward. Her body hit the ground with such force that her breath was knocked from her. The last sound she heard was her own desperate gasp for air.

2

Mary opened her eyes to a darkness almost as black as her dreamless sleep. She thought for a moment it was nighttime before her eyes began to adjust and the brain fog to clear. The shadows were replaced with the blur of overhanging trees whose full, outstretched branches blocked the sun, plunging the forest floor into obscurity.

Her head swam and she closed her eyes against the swaying branches while she fought a wave of nausea.

She lay there for a long moment, feeling the earth beneath her body, breathing the thick air laden with soil and decaying leaves and a musky odor she couldn't quite place, trying to stop the spinning and orient herself.

When she opened her eyes again, she detected a slight movement. Slowly, she attempted to turn her head to peer in that direction, but the side of her face erupted in pain.

Though her first instinct was to scream for help, she knew her life might depend on her ability to remain quiet. She'd spent her brief lifetime as a pioneer, moving hundreds of miles west as her years progressed. The wilderness was plentiful with bear, deer, boar, and wildcats—in fact, just about any kind of wild animal one could imagine. But it was woefully short on people.

And there were Indians about.

She lay there silently, her eyes closed, listening. There were no screams. No gun shots. No war cries. Was it over? Had they left?

She began to raise her hand to her left eye where the pain originated, but she found her wrists were tied tightly together. Opening her other eye and trying to focus, she attempted to move her body into a seated position, but her ankles were bound together as well, with one ankle over the other. Every movement caused her bindings to cut into her flesh.

Slowly, she raised her bound hands. Her fingertips found the side of her head, and felt an icky substance plastered against her. She removed her fingers and tried to peer at the matter in the waning light. Was it blood? Had the warrior bashed her eye sightless, was her face caved in?

No; it was a mixture, a poultice of some sort. She recognized the sweet smell of comfrey leaves. She rubbed the mixture between her fingers. She thought she recognized calendula, and there was no mistaking the beeswax thickening it. Her mind snapped back through years of herbal remedies. This was not a poultice made by settlers.

A soft voice broke the silence with a single word Mary did not recognize.

She turned her head toward the sound, but her skin exploded in a burning sensation so painful she thought she would faint.

The female figure came into her view. Gently but firmly, she pressed Mary's hands downward to her waist, away from her face. She held a gourd above her. "Nepi," she said, holding it to Mary's lips.

"Nepi," Mary repeated. It was not a word she'd heard before.

She sipped the liquid. Once her brain registered it as water, she hungrily devoured it, as if her body was as dry as cured tobacco.

Her eyes began to adjust in the dim light. The Indian who held the gourd for her had thick black braided hair streaked with gray.

She was compact and muscular, her frame built for hard work. She wore moccasins and a buckskin skirt almost the color of her tawny skin, but nothing above her waist except a necklace of multi-colored beads.

After Mary had her fill, the squaw disappeared for the briefest of time, returning with a fresh poultice. The coolness calmed the burning.

Mary's mind was racing. Had this squaw been part of the raid? The images of her father dying alongside the river flooded her mind and the tears stung her eyes as she fought them back. She struggled desperately to calm the dizziness that still threatened to sweep over her.

She wondered if the raid had continued from the salt lick to the homestead, where only womenfolk were there to defend themselves. And somewhere in between were Sam, George, and the men from Mansker's Station, hurrying to get back to their families and the safety of the fort.

The irony hit her as she struggled to rise that they'd given her a poultice to heal her wounds. First they killed her father and God only knew how many more, and then they attempted to heal her!

She struggled to a seated position, teetering slightly. She placed her bound hands awkwardly on the ground in an effort to steady herself, her eyes focused on her bloodied fingers. How had they become so bloody? she wondered.

As she sat there staring at them, two large feet came into view, stopping inches from her. The feet were bare, each toe as big around as her father's thumb. They were spread wide and were as brown and thick as leather. Around one ankle was a band of raised skin in a feather pattern as though a bracelet had been permanently tattooed on it.

Her one good eye followed the ankles up to sturdy calves. Her heart was pounding wildly in her chest, but she forced herself to raise her head as though she had no fear.

His chest was oiled and covered in red and black stripes that reached upwards across a thick neck. His facial features were obscured by the darkness, but his head appeared huge.

He spoke to the woman, who quickly rushed to Mary's side. She untied the hemp around her ankles and then quickly retied them, this time with a stretch of rope about three feet between her legs. Then with one swift movement, she'd grabbed her and hoisted her onto her feet.

By the time the forest stopped spinning around her, the brave was gone.

They marched through the wilderness in single file, each person stepping in the footprints of those before them. Mary tried to determine how many there were, but she'd already learned by a lash across her back that she must concentrate on placing her feet squarely in the prints. The brush was thick here, the bodies before her winding around trees, so it was impossible to get an accurate count. From what she could tell in those brief moments where the underbrush cleared, the Indian with the ankle tattoo was leading them, his band of feathers visible only slightly through the vegetation. At least a half a dozen braves were between them. They seemed not to look at the ground at all, but their flat feet landed directly in the prints each time. She had no idea how many were behind her. They all moved with complete silence, neither slow nor fast, but at a measured, steady pace.

As the hours dragged on, she heard nothing but the birds. If they had captured others and they were somewhere behind her, she might have heard a whimper or a voice, but she heard nothing. She had no idea how many they had captured—or how many they had killed.

These were not Cherokee.

She knew the Cherokee; they traveled the river, often stopping to trade. They'd learned the Neelys were a sociable lot, ready to share whatever they had. It was the plentiful bounty that attracted them: there were no Indians who made these parts their permanent home. They used it instead for hunting grounds. And when they left, they often had salt from the Neely Salt Lick and vegetables from the settlers' gardens and often cloth, blankets, and the occasional piece of jewelry. It was the custom to trade, and when they could, the Neelys, like other settlers in these parts, kept trinkets that were not of much value but which the Cherokee would covet. It was far easier to live alongside in peace.

It had been five years since the Cherokee had sold the tribe's claim to the land on which Fort Nashborough now stood, an agreement known as Henderson's Purchase, since Pa's friend Richard Henderson had orchestrated it. One Cherokee, Dragging Canoe, had vehemently disagreed with the sale, claiming the white man's incursion into their hunting grounds would mean the end of the Cherokee Nation.

It took another four years for the white settlers to move in and build Fort Nashborough. Several expeditions had traveled into the area, surveying it and planning for the settlers' futures, including another of their acquaintances, James Robertson, when he arrived just last December with others from the Watauga Settlement to inhabit the French Lick.

It was rumored that Dragging Canoe had settled along Chickamauga Creek to the east, downriver from Watauga; his followers were now known as the Chickamauga band of Cherokees. Mary glanced up as she stepped from one footprint into the next, trying to determine if these were Chickamaugans. If they were, her fate was sealed: she would be tortured or killed and most likely both.

She tried to remember the conversations amongst the settlers about the raiding Indians. It was mostly the men who would get together while the womenfolk talked about cooking, childrearing, sewing, and God. But Mary preferred to sneak within earshot of the men and listen in on their debates about the tribes and the future of the Cumberland.

Now she struggled to categorize them: besides the Chickamaugans, there were smaller parties of Creeks and Chickasaws. She quickly ruled out the Chickasaws. Pa had said their leader, Piomingo, was in talks with the white settlers and had made it clear he wanted peace, if for no other reason than to have allies if they had to fight the Spanish government's invasion into their lands.

She'd heard the men speak of Shawnee and Delaware Indians, neither of whom made the Cumberlands their home, reaching down like fingers from the north and northeast, orchestrating raids with precision, only to vanish into the wilderness. Even the river had obtained its name from the legendary battles between the Shawnee and Cherokee: it had been some thirty years since Dr. Thomas Walker had learned this area was a bloody land because of their tribal wars. It reminded Dr. Walker so much of the Earl of Cumberland's treatment of British subjects that he promptly named the area Cumberland and the water that flowed through it, the Cumberland River.

Mary could see the river every now and again; they appeared to be following its course northward. And with every footstep, she was taken farther from home.

3

They stopped at dusk in a small clearing in sight of the river. A brave pulled her out of the single-file line and pointed to the forest floor. Mary hesitated, trying to understand what he wanted her to do. But before she could respond, he pulled her to the ground by a fistful of hair. A hemp rope was placed around her neck and tethered to a sturdy tree trunk, providing her with only a few feet of clearance. As Mary sat on the ground with her back against the tree, she knew an escape attempt, even if she wasn't securely bound, would be suicide.

They had walked for hours, until the act of putting each foot into the other's footprints had become nothing more than a blur. She had no longer seen the footpath or the bodies in front of her, weaving their way through the underbrush. She thought several times that she had simply closed her eyes, almost falling asleep while her feet continued to move as if they had a mind of their own. It was apparent to her now that they followed a well-established trail. Though it was barely wider than a wagon wheel and frequently obscured with overhanging fauna that blocked it from view until their bodies parted it, the Indians walked it as though they had memorized the route.

Her feet ached. The shoes that were reliable for her chores were proving to be unsuited for a forced march such as this one, and blisters had formed where the leather rubbed the top of her foot. Gingerly, ever cognizant of the ropes around her neck and wrists that impeded smooth movement, she removed her shoes and held each foot in her hand, clumsily squeezing and kneading them.

She moved her hands to her ankles and slid the rope upward until the natural curve in her calves stopped it. The rope had worn completely through her skin. Dried blood ringed her ankles like bracelets, and she found herself swatting away flies and gnats that would make a meal from her blood. The pain had steadily intensified to the point where she'd bitten her lip in an attempt not to cry out with the pain of each step.

She glanced around for the woman who had placed the poultice on her face, but she was heading into the underbrush with another squaw.

Mary turned back to her legs. She kept the rope held high and wondered how she could endure the pain when she was forced to move again.

Her calves, too, ached with a heaviness that was almost beyond endurance. She didn't know how far they had walked, but it was obvious from their pace the Indians planned to put as much distance between them and the salt lick as possible. And to add to her misery, the sweat that ran down her calves had gotten into her ankle wounds, the salty sweat stinging her wounds.

She ran her tongue over her parched lips. Her bodice, boiled just yesterday, was already drenched in perspiration and streaked with dust. She longed to rip the clingy material away from her skin, as if that would enable her to feel a non-existent cool breeze.

The mosquitoes became vicious as the sun set, but with her hands tied in front of her, she was limited in her ability to slap at them. They didn't attack the Indians; their skin shimmered with bear fat, which kept them at bay. Her unprotected skin attracted them like bees to honey.

Somehow through her pain, she steeled herself and surveyed the movement around her. There were fourteen of them: nine braves and five squaws. A dead brave was laid on a litter. She watched as the men wrapped the dead man in hides, covering him from head to toe and securing him with hemp, and laying him gently at the edge of the riverbank. The litter, which appeared to have been made hastily, was discarded.

She never saw the litter as they'd marched through the woods; it must have been behind her. What else could she have missed while she concentrated on filling the footprints in front of her?

Her eyes fell on the large Indian she'd seen earlier. She could now see his face more clearly; it was striped in war paint. He wore a narrow, beaded headband with two eagle feathers, and appeared to be grunting abrupt orders in a language she didn't understand. From his stature and demeanor and the way in which the others responded, he had to be their leader.

The squaw who had helped her returned with the other woman. They carried a cloth between them filled with wild grapes and berries. The other squaws had busied themselves with what appeared to be a dinner preparation, though they did not start a campfire. Amidst all the activity, it was amazing to Mary how very little was said.

Her eyes followed two braves as they left the camp, their bodies disappearing into the gathering darkness like ghosts on the wind. Just when she thought they would not return, they reappeared and conferred with the leader in low voices.

There were no signs of other captives. She felt the tears welling up inside, felt them shake her very foundation, but she knew she could not allow them to escape from her. She had heard tales of children who were killed for no other reason than the fact that they made noise. Or even worse, they cut their tongues out but they did not die; instead, they were cursed to live a life without the benefit of speech. Above all else, she knew she had to stay alive and intact. She must survive.

She had to force herself into believing the Indians did not reach George, Sam, Ma, or the rest of the family. That would mean one or all of them would attempt to reach the safety of Fort Nashborough. Even the men and the families at Mansker's Station would rally to the larger fort, and once they were there, they would prepare to defend themselves. If an Indian attack did not come, they would form a rescue party. Unfortunately, this had become all too common.

She calculated the distance from the salt lick to Fort Nashborough. From what she could determine, the Indians were headed north, which would take them right into the path of the fort. She wondered if this savage group would attempt to attack the fort itself.

And if the settlers traveled all night, they would reach it sometime late tomorrow—if they didn't stumble upon them during the night. Now she understood why they didn't start a campfire; the smoke would threaten to give away their position.

She watched two of the younger squaws walk down to the riverbank. They removed their moccasins and waded into the shallows, their feet easily traversing the rocks as if their soles were made of thick leather. The water lapping at their ankles only reminded Mary of her thirst, especially when one stopped to cup her hands and drink.

She heard a movement to her left, and she turned. The eldest squaw stood only inches from her, yet Mary had not heard her until she'd almost been upon her. She knelt beside her and untied the rope from around her neck. Then she offered her a drink of water.

"Nepi," Mary said as she reached for the gourd.

The squaw appeared pleased that she remembered the word.

Mary sipped the fresh, cold water. She held the gourd with both hands, the only way she could securely grasp it with her hands still tied at the wrists. Oh, what she wouldn't do to have them untied, to be able to massage her wrists and stretch her arms!

She felt the squaw's presence beside her, though she was careful not to look directly at her. One never knew what could be misconstrued as insolence. Still, this squaw was perhaps her only ally. She'd given her a poultice that deadened the pain in her face, even if the sight in her left eye was still blurred from the assault. And she'd given her water, not once but twice.

Trying to appear casual, she glanced out of the corner of her eye toward the squaw. She was definitely older than the others. She wondered if they were somehow related. As she became braver and looked more in the old squaw's direction, she saw a movement behind her. At first, it was almost imperceptible and she thought she'd imagined it. But as she continued to peer through the shadows, she saw the unmistakable golden fur of a cougar.

She leapt toward the squaw as the big cat hurled itself from the safety of the trees, its huge paws outstretched and its mouth curled in a vicious snarl. She shoved her to the ground, falling over her body, as a shot rang out.

The silence enveloped them. Then Mary was struck by the pounding of both their hearts, sounding as one against each other's chest. Strong hands grasped her shoulders and ruggedly pulled her to a standing position, but her eyes were fixed on the squaw. There was a mixture of terror and bewilderment in the woman's eyes. The squaw came to a seated position, searching first Mary's eyes and then the brave's, and then falling on the cougar that lay dead at her feet.

There was complete silence, as if time stood still. Somewhere in the back of her mind, Mary felt the women at the river, the braves, standing at the ready, and the old squaw, staring at the cougar.

Mary felt suddenly weak, and slipped back to the ground, resting her back against the tree. The gourd was broken now, the water spilled across the ground. It was only fate that the Indians hadn't thought she was trying to escape. When she realized how close she might have come to being shot or killed, she placed her head in her hands. Her insides felt wracked with sobs but they would not pass her lips.

A brave awakened Mary and hauled her to her feet. She cringed as her sore and blistered feet hit the ground and she bit her tongue to keep from crying out. She was led to where the Indians had gathered in a circle and directed through gestures to sit down.

There was no apparent order to the seating: squaws and braves sat side by side. The old squaw and the leader, whom Mary supposed could be a minor chieftain, sat across from each other. It was like gathering around a dinner table, only the table and chairs were replaced with the hard earthen forest floor.

This could not be a war party, she thought. War parties didn't travel with their squaws. The women would be left at a camp at least one day's travel away while the braves would go through the ritual of painting their faces and preparing for a battle or raid. They would not run the risk of the white man following them and massacring their women.

The Indians ate a meal of venison jerky, grapes, and berries. Though Mary was not hungry and the thought of food was enough to make her nauseous, she forced herself to eat the venison, chewing it thoroughly. It was tough and leathery; she gnawed off a piece and allowed it to soak in her saliva until it was pliable enough to chew and swallow.

She glanced up every now and again, only to catch one of the braves or squaws watching her. Occasionally, one of them said something and the others would nod or laugh and watch her more intently. She wished she knew what they were saying.

Behind them was the cougar's pelt, already removed and cleaned and hanging in the branches, presumably to dry. She supposed they would use every last morsel of the animal's meat, including its organs. It seemed to be the Indian way.

Strung over another branch nearby, she caught sight of the rabbits Sam had left for her and Pa. It felt like a lifetime ago. She fought back the tears that stung the corners of her eyes.

The old squaw placed several grapes and berries in front of her and nodded as if to direct her to eat them. Mary forced herself to smile at the squaw in an effort to show her captors she would cooperate, but the Indian only returned her smile with an expressionless gaze. Gone were the terror and the bewilderment Mary had observed earlier; now her eyes looked like nothing more than two bits of coal.

After they had eaten in silence for awhile, the chief spoke. Mary tried to place any of the words, but she did not understand their language. They were definitely not Cherokee; she knew enough of that language to be able to grasp words and meanings here and there—it was essential for trading.

"Warioto," the chief said. All of the braves nodded. The squaws continued to eat.

Warioto.

Mary's hair stood up along her spine and she fought the impulse to jerk and stare at the chieftain. It was the Shawnee word for the Cumberland River. She glanced beyond the circle at the swirling water a few yards from them. Warioto. The Cherokee word for the same river was Shawanon.

She had been captured by the Shawnee.

Her mind was flooded with doubts: what did they plan to do with her? She had heard tales of the savage Shawnees raiding camps, killing men and capturing the women and children. More often than not, the captured were never seen nor heard from again. Occasionally, word would travel back, usually from the Cherokee with whom they traded, of a white captive who had been tortured and killed, or forced into a life of slavery. What was to be her fate?

She felt a scream rising within her, and she quickly subdued it. She couldn't think of anything else right now except getting through the coming night. She would have to memorize everything she could: the terrain, the direction in which they traveled, and the Indians' faces. She would have to know at all times where each of them were. And she would have to bide her time and plan her escape.

It wouldn't be enough to simply run away, even if her legs were not still tied together. The Shawnee, like all Indian tribes, were expert trackers. They would be able to follow her over soil, rocks, or even through water. They could move silently, stealthily, and they would hunt her down and kill her.

She had to hope that Sam and George had gone for help. And that some time during the night, as they slept on the ground here, the settlers would surround them and attack. She thought of scenarios in which the settlers would rush into the camp, and wondered how she should best react: lie still on the ground? Crawl to a safe place? Surely not get up and run, lest she come into the line of fire?

It did not escape her how quickly the cougar was killed. In the fraction of a second, it had become airborne in its attack and just as quickly, an Indian had aimed and fired. Oh, thank God, she thought wildly, thank God that hadn't been George!

After they had eaten, the Indians continued to sit in their circle. Occasionally, they would speak, though now it appeared as if they were talking of something other than their captive.

Then one by one, they left the circle to retrieve bloody scalps and washed them in the river beneath the moonlight. They returned to the circle and combed each scalp with their fingers, appearing to talk about their exploits. They became more animated, thrusting their arms and hands in the air as if to illustrate their actions in the raid and jabbing the air, and occasionally all eyes would turn to her.

She felt sick. She fought to keep the venison from rising in her throat as she recognized the scalp of her father.

There were other scalps, some bloody and some not. She forced herself to look at each one, as if each would help to tell the story of the raid: where they had gone, who they had attacked. But she recognized none of the others.

As if one of the braves were watching her and studying her reaction, he cut a piece off her father's scalp and tossed it at her feet. The circle was silent. She knew the Indians were watching her. She stared at the shiny black hair, the only thing she had left of her father. Then silently, she dug a small hole in the dirt with her bound hands. She lifted the scalp and ran her fingers through his hair, caressing it one last time. With a silent prayer formed on her lips, she gently laid the scalp inside the hole. With her heart heavy, she quietly covered it up. She took two twigs and broke them, then laid them in the shape of a cross upon the tiny grave.

The Indians burst into laughter. She bit the inside of her cheek in an attempt to squelch the desire to kick dirt in all their faces and scream at them to shut up. In time, she told herself. In time, I will escape.

Mary stirred beneath a fine drizzle that swiftly coated her face and body. The ground on which she lay had been hard and dusty; now it began to take on the floral scent of wet flowers and fauna, tickling her nose. After their meal, the Indians had not bothered tethering her neck to the tree again, but the ropes that bound her wrists and ankles rudely reminded her of her situation, and she groaned softly and tried to clear her mind of her nightmare reality.

The air was heavy and warm and the first droplets of rain felt refreshing on her parched skin. But the drops quickened and grew in size until a downpour had developed, quickly saturating her body and her clothes and leaving her hair hanging in wet strands around her face.

Somewhere in the distance, a wolf howled, its soulful cry carried on the wind, eventually disappearing in the gathering storm.

As its voice faded, another mournful cry answered. Her eyes flew open. Just a few feet from her, she could barely make out the silhouette of an Indian brave standing near the edge of the woods, his hands cupped, his voice raised in a perfect howl. He stopped, his arms falling to his sides, his head cocked as if listening, the beads of rain running unheeded along sinewy muscles and glistening skin.

In a moment, he received his response.

Mary attempted to sit up but her bones were stiff from her bondage and her awkward sleeping position. She managed to turn onto her side and partly raised her torso. She tried peering through the darkness in the direction of the howl, which originated across the river. The moon had disappeared behind gathering storm clouds and the rain was intensifying.

Through a fine cloud of fog and mist, she could barely distinguish ghostlike figures along the riverbank. As her eyes adjusted, she recognized the braves from her day-long march. Now they were toiling over a half a dozen canoes that had been pulled onto the riverbank. The body of the Indian slain at Neely's Salt Lick, still wrapped in hide, was placed inside one of the canoes. Meats were packed in another, along with the leftover berries and grapes.

One of the braves broke away from the others and came to her side. Unceremoniously, he wrenched her upwards to her feet. She groaned as the ropes scraped her raw skin and quickly bit her lip lest she cry out. Without a word, he grabbed her wrists and led her down the riverbank. She stumbled on the protruding tree roots. Her ankles were tied so tightly that she struggled to shuffle quickly along behind him to keep from being pulled right off her feet, the fog obscuring the ground until the earth attempted to ensnare her.

They stopped beside one of the canoes. He gestured and said something she didn't understand, but the meaning was clear. She pointed to her ankles and looked at him with what she hoped was an imploring look. Surely he didn't expect her to climb inside with her legs tied together!

Before she could answer, she felt her feet swept out from under her as another brave lifted her off the ground and laid her inside the canoe. The wood underneath her was hard against her spine and the quarters cramped. Though she couldn't understand their language, it was clear to her from their gestures that she was to remain perfectly still.

Her range of vision was now obscured by the sides of the vessel. Their voices were muted as their words were carried away by the wind and rain.

It seemed as though she lay there at the bottom of the canoe, her bones stiffening and the rainwater soaking her thin clothes, for an unbearably long time. Finally, one of the braves slid it into the river and climbed into the opposite end. He grabbed a paddle, pushed off from the shore and settled into a seated position.

She watched him row, his forward stroke causing them to quickly gain speed. From the easy movements of his arms and shoulders, she knew they were moving downstream.

She stared at the night sky through the rain and mist. Downstream meant they were moving north. This would take them right past Fort Nashborough.

She'd been through the fort just six months earlier on the family's journey from their previous home in Augusta County, Virginia to their present home along the Cumberland. They'd been accompanied by several other families, who all lay claims to other lands in the vicinity. The fort was surrounded with a sturdy stockade fence, built primarily to keep marauding Indians out, but which also provided safety from wild animals. Pa said it was two acres, but it seemed smaller because of the number of families there at the time sharing space with their domesticated animals.

She thought of the twenty-odd homes inside and of the warmth the fireplaces gave her when she'd first arrived here in early spring. Her blood froze.

They were moving toward Fort Nashborough.

It suddenly struck her what that could mean. She peered through the darkness at the brave in the opposite end of the canoe. His eyes were riveted on something ahead of them. She tried to sit up but he sternly shoved her back with the paddle and motioned for her to stay down.

Would they try to take Fort Nashborough?

From memory, she recounted the number in their party. Fourteen of them, but only nine braves. Were they still traveling with the squaws? She tried to think, but she realized she had been forced into the canoe before she'd had time to adequately assess their situation. Surely they would not take a captive with them on a raid. Unless—no, she couldn't think that way. She couldn't think about the stories she'd heard of these savages and their propensity for violence and torture, the way in which they killed children before their parents' eyes and women in front of their husbands.

She closed her eyes tightly as if to ward off these demonic thoughts. Her heart pounded, seeming to reverberate in the small vessel. She tugged at the ropes around her wrists and ankles; they were so tight she could barely move. And if she struggled too forcefully, the brave would be alerted to her efforts. Yet she knew she had to warn them.

There would be as many as twenty families inside that fort, Colonel James Robertson amongst them. He was a tall fellow, over six feet, a native Virginian who moved south and eventually further west ahead of the Neelys. His parents, like Mary's, were a mixture of British, Irish, and Scot, evidenced by his thick dark hair, fair complexion, and stunning blue eyes. He had been the one to convince the Neelys to leave Virginia and travel westward to the Cumberland Valley, even paying Pa to assist in clearing lands around the Fort to reduce the Indians' hiding places.

Robertson was no stranger to Indian attacks; as early as his childhood, his home had been attacked and some of his mother's relatives had been killed. They settled for a time along a tributary of the Roanoke River before moving southward to North Carolina.

He was only nineteen years old when his father died, leaving him with the responsibility of providing for his family. He raised cattle for a number of years, during which time he met and married Charlotte Reeves, a minister's daughter. Mary realized with a sinking heart that Charlotte would also be at Fort Nashborough, along with their children. She tried to remember their faces, but could only picture the eldest, Jonathan, who was barely 11 years old.

They would be in their beds right now, fast asleep or perhaps listening to the rain pelt their rooftops, with a false sense of security on this fateful night.

The river fog encased them in a blanket so thick that at times the brave's face was obscured, though he was only a few feet away. She turned her head toward the side of the vessel. If she could only find a slit in the side, something she could peer through, she might be able to determine their whereabouts. She turned her head from left to right, trying to be as silent as possible, but the bottom of the canoe was as black as a tomb. If there had been any seams in the wood, they had been effectively covered with pitch.

She would have to calculate the distance down river from Neely's Salt Lick, and when she thought they were near, she would have to take a chance and sound an alarm. She lay in the boat for what felt like an eternity, at times believing she was far from the fort and other times, ready to bet her life that they were upon it.

In the end, it was the brave who unwittingly signaled their approach. His pace quickened; though the current was naturally carrying them downstream, he was obviously forcing it to speed ahead, his arms moving faster and more rhythmically. Mary also felt, from the movement of the canoe, that they were moving closer to the bluffs just below the fort.

Then the brave abruptly stopped, pulled his paddle inside, and leaned down. His body was so far forward that his chest touched Mary's knees, and she stiffened and fought the impulse to push him away.

As they floated downstream, she knew he was hiding from sight, lest the sentry at the fort see them. They had to be close.

She offered a silent prayer and then steeled her body. She wouldn't be able to escape or even move from this confining location in this stinking boat, but she could sound the alarm.

She screamed as though the Indians were attempting to kill her. She screamed and screamed again, her voice carried on the currents and lost in the wind.

The brave was upon her, staring into her eyes with a murderous rage. He pulled her upward and slapped her across her cheek, but she continued to scream. Somewhere in the fog, other canoes emerged, the braves leaning forward and pushing them downstream, their heads barely visible above the sides of their vessels.

The brave struck her again. Her head lolled backward and the clouds parted, leaving a white moon staring down at her in its brilliance. She quickly turned toward the western shore. There was Fort Nashborough—there in the distance—but it was behind them. They were speeding away from it, continuing downstream, and now there were not six canoes but at least twice that many, all moving as though they were empty, with not even a feather peeking above their sides.

The brave shoved her downward, and as her head hit the wood bottom, she realized with a sinking heart that she was beyond help now. As they rounded a bend and Fort Nashborough faded into the river fog like an apparition, she knew although it would not be attacked—not tonight—she was now at the mercy of the Indians.

5

The sun found them at daybreak still on the river, its warmth welcome to break the chill from Mary's rain-soaked clothes. But as the day wore on, it beat down on them unmercifully, its rays bouncing off the surface of the water and searing through her closed eyelids. Though the brave did not change his expression, he stopped rowing now and then to cup his hands in the fast-moving current and drink from the refreshing liquid, but he did not offer Mary anything to ease her misery.

At last, she motioned to him in an attempt to convey that she wanted to sit up. When he only stared at her with expressionless eyes, she gingerly and painfully eased herself to a seated position. He did not stop her. Her back felt as though it would break in two from the hard wood and cramped position she'd found herself in hour after hour. She stretched her neck to the left and then to the right, pulled her shoulders into a hunched position, and leaned forward to stretch out her lower back. When the brave only showed minute interest in her, she became bolder, turning first to the left and then to the right, as though she was continuing to stretch.

The sight astonished her. At least a dozen canoes were in front of them and a dozen more behind them, each filled with two to four people. When they reached the spot where another river flowed into the Cumberland northwest of Fort

Nashborough, still more canoes joined them. The river then meandered in a general northwesterly fashion, sometimes dipping to the south before heading back to the north.

As she studied the people in each vessel, she realized the group that had attacked Neely's Salt Lick had been only a spoke in a much larger wheel. She was now one of perhaps seven or eight captives—all women and children.

As the day wore on, she became still braver, staring for long periods at the other captives, wracking her brain for any place or time in which they might have crossed paths, but she didn't recognize any of them.

They were nearing the mouth of another river, its distinctive ruddy color identifying it as the Red River. Mary heard an infant wailing continuously even before their party joined them on the Cumberland and she spotted the young mother seeking to calm the child. As they joined them, the braves turned and stared sternly at the mother and child.

Mary closed her eyes and silently prayed. The infant was dangerous to the Indians; it could alert settlers to their approach, just as it had alerted them. She thought it sounded colicky and no amount of soft singing or bouncing by its mother could stop its fretful cries.

Moments later, Mary heard a shriek like a wounded animal, the sound ripping through her senses like the sharp blade of a knife tearing into her heart. When she opened her eyes and started to turn, a small body floated past them face down, its blood turning the water red, its tiny arms jerking spasmodically. As it approached each canoe, the brave batted it with his paddle on to the next one, until it was nearer the shoreline and caught up in the reverse current.

The mother continued to wail until the Indian in her boat hit her alongside her head with his paddle. Her head lolled back and she sank down into the boat, mercifully unconscious.

From somewhere behind her, she heard a soft whimper and turned to see two young girls huddled together, their eyes wide and unblinking as though their souls had separated, leaving only the shell of their bodies behind. She wondered if her own face looked the same.

When dusk arrived, they had traveled so many miles from Neely's Salt Lick, she wondered how Sam and the other settlers would ever find her. It was obvious from their rapid descent downstream and the lack of breaks the Indians were striving to put as much distance behind them as possible.

At last, the old Indian in the first canoe held up his hand. In a silent response, the canoes slowed and the paddles were used now to steer them toward the bank. They arrived in rows of six, each canoe's occupants hopping out as they reached shore, pulling their vessels behind them to make room for the others.

When it was her turn, the brave motioned for her to stay in the canoe. Once he had pulled the vessel out of the way, he returned to her and untied her ankles. She followed his instructions, rising to her feet as though her bones were a hundred years old, and stepped over the side onto the ground.

She felt as though she was still caught up in the river's current, and she struggled to maintain her balance. The brave led her to a tree and tied one end of a rope around her neck and the other end around the tree trunk. She was able to sit and move about the tree as much as six feet in any direction. She found a relatively private clump of bushes in which to relieve herself and then stood near the tree, using its girth to help steady her.

She watched as the boats were unloaded and the remaining captives were bound to other trees, too far apart to allow conversation. The young mother sank to her knees in the soft earth, her forehead touching the ground, and sobbed, her body shaking.

There were no adults with the children, and Mary longed to be near enough to offer them a reassuring word. She caught the eye of a young girl of perhaps eight or nine years old, and she smiled to let her know that everything would be okay, but the girl's face was expressionless, as if Mary was not even there.

Mary eventually sank to the ground.

Some of the squaws, like the night before, busied themselves by gathering nuts and wild berries. They returned a short time later with a blanket filled with wild blackberries and gooseberries, enough to set Mary's mouth to watering.

She watched as some of the squaws started fires near some rocky bluffs, expertly arranging aged dry grass, leaves, and small chunks of bark. A minimal amount of smoke softly curled around the bluffs and dissipated quickly before it rose above them.

They cooked meat that Mary guessed was venison though it could have been the cougar, along with a mixture of corn meal and water formed into patties that resembled hoe cakes. She was thirsty, hungry, tired, and sore. And she wanted to go home. She thought of her family and imagined them at Fort Nashborough, the women sheltered by the fort while the men readied a search party.

The sun was setting by the time the food was ready. Unlike the night before when the squaws and braves sat together, they silently divided into groups. The older men with more feathers, whom Mary presumed to be the leaders, sat around one campfire. The remaining braves huddled around another. As the sun sank behind the mountains, the young men's stories became louder and more boisterous, their motions exaggerated as if to demonstrate their bravery or actions as they undoubtedly recounted tales of attacking the settlers and seizing their captives. The brave who carried Pa's scalp pointed to her and gestured excitedly, causing all of the others to stare in her direction. She wondered what he could be saying and whether his story could seal her fate—something she truly did not even want to think about.

The squaws sat in another group, listening intently to the men and occasionally speaking quietly amongst themselves. Mary caught the old squaw looking at her more than once, but her face was expressionless, her eyes bathed in the shadows.

Once their meals had been devoured and Mary felt as though the sides of her stomach were rubbing together, they offered the remains to the captives.

A young squaw from Mary's original group brought her corn meal, meat, and berries. She offered her thanks and tried to make eye contact, but the squaw appeared not to notice her overtures, and left her almost immediately to eat her meal in silence. Her stomach churned and tumbled, but she did not know when or if she would be offered more food. And she knew if she were to attempt an escape, she would need as much strength as she could muster.

She was finishing the berries when a brave stood up from the circle of elders and made his way across the clearing to her. She watched him curiously; he had not been with her original group, but must have joined their party at the Red River. He was tall, his body firm and muscular. His hair was straight and long. But as he stepped out of the shadows, the moonlight caught his hair and Mary gasped. It was not black, as the others' were, but a warm brown.

He walked silently, like a cat, his feet seemingly barely touching the dirt beneath him. When he reached her, he knelt, resting back on his haunches.

His eyes were fixed on hers as though they were searching for a story within their depths. She knew her own eyes mirrored his: they were both imploring and guarded, wanting information tempered with a reluctance to reciprocate.

As she returned his gaze, she realized his eyes were hazel.

He nodded slightly toward the elder brave who she suspected was the leader of their group.

"Eagle Feathers wants to know why you screamed," he said. His words were measured but he had a command of the English language that was startling, given his appearance.

"Eagle Feathers?" Mary said.

"He is your chieftain."

"*My* chieftain?" she repeated, bristling.

"He wants to know why you screamed."

She glanced at her lap. She couldn't tell him the truth; for all she knew, it could cost her her life. She looked into his eyes but saw no answer there.

"I screamed for the spirits to help me," she said.

She thought she detected a slight smile. "They did not come," he said.

"No. They did not."

"Eagle Feathers says you are a goshawk," he said.

"A what?"

"You sing like a bird but you attack from the safety of the woods, like a goshawk." When she didn't respond, he added, "They believe you are a great warrior."

She would have laughed had the statement not been so ludicrous. "How could they possibly think that?"

"You attacked them from the woods?"

"I was defending my Pa."

He nodded. She waited for him to respond but he continued to look at her silently.

"Who are you?" she said at last.

"The English call me White Messenger."

"You *are* white, aren't you?"

His eyes did not waver from hers. "I am the son of Eagle Feathers and Medicine Woman."

She looked across the clearing at the old squaw. "They can't be your parents."

"Some day you will learn."

Mary nodded toward the old squaw. "She healed my face."

She watched as his eyes followed the curve in her face, settling for the briefest of moments on her eye, which was beginning to open now that the swelling in the side of her face was diminishing.

"My people will often heal a warrior," he said, "sometimes even before they are led to their deaths."

He rose and turned to leave.

"Wait," she said.

He stopped and turned back to her.

"What will happen to me?"

He waited a long moment before answering. "You can be a songbird or a goshawk; it is your choice."

"But I am no fighter," Mary said.

"Tell that to Bear Claw."

She looked at the braves, some of whom were telling stories while the others listened. "Which one is he?"

White Messenger pointed to the bodies wrapped in hide that they had carried down the river.

Mary was dumbfounded.

"Bear Claw was a great warrior," White Messenger said. "Only another great warrior could slay him." He nodded toward the others. "They tell me you came from the woods and fired one shot, killing Bear Claw. Then you fought the others. It took many to subdue you."

Mary leaned against the tree and stared for a long time at the stilled bundle. At some point, White Messenger moved into the shadows and the talk among the braves quieted. Later, the Indians prepared their beds and the captives huddled on the bare ground while Mary sat against the great tree trunk, her eyes still on the bundle.

6

The sun had barely begun to cut through the darkness when Mary was awakened by a flurry of activity. The squaws worked silently, their figures barely visible in the early morning mist, as they packed the meager possessions they had used overnight. The braves were gathered at the river, inspecting the canoes.

Mary's eyes searched the terrain. Some of the captured children were still asleep, tethered to the trees nearest them. Others sat with wide, startled eyes as they watched the Indians. The woman who had lost her baby was staring straight ahead as if in a stupor. Mary had never felt so helpless in her entire life.

Some of the canoes were carried deep into the underbrush, perhaps determined to be in an unacceptable condition for the journey ahead. The Indians loaded their possessions into the remaining vessels.

The brave who had proudly displayed her father's scalp approached her. It took all her willpower not to recoil from him, but she forced herself to raise her head and look him squarely in the eyes. Roughly, he untied the hemp from the tree and walked her to the edge of the water as if she were a horse on a lead. She knew before he began to gesture that she would be expected to climb into the canoe and remain seated and still. Silently, she complied.

She watched as the other captives were similarly led and loaded. Then the canoes were pushed from shore. There would be no breakfast. Their day had begun.

The sun was high overhead when they came across a stunning landscape. The water had been a clear, placid blue but now it reflected an expanse of golden and green fields. And as they rounded a bend in the river, Mary found herself staring at hundreds of bison.

She had never seen animals this large. Some of them appeared to be as tall as a man and twelve feet long. She imagined just one of them had to weigh as much as a half dozen men or more. They were grazing amongst prairie grasses that rose to their massive chests. Above them soared bald eagles on wings spread wide, no doubt inspecting the ground below for prey.

Upon spotting the bison, the braves began talking and gesturing excitedly. Several reached for their muskets or bows. They stopped rowing and the procession began to slow, moving closer to the shore. Mary wondered if they planned to stop and if the rest of the day would become a hunting expedition for the braves. Her legs and back ached and she longed for a rest along the grassy shores.

Then one brave's voice rose above the rest: it was White Messenger. He was speaking now in the Shawnee language, and pointing. His face was solemn and as he spoke, Mary saw the smiles fade from the others' faces.

She peered across the water to determine what White Messenger had brought to the others' attention. The herd was parting like two waves to make way for a lone white bison.

It was larger than the others. It moved with the ease of an animal confident in its superiority.

The sighting hushed the Indians. Those with weapons laid them down quietly. It was almost as if a god had materialized before them. They remained perfectly silent as they floated past the herd, all heads turning as though they could not tear their eyes away from the massive white creature.

The animal reached the edge of the shore and watched them as they floated past. They were so close that Mary could see its deep brown eyes. It seemed to look directly at her as if it contained a depth of wisdom.

Even after her canoe moved past it, she turned to gaze at it. It had the same effect on the Indians as it had upon her. Each person stared into its eyes until they moved further downstream.

They did not speak again until they reached another river several hours later.

The sun was low by the time they reached a much wider river. Here, the Cumberland abruptly ended, its waters emptying into a body of water the Indians excitedly referred to as "Spaylawitheepi." Mary had never heard the term before, and had no idea where they were.

Where the rivers converged, she could barely see dilapidated rooftops of long wooden structures set back from the waters. The Indians were obviously familiar with them, as they pointed and chatted excitedly.

Then the braves began to call out in strange voices that sounded like a cross between a human and an animal. It was different from their war cry; Mary knew she would never forget that sound as long as she lived. This was almost like a howl. As they continued, she realized that some braves added the last syllable multiple times, while those who had captured her only sounded the last syllable once.

They appeared to be listening for a response as they guided the canoes to the shore, but they received none.

The Indians disembarked as they neared land, pulling the canoes out of the water. They motioned to the captives to follow them.

After hours on the water, Mary fought to maintain her balance on land and marveled at how well-adapted the Indians appeared to be with their changing environment. White Messenger gathered the captives in a group along the shore. It was the first time Mary had been this close to the other captives, and she couldn't stop herself from staring into their faces. She longed to know where they had come from and of their experiences, but she was afraid to speak while the Indians remained within earshot.

White Messenger untied her hands. Instinctively, Mary rubbed the skin where the ropes had bruised and chafed her. She immediately regretted the action: the salt from her sweaty palms stung the raw flesh.

"Untie the others," White Messenger directed. "Empty the canoes. Put everything there—" he pointed near a fallen tree "—and tell them do not try to escape."

Mary nodded. She went first to the woman who had lost her child. The ropes were tighter around her wrists than they had been around Mary's and she struggled to remove them.

"What is your name?" Mary asked.

The woman looked at her without responding.

"Your name?" Mary repeated.

She shook her head.

"Do you speak English?"

The woman's eyebrows were knit together, and Mary realized she did not understand her. She motioned to the other captives' ropes. "Untie," she said, motioning to their wrists. "Untie."

The woman nodded and went to work on the nearest child.

Mary asked each of the children if they understood her. Most of the captives spoke English, though Mary suspected the others were of German or Dutch descent.

She tried to reassure them as she removed their bonds. She glanced up once to see White Messenger watching as he leaned against a nearby tree. He nodded once in her direction, and then pointed to the canoes.

"Hurry," she said, ushering them toward the river. "Empty the canoes. Put everything there—" she pointed to the location White Messenger showed her "—and do not try to escape. We are in Indian Territory now. They will kill you if you run."

She didn't know how many of them understood her directions, but they all watched her actions and didn't hesitate to help. The smaller children were almost useless in their efforts, and Mary found the brunt of the work falling on the young mother and herself.

She noted that only a couple of braves had stayed behind to guard them, while the other Indians had disappeared in the direction of the wooden structures, which were now blocked from her view by thick woods. She knelt more than once and dipped her hands into the cool river, then drank out of her cupped hands. The water was refreshing, and she hoped by drinking enough of it, she could fool her stomach into thinking it was full.

They toiled for the better part of an hour, emptying the canoes of such diverse items as furs, meats, cornmeal, blankets, clothing, moccasins, weapons, shot and powder, and even jewelry, china and figurines they had either stolen or acquired in trade.

As Mary unpacked, she felt a sinking sensation. They had come too far and traveled into territories with which her family— and all the frontiersmen she knew—were unfamiliar. And with every hour that passed, every mile they had traveled further northward, she knew her chances of ever being rescued diminished.

She studied the faces around her, considered the numbers of Indians and the other captives. How would she ever manage to escape? And if she did, assuming they did not hunt her down and capture her again, how would she ever find her way home again?

She had no chance on foot. The terrain was too foreign. Even if she managed to remain close to the river, there would be times when she would have to cross it, and she would not have the means to do so. She was a strong swimmer, but not nearly strong enough to navigate these waters, even just to cross from one shore to the other.

They had also crossed other rivers and tributaries, most of which they did not take. How would she ever remember which one to follow?

Two and a half days had passed. Two solid days of constant rowing. How many days would that equal on foot?

She stared at the expanse of trees beside the river. One day of walking had left blisters that were still open and raw. But without her shoes, the forest floor would rip her feet to shreds.

Food would not be a problem, she surmised. Not at this time of year. Berries were plentiful, even if she didn't know how to fish or hunt or trap without the proper tools. She could survive on berries and wild fruits, knowing at the end of her journey, she would be reunited with George and her family—what was left of her family.

She thought of the bison and wondered what the massive creatures would have done to her had she stumbled upon them without the water providing a buffer. Would they have allowed her to pass? Or would the bulls have charged her and trampled her? What other wild animals lurked there? She thought of the cougar and shuddered to think what would have happened if it had come upon her while she was alone and unable to defend herself. There were bear in these woods and other big cats, and perhaps wild boar and other creatures that would not take kindly to a human walking through their territory.

The longer she thought of her potential journey back home, the deeper her heart sank. Would she ever see her family again? Oh, Sam, George, are you both looking for me even now?

Once the canoes were unpacked, White Messenger and the other brave escorted them through the woods on a trail that was barely visible through the underbrush. The captives swatted at gnats and flies but the braves seemed unaffected, even amused at their attempts to brush off the nuisances.

They came to the edge of the woods. The brave led their group into a large open clearing, beyond which were a row of long bark-covered structures. Smaller structures were along the outer edge of the clearing, but those appeared to have been abandoned some years earlier and now the woods were quickly overtaking them.

Mary stopped, allowing the others to pass her. White Messenger was in the rear; as he approached, he motioned for her to continue.

"What is this place?" Mary asked.

"Eagle Feathers says that once it was a great village," White Messenger responded, "filled with Shawnee and French traders."

"What happened?"

"War."

She swallowed. "With the white man?"

He turned to look at her. "Cherokee."

As they neared the long building, the squaws had already started a fire and were intent on preparing a meal. She hoped it would not take long.

There was a festive atmosphere. The Indians were obviously familiar with the village and almost acted as if this was a homecoming. They ran about, inspecting the buildings, pulling out items that had been left by prior occupants, laughing, and talking excitedly.

Mary was soon put to work. She was sent with a squaw to fetch a large package she had unpacked from one of the canoes. It turned out to be a rather large bear, and it became obvious it would serve as the night's meal. It had already been skinned and divided, and the squaws went through the remains and selected the cuts of meat they intended to prepare. Then Mary was tasked with repacking the rest of it and returning it to the shore.

Two squaws accompanied her. Mary carried the package alone; she figured it must have weighed as much as seventy pounds. As they walked along the trail, each squaw left in turn, batting about the underbrush. By the time they reached the shoreline, they had about a dozen tree limbs, each one taller than they were.

She had heard the horror stories of people burned alive and now she wondered what was to become of her and the other captives. Would the Indians use these limbs to start a bonfire upon which to roast them?

If it was their intent to kill her, she would stand no chance at escape. She began to pray that any fate that should befall her would come mercifully swift.

The squaws motioned for her to add the bear to the pile she and the young mother had made. Then they set about erecting a structure. It was difficult to understand what they wanted her to do, but Mary tried very hard to pay attention to their words and motions. When they were done, they had placed some of the limbs into the ground to form four corners. After a short trip into the woods to obtain more branches, they laid them from one side to the other, forming a bed almost six feet off the ground. More branches were then laid in the opposite direction.

When they were done, they walked around the structure and tested for sturdiness. Once a few adjustments were made, they appeared pleased.

One of the squaws bent down to the pile of belongings and pulled out a package. She held it up and said to Mary, "Mie-ken-whe."

"Mie-ken-whe," Mary repeated.

"Mie-ken-whe." She then placed the package atop the structure.

Mary reached for one of the packages, but the squaw motioned for her to put it down. The squaw reached for another package instead and repeated the word. After a few attempts, she realized they were referring to the meat. With a sigh of relief, she understood: they wanted the meat placed high above the ground.

"Mie-ken-whe," Mary said excitedly, pulling out all of the packages containing meat. They nodded and again appeared pleased as she placed each one atop the structure, careful not to overload one end and cause the whole thing to topple.

She was famished by the time they joined the others. The other squaws had been busy preparing the meal while the braves lounged around talking and smiling.

At long last, each person was provided with a wooden bowl. One by one, they passed their bowl to Eagle Feathers, who placed the same amount in each person's bowl. He then held it over his head and said a few solemn words. The bowl was then passed back down the line to the person from whom it originated. Mary noticed they all waited until each person had his or her bowl before they commenced to eating. Thankfully, she dove into the meal of bear meat, corn, cornmeal, and berries.

After the meal, they walked down to the river and washed their bowls. Mary noted that each person kept their own. Then the captives were again separated, each returning to the old village with their original captors.

Mary was brought to one of the smaller structures with Medicine Woman. The old woman spread a hide upon the dirt floor. She then handed Mary a deerskin and motioned for her to do the same. Then the old woman lay down and curled up as if to sleep.

Mary lay upon the deerskin, her bowl still in her hands. Her wrists and ankles were untied. There was nothing to keep her here except the possibility the Indians would hunt her down and torture or kill her if she tried to escape. She resolved to sleep a few hours and then, in the dark of night, she would awaken, creep to the river, steal a canoe, and try to make her way back home.

7

ieutenant James J. Hawkins sat tall atop the black stallion, his bronzed chest gleaming with perspiration in the August sun, his long, sun-bleached hair pulled into a single tail. Though dusk was still hours away, the mosquitoes were already out in full force. As he slapped at one on his bare arm, it briefly crossed his mind that, were his family to cross his path at this very moment, they certainly would not recognize him. He was half-naked in the Indian custom, as was often the practice among the men in Colonel George Rogers Clark's forces.

His sharp blue eyes surveyed the valley below. With the grace of a man accustomed to long hours on a horse, he reached into the buckskin pouch strapped to his thigh and pulled out a well-worn telescope.

Only a few weeks earlier, a force of British soldiers and Indian braves led by Captain Henry Bird had attacked Ruddell's Station. The result was almost a total massacre. It was suspected the Indians were mostly Shawnees, since they were well known for their brutality and their allegiance to the British. Those they didn't kill at Ruddell's Station were reported to have been marched to the British-controlled Fort Detroit, where they most certainly faced torture, death, or slavery.

Under the command of Colonel Clark, Jim had traveled to Ruddell's Station and then on to Martin's Station, which had fared no better. Then word came that bands of marauding

Shawnees were raiding as far south as the Cumberland River, killing male settlers and capturing their women and children. Word traveled quickly throughout the western frontier, swelling the ranks of Clark's militia to more than one thousand men thirsty for revenge.

Jim had been with Clark since the early days, having joined his militia in Virginia in the summer of 1777. Most of the folks on neighboring farms had enlisted in the Continental Army and marched to the north or east to fight the British. Jim's two older brothers joined the 14th Virginia Regiment and moved northward to Pennsylvania, leaving him and his younger brother, Teddy, at home among three sisters, a circumstance he thought might be worse than battle.

As time passed, he felt drawn to the west and to Indian Territory, but leaving had not been easy. He'd asked for Susannah Davidson's hand in marriage; she and her family had expected them to settle in Augusta County and raise cattle as both their fathers had done before them. But as the weeks swept past, he felt a tug-of-war within his heart, within his very soul; and when his old friend Clark had personally asked him to join his militia, he had not hesitated.

In the summer of 1777, Clark helped to orchestrate the formation of the County of Kentucky, giving Virginia the power and the right to defend the land against the British and the Indians, all the way to the Mississippi River. And so Jim had left Virginia and Susannah behind with nothing but a promise that he would return for her once the war was over.

It hadn't been an easy fight. While the war raged on in the east, too few recognized the need to defend the west. But the visionary Clark knew. He'd always known. He'd traveled to Williamsburg and successfully made the argument that even if they were to win the war in the east, they must secure the western frontier or the British would always be at their backs and recurring disputes would rage on for future generations.

Though the Virginia government had given him the official power to fight the British and their allies west of the Cumberland Gap, raising an army had been a different matter. Jim had joined Clark when he had less than a hundred and fifty men; their ranks would rarely swell to three hundred. But now things were different. Now the British and the Shawnees had marched upon two forts and killed or captured almost every soul, and they were continuing to wage a bloody war against the settlers. Now a thousand frontiersmen were screaming for revenge.

And they would have it.

Jim peered through the telescope. Below him, nestled into the Miami River Valley, was the Shawnee village of Chillicothe.

Jim had expected to see Indians milling about. There should have been squaws harvesting the corn in the fields just beyond the village; children playing along the riverbank; scores of Shawnees going about their daily chores. But there was none of that. As he patiently surveyed the village, he saw only one sign of movement: a dog wandering past silent buildings. He followed its movements until it was out of sight behind a communal building; it was a yellow dog, no doubt a mongrel, who was so thin that when it turned away from him, the body looked barely wider than it's tail.

Moving his attention away from the dog, he noted the large, bark-covered council houses and rounded dwellings of individual families appeared to be deserted.

His eyes followed a trail of smoke ascending from a single fire. It could be a trap; Shawnees were known for their tricks. There could be hundreds of braves hiding inside those structures, just waiting for their forces to attack.

He maneuvered his horse in an attempt to reach a better vantage point. He stopped abruptly when he was able to view the source of the fire: three men were tied to stakes, their charred remains smoldering in the summer sun.

He heard a movement behind him, and he turned his horse partway to face the other scouts.

"Best get back to Colonel Clark," he said. "Chillicothe appears to have been deserted, but we shouldn't count on it."

"Yes, sir," one said, digging his heels into a dappled mare. The other followed.

Jim collapsed his telescope and returned it to his buckskin pouch. His eyes studied the village one more time before falling on the corn fields. At least there would be a good dinner tonight—for those who survived.

The cannon boom echoed across the valley, the volley landing squarely on the council house where it erupted in a mass of black smoke, flying debris, and fire. In years past, the structure had been the site of Indian gatherings that had numbered into the hundreds—some said thousands. Now the weather-beaten bark burned easily, the flames climbing ever higher amidst the shouts of appreciation from the scores of men gathered about.

"Told you that cannon was worth saving," Colonel Clark said with a grin.

"Yes, sir," Jim said appreciatively.

"Let that send a message to them," came a weathered drawl.

Jim turned to face Daniel Boone. He was a slender man of medium height, his cheekbones high and almost fragile, but he was legendary in these parts.

"How many months you been dragging that thing around?" he chided.

"Just since Vincennes," Clark answered smoothly. "Courtesy of the departing British."

Jim peered through his telescope. He did not see any signs of life—even the dog had disappeared. He searched the horizon for any evidence of Indians lurking about, readying themselves for an ambush, but could find none.

They waited until the smoke cleared. The air was filled with a militia ready to assault Chillicothe on foot and on horseback. All eyes were riveted on Jim's companions.

Boone spoke first. "That building over there," he said, pointing to a structure relatively close to the council house, "that was Blackfish's home."

Clark nodded to the captain at his elbow. The captain responded by issuing a command to fire at the structure. The single brass cannon was maneuvered into position.

Jim knew before the shot was fired that it was symbolic. Blackfish would not be there. He had died the previous May when Boone had attacked this very village. At that time, Blackfish had been able to defend the village and prevent its capture, but he'd suffered a gun shot in the leg. They learned last summer from French traders that he had died after waging a protracted battle against the infected wound.

Boone pointed out other targets. Each time, Clark instructed the captain, who in turn ordered the privates, to bombard the designated targets. Each time, they waited until the smoke cleared. There was no return fire and no signs of life.

Jim sat quietly, listening to Boone's strategy for surrounding the village and overtaking it. He knew Chillicothe well: he had lived here for several months as Chief Blackfish's adopted son after having been captured, along with other settlers, while gathering salt near Boonesborough.

It would have been easy to march upon the seemingly deserted village, only to encounter an ambush.

While Clark and Boone conferred and two other colonels joined the quiet discussion, Jim tried to rein in his desire to charge down the hill into the open field, a battle cry on his lips, his longrifle cocked and ready. Almost in tandem with Jim's thoughts, his horse pawed the ground.

He could feel the tenseness in the air, the impression that hundreds of men on foot and on horseback were at the ready, their spines rigid and their eyes focused. He peered behind him. As far as he could see, faces stared out from the woods, intent on Indian blood this day.

"Lieutenant," Clark said as those gathered around him pulled back, "advise Colonel Logan we are ready for the charge."

"Yes, sir," Jim responded. With a swift kick, his horse was off and racing along the perimeter of the woods. He was thankful for the mission; the feel of air rushing past his face and the sound of his horse's hooves along the ground kept time with his pounding heart. He could feel the eyes of the men boring into him, waiting expectantly for their orders.

He reached Colonel Benjamin Logan and relayed his message. Then he dropped his horse back to await additional orders.

It was as if the men held their breath simultaneously. Then Jim felt the ground shake under him as swarms of horses galloped at full speed from Clark's vicinity. Through the dust that swirled about them, he could barely pick out Boone's slim figure, but there was no mistaking the legendary backwoodsman's blood-thirsty scream as they advanced on Chillicothe.

"Permission to join them, sir," Jim said.

"Permission granted," Logan responded without wavering.

A long moment passed. Jim could feel the horses behind him pressing in.

Logan raised his left arm. He kept it high in the air for what seemed an eternity. When it dropped, it was like a gate opening: the horses thundered down the hill and across the open field, their hooves racing through the tall grasses, their muscles taut as they sped toward their target.

The village became a blur of men and horseflesh, the chilling war cries filling the hot August air.

They rode headlong into the village, rumbling past the rounded wigwams, pulling hides and bark off the structures and crashing them in heaps that sent dust clouds rising.

Jim rode his horse straight through one of the larger homes, crashing tables that were set as if it were mealtime and breaking pottery filled with corn and beans and meat as he went, bent on destroying every last Shawnee possession. Oh, what he wouldn't give to have just one Indian pop his head up right now!

Everywhere around him there was mayhem—the sound of wood splintering, of men shouting, of utter destruction. The air was thick with debris that blocked out the remaining rays of sun as the village of Chillicothe was ravaged.

In the space of a few minutes, the destruction ceased and the men grew quiet. There were no Indians here. There had been no ambush. It was now apparent that someone had sounded the warning of their advance just as the Indians had begun to eat their main meal, and they had dropped everything and fled.

Now they picked through the remains of the village, their horses stepping past littered pots and broken wood. Jim paused in the center and watched as men climbed down from their mounts and entered structure after structure, sometimes emerging with armloads of furs and possessions. He knew that more than one man was searching for evidence that a loved one had been here—perhaps a piece of cloth, a shoe, a treasured doll or piece of jewelry—anything to give them hope that their women and children were still alive.

As he turned and surveyed the scene before him, Clark's tall figure swept through the crowd, his eyes fixed on the three men still tied to stakes. He dismounted when he reached them and stepped quietly into the circle, kicking dust into the dying embers around their charred bodies. He stopped and stared at each one as though memorizing what was left of their facial features.

Jim felt an emptiness begin to creep over him, a sense of loss that he seemed to experience more frequently these days. He knew he should discreetly turn about and give Clark his privacy, but he continued studying him as his chest grew heavier. Perhaps he was waiting for a reaction, a sign that Clark recognized one of the men, but he got none.

He sighed deeply. It had been just about three years now... They'd been delivering much needed gunpowder to the settlers here when the Shawnees attacked a part of their forces that had become separated from the main body. One of the men who had been captured was Clark's own cousin, Joseph Rogers. For the past three years, Jim had watched Clark every time they discovered a dead white man or an escaped captive. And every time Clark had turned his back, his shoulders just a bit more slumped, Jim knew he continued to carry the burden that his cousin was still out there, perhaps still awaiting his rescue.

This time was no different.

Clark returned to his horse, mounted it easily, and squared his shoulders. When he spoke, his voice rang out, strong and solid, hushing the commotion around him.

"Cut them down," he said. "We'll give them a proper funeral."

He turned his horse to face his immediate subordinates, who had gathered around him.

"Assign some men to gathering as much food as they can," he directed. "I want that corn field stripped almost bare—just leave enough for our return home. I expect to come back through here.

"We stay here tonight. Tomorrow, prepare to resume our march. We will track down the Shawnees and we will rid this country of them once and for all."

9

Mary awakened to a drowning sensation. Her breath felt cut off and her body sucked ever deeper into a pit of blackness.

She instinctively raised her hand to her face only to find a firm leathery palm pressed across her mouth so close to her nostrils that she could barely breathe. As her eyes adjusted to the darkness, she realized the old squaw was sitting squarely across her chest, pressing down on her with bones that felt like iron.

"Silence," she hissed in broken English.

Unable to speak, Mary nodded, her head only able to move a fraction of an inch under the woman's weight.

A knife's cold blade was pressed under her chin. In the filtered light that crossed the threshold, she could see the intense resolve in the squaw's black eyes. She had no doubt she was capable of killing her.

She tried to feel the location of the squaw's hands, arms, legs and feet. She fought to quiet the rapid beating of her heart, to calm her nerves as she readied herself. Mary would defend herself; she would not die simply by laying bare her throat to her captor.

She moved her hand just inches away from the squaw's right hand and braced herself for the right moment. She would have to be faster than this old woman. She had no choice but to believe she would be.

But the moment did not come. The knife remained pressed against her skin but the old squaw was still.

Mary caught the scent of charred bitternut hickory in the warm summer breeze as it drifted into the tiny hut. Had it been just a few hours ago that she had eaten with the Indians, passing her bowl down the line for it to be filled and presented to the gods for their blessings before returning it to her? Ah, yes. It had happened for the past three days now...

For three days they had remained in this abandoned settlement. Three days of hard work, of repairing moccasins with bone needles, of plucking quail and duck, of skinning fish. Three days of washing clothes for all the squaws in the camp. Three days of combing the old squaw's hair, of learning to fashion it into braids just like the old woman wanted. Three days of cleaning their hut, of starting fires for their meals, of cooking and gathering food. Three days of enslavement.

And one day in which she was certain she would die.

She had been forced to dig a grave with her bare hands. Periodically, she would be instructed with jabs and gestures to lie prone in the grave; each time, she would pray fervently that the braves would not suddenly begin to toss earth on top of her and bury her alive. They had not, and whether they only wished to judge the size of the grave by measuring it against Mary's body, or whether they took sadistic glee in torturing her, she would never know.

It took her from sunup to sundown to dig the grave. She had neither food nor water. When she was finished, the Indians conducted a ceremony in which they buried Bear Claw.

Mary had been forced to sing over the grave. Not knowing what they wanted her to sing, she had broken into a rendition of Amazing Grace. She'd sung it long after the body was covered in mounds of soft dirt, and long after the others had retired to their beds.

Each day after that, she had been forced to sing again. She sang as she cooked and cleaned and went about her chores. She sang every song she could remember from the old church hymnal.

The children were gone. They had vanished with their Indian captors sometime during the second night. The young mother was only a shell now, her eyes distant and unseeing, her movements mechanized like the wheels in a grist mill: moving without feeling, existing but not living.

Mary heard a lone wolf howl in the distance. Oh, to be a wolf and free! she thought.

Then her heart stopped. No, it was not a wolf. She listened more intently. An owl hooted in the darkness, just beyond their room.

They were Indians, communicating with each other, just as they had when they'd been on the trail.

Mary peered through the darkness at Medicine Woman. Her head was cocked slightly as if she, too, were listening to them.

She felt her heart quicken. Could it be George and Sam? A search party come to rescue her? she thought.

Her mind raced. Did she dare cry out? It was obvious that the squaw was intent on silencing her; that was clear by her hand still pressed upon her mouth and the knife against her throat. That would have to mean that someone—someone other than an Indian—was afoot nearby, near enough for her screams to be heard.

She would have to risk it, even if it meant sure death. Better to die here in a struggle for freedom and within earshot of white men than to be tortured and killed in some Shawnee village.

She braced herself for the coming clash. Her hands were free, though Medicine Woman was still perched securely on her chest, bearing her full weight upon her.

She would grab the knife. Though it could slice through to the bone, the squaw would not be expecting her to grab the blade. Once she had it in her hand, she would not let go. She would continue to hold it until the old woman realized she had no other weapon and would be forced to let go.

But how to keep the squaw from crying out, from summoning the others in the tribe? she wondered.

Her cries could warn the people nearby, the very people she sought to keep Mary from alerting with her own voice.

On the count of three, Mary thought. She closed her eyes and prayed silently. Then she opened her eyes and focused on the old squaw's face, still cocked to one side. One... two...

A figure burst through the doorway, reaching them in a split second. Mary felt his presence even before she saw the shadow of broad shoulders, long flowing hair, and a single feather.

"Come," White Messenger said quickly. Medicine Woman was off Mary so hastily that she didn't know whether she'd been pulled off or had jumped off her.

Mary sat up, her hand instinctively moving to the area under her chin where the knife had pressed. It was damp with perspiration but she did not believe she was bleeding.

"Come," White Messenger said again, signaling rapidly for Mary to join them.

He reached the doorway in two quick steps. He stopped a brief moment, his head cocked as Medicine Woman's had been. Then he stepped through the doorway to the heavy night air.

Medicine Woman followed.

White Messenger said something to her in a hoarse whisper, something Mary did not understand. The old squaw began to run down the path toward the river.

As Mary stepped outside, White Messenger halted her.

"You are not bound," he said. "Your voice is not stilled. You can remain thus, and you will remain unbound."

Mary swallowed. "Yes."

"If you make any noise—*any noise*—I will bind you myself and you will wish you were dead. Do you understand?"

"Yes," she said shakily.

"Now go," he said with a shove. "To the river!"

Mary sprinted along the same path that Medicine Woman had taken, over roots that reached up from the ground and threatened to send her sprawling, over cockleburs and pine needles and the soft velvet touch of moss. She felt others running through the woods in front of her and behind her, all racing for what they must have felt was the safety of the water.

They reached the edge of the river. Without a word, the Indians were working in tandem to pack a large boat—one much larger than the canoes in which they had arrived.

Mary counted the Indians: five squaws, the same squaws who had been in her original group. And eleven braves. Eleven.

She tried to view their faces in the moonlight. Nine had been in their original group. Now there were two that Mary did not recognize—two who had not been part of their group at any time.

And where were the others? The young mother and her group?

White Messenger joined them and directed Mary to help them pack the boat. She busied herself with carrying sacks of cornmeal and meats wrapped in buckskin.

White Messenger approached the two braves she did not recognize and they broke away from the group. They spoke in hurried whispers. Mary strained to hear them, but she only caught a word here and there, words that meant nothing to her— Chillicothe, Spaylawitheepi, and Piqua.

Then she gasped, her feet frozen.

Daniel Boone.

She couldn't have imagined it. They spoke his name, followed by Sheltowee. Sheltowee, Mary thought. She'd heard that word before. Sheltowee. Then it dawned on her: at Fort Nashborough, Pa had been deep in conversation with other settlers as they recounted Boone's capture and adoption by Chief Blackfish. That was the name he had been given: Sheltowee. It meant Big Turtle in the Shawnee language, a detail that many of the frontiersman found both puzzling and humorous.

Was Daniel Boone at Chillicothe? Piqua? Spaylawitheepi?

She went back to loading the boat, afraid she would rouse suspicion. Spaylawitheepi was the water, the name of the river. Could he be here?

The boat was packed. One of the braves directed the small tribe into it. Mary found herself seated between two squaws on a sturdy wooden bench.

White Messenger broke away from the two strange braves and joined them, helping to push the boat away from shore. Then he jumped inside, grabbed a paddle, and helped to silently row the boat into the main current of the wide river.

Mary's thoughts were jumbled. A year or so ago, Boone had pursued his daughter's Indian captors. Could he be pursuing hers? Did this mean that George and Sam had reached Fort

Nashborough and had been successful at raising a search party? Boone should have been hundreds of miles away in a settlement called Boonesborough—but had he, by chance, been traveling through Fort Nashborough?

Her eyes fell on the squaw's lap beside her. The attractive young squaw sat silently, her hands folded in her lap. Mary realized her lap contained her bowl, the same bowl used at every meal. For some reason, that made her heart sink. She'd been roused and pushed along the path so quickly that she hadn't the time to gather her meager possessions. Her bowl, then, had been left beside the bed she'd made with old buckskin. Now even her bed was behind her.

She glanced down at her feet. Her shoes had been left as well. She was barefoot, her tender white flesh now unprotected against the harsh terrain.

She glanced behind her, yearning to go back, to gather her shoes, her bowl, and her buckskin. They had been all she owned besides the dirty tattered cotton dress she wore. And now even those were gone.

10

Jim poured a cup of coffee from a battered tin pot. It was black as pitch and strong enough to grow legs. He sipped the bitter brew as he stepped toward Colonel Clark's tent.

He needed the brew. He'd had a sleepless night. Every time a wolf howled or a twig snapped, he was wide awake. Though there were double sentries posted in anticipation of an Indian counterattack, his body remained at a heightened state of alert, his rifle within arm's reach and his boots at the ready.

The tent flap was open and as he neared, he heard voices from within. He stepped inside and hesitated for a brief moment while his eyes adjusted to the dim light.

"Jim," came a youthful voice.

He turned as a freckle-faced young man leaned toward him. Jim groaned inwardly. He knew he should have more patience with Tommy Buckingham. He was conscientious and honest, never complained, and would volunteer for just about anything. But he was a lieutenant—same rank as he—and Jim knew he hadn't earned it. He was as green as spring grass, totally untested in battle and he should have been a private were it not for his family connections.

"Tommy," Jim said before moving toward the center of the tent. To his chagrin, Tommy remained at his elbow.

Jim found a space where he could peer past shoulders to a map spread across a portable wooden table.

Clark's finger rested at Chillicothe. Jim recognized the Little Miami River snaking alongside the village; its powerful current would empty into the Ohio River, which stretched almost a thousand miles from east to west. He'd traveled much of the Ohio, from its beginnings at Fort Pitt past the Cumberland River roughly five hundred miles from where he now stood, all the way to the newly established Fort Jefferson at the Mississippi River. A beautiful river it was, and one of the widest he'd ever seen but it could be treacherous and unforgiving as well. The Shawnees referred to the Ohio as Spaylawitheepi, though he was never able to figure out why.

"The scouts report the Shawnees are massing on the bluffs at Piqua," Clark was saying, moving his finger northwest along the map.

"More than the Shawnees, Sir," Colonel Ben Logan interjected. "It's also the Delaware tribes, Wyandot, and Miami Indians."

"Do we know who is leading them?" Clark asked.

"Scouts tell me it's Chief Black Hoof, sir."

"Who is Black Hoof?" Tommy whispered, his face so close to Jim that his meager mustache brushed his ear.

"Shawnee. Mekoche division," Jim whispered curtly.

"Is he a savage?" Tommy asked, pressing closer.

He wished he would be quiet long enough for him to hear what Clark was saying. He half-turned to Tommy. "He's a Shawnee; they're all savages."

"Has he killed many white men?"

"He was with Blackfish at the siege of Boonesborough, and he was at Chillicothe when Boone fought here a year ago."

Tommy moved a half-step away. Jim noticed out of the corner of his eye that his face had grown a bit pale. Jim leaned toward him. "He's no fiercer than you or I."

Tommy nodded and Jim turned his attention to his commanders.

"Three units," Clark was saying. "I'll move due west across the prairie and engage them at Piqua. The cannon goes with me. Colonel Logan will cross the Mad River here and flank them."

He moved his finger to a point just northwest of their present location.

"A third unit will come around this way—" he moved his finger to the north "—through the hill country."

Jim leaned in closer.

"Lieutenant," Clark said, his eyes meeting Jim's. "You'll travel ahead of my unit; report back to me. You know the information I'll need."

"Yes, sir." Jim began edging his way to the tent flap.

"Oh," Clark said, "and Lieutenant Buckingham, go with him."

Jim stopped short and gaped at Clark. Moving ahead of the main army meant he would be engaged in the most dangerous assignment of the march: scouting for Indians. If they lay in ambush, it would be Jim who they would engage first. And now he was ordering him to babysit a greenhorn?

Clark had turned back to the map and was conferring with the others now.

Jim sighed and stepped outside, where Tommy immediately joined him.

"How far is Piqua?" Tommy asked excitedly.

Jim stopped at the coffee pot and poured another half cup of the black brew. "If I traveled alone, I'd reach it in short order. But with an army of close to a thousand men, this march is not without risk."

"What do you mean? What could happen?"

"Tommy, we need to find the best route for the unit. The cannon could easily bog down in the willow swamps."

"If it could bog down, why doesn't another unit take it?"

"Colonel Logan is crossing the river; that poses a different set of problems. And the hill country is heavily wooded. Anyway, we're going to need it when we fight them at Piqua." He paused. "Tommy, stay close to me, you hear? We'll be easy targets crossing the open prairie."

"But they don't know—"

"They know." He gestured toward the terrain just beyond the village. "They're out there now, watching us."

Tommy stared at the horizon, his eyes searching for any movement. But Jim knew they could be completely surrounded and they'd not even realize it until the Indians were ready to engage them in battle.

Someone shouted and the two men turned back toward camp. A private was shooing away the stray dog Jim had seen the day before. When the young man made a movement as though he was aiming to kick it, Jim shouted at him to stop.

"That's my dog," he bellowed, striding to the man's campfire. "I'd better never see you raise a hand or a foot to this dog again!"

"Yes, sir," the private mumbled. "I didn't know it was yours, sir."

"Well, now you do." Jim reached into the buckskin pouch he kept on his side. It was generally filled with jerky, food he used to sustain himself on long marches. He knelt down, holding a piece of jerky out to the dog.

It bowed its head and cautiously approached him. He did not make a movement to pet it. Instead, he remained perfectly still, the jerky extended well beyond his torso. As it gingerly took the jerky, he noted it was a female. When she'd finished eating, he held another piece to her, and then another.

"That's a good girl," he cooed.

The others were leaving the tent now, still deep in conversation. Reluctantly, Jim rose. Clark stopped a short distance from him and turned to the men near his right.

"Torch the village," he said. "Every building, every possession, no matter how small—I want it destroyed."

"The fields too, sir?"

Clark's eyes moved to the cornfields, the tall stalks shifting in a slight summer breeze. "Leave enough to feed us on our return trip," he said. "Burn the rest."

Jim slipped on his hat and started through the village to the hut he'd slept in the night before. He paused only long enough to return his meager possessions to his haversack: his shaving mirror, cup and razor; a well-worn Bible; a few yellowed papers with a goose feather quill pen and powdered ink Susannah had given to him when he'd gone off to fight. He paused before packing them; he'd meant to write a short note the previous night but had fallen asleep. It had been too long since he'd last written. Too long.

He'd received his mother's last letter months ago. He'd read it so many times, it had begun to fall apart along the folds. Someone else had asked for Susannah's hand in marriage.

He touched his mother's letter, almost succumbing to the temptation to read it again, but stopped himself. He'd waited too long, and now Susannah was betrothed to another man. Might have married him by now. She may even be heavy with his child. It was almost too much for a man to bear.

The sound of horses roused him from his thoughts and he shoved the rest of his things into the haversack, grabbed a blanket, his longrifle, shot, and powder, and headed outside. He was surprised to see the dog outside his hut. He bent to scratch her behind the ears and give her another piece of meat.

"You're the color of brandywine," he whispered, running his hand over her golden fur. Her ribs were clearly visible and her coat showed signs of injuries that had since healed—perhaps from long ago fights with other animals. He rose to his feet and patted his leg. "Come on, Girl," he said. "Come on, Brandy."

Tommy was waiting for him at the edge of the village, his own horse saddled up while Jim's waited for him. He quickly tacked his horse and then mounted it easily. Wordlessly, he turned toward the prairie, the smell of burning wood tickling his nostrils. He'd ridden out a short distance from the village before pausing to look back upon it once more. There were too many fires to count now. Every structure was ablaze, the flames reaching skyward as men fed them with a myriad of Indian possessions. The sky turned black behind him as he clicked his heels against the horse's belly, spurring him toward Piqua, Brandy running a short distance behind.

11

It was the moment just before dawn, when the sky was still black but the faintest of blue-gray began to appear on the horizon, when the Indians steered the large boat into the shallows. Mary peered ahead, trying to recognize the surrounding terrain.

They were at the mouth of the Cumberland River. Days before, they'd turned south on the Spaylawitheepi; now they were back. Her heart quickened as she wondered if they would start back on the Cumberland, if they perhaps would head southeast toward Fort Nashborough, bringing her closer to home.

All but one brave leapt off the boat and disappeared into the heavy woods. The squaws and the remaining brave remained still as statues. Mosquitoes converged, hungry for human blood, and while they did not appear to bother the Indians, they descended on Mary with a vengeance. She tried discreetly batting them, afraid to bring attention to her movements, but before long her feet, legs, and arms were covered in bites. They were even beginning to bore into her forehead, her cheeks, and her neck.

Finally, what sounded like early morning songbirds reached her ears. The brave responded in a perfect imitation of a whistling swallow-tailed kite.

With that, the brave used a paddle to push the boat away from shore. Without a word exchanged, three squaws assumed positions in the boat to help paddle and Mary was directed to join them. They stayed close to the shore, just outside of the reverse current but effectively concealed by the shadows.

They passed the mouth of the Cumberland and headed further north along the Spaylawitheepi. Despite herself, Mary turned to stare at the Cumberland until it was out of sight, her heart sinking deeper.

When she was a young girl, Ma would recite nursery rhymes to her. Mary often suspected many were conjured up at the spur of the moment, and now she felt her mind wandering to rhyming words. An idea hit her like the sudden glow of the sun breaking through storm clouds: she would memorize a poem to keep track of her journey. Remembering details and their sequence would be difficult without some sort of order, she reasoned. And what better order than a rhyme?

> *Mary Neely is my name,*
> *At the Salt Lick when they came;*
> *North on the Cumberland past the Fort,*
> *Joined at the Red River by additional escort.*
> *North on the Spaylawitheepi…*

The lone brave spoke to her, breaking her train of thought. She glanced at him, almost recoiling from the sight of her father's thick black hair hanging from the waist of his breechcloth.

He pointed to his chest and repeated the word. "Msipessi."

"Miss Pessi," Mary repeated.

"Msipessi!" he said louder, pointing to his chest more vehemently. "Big Cat! Msipessi!"

"Miss Pessi," she said, realizing he was telling her his name. Then she placed her hand over her chest. "Mary."

"Ma-ree," he repeated. Then he shook his head. "Nuc-kum-mo wie-skil-lo-tho."

"Mary," she said firmly.

"Nuc-kum-mo wie-skil-lo-tho," he corrected. "Song Bird. Nuc-kum-mo wie-skil-lo-tho."

They fell silent. The minutes passed by and the sun slowly rose, burning the dew off their clothes and skin and eventually burning Mary's chapped lips. It was going to be another scorching day. Her arms moved rhythmically, the paddle slicing through the water, placing them further and further from her home.

She looked at Msipessi as he navigated the boat northward. He glanced at her and smiled with even white teeth.

Mary was aghast. He still wore her father's scalp proudly. What was he doing now, attempting to win her admiration?

"Nuc-kum-mo wie-skil-lo-tho."

"Mary," she said sternly, her back stiffening. She didn't know what this savage had in mind, but she was determined it would not involve her.

The monotonous rowing was soon interrupted by a gaggle of geese. Mary peered upward, squinting to protect her eyes from the sun as she sought to spot them.

Msipessi laughed and returned a goose call.

Almost immediately, three fast moving canoes came into view behind them. Mary's blood went cold with terror. They were quickly surrounded by savage Indians, their bodies and faces covered with war paint in shades of red, orange, black and blue, the patterns causing their faces to appear grotesque.

As they sped past them, one turned to face her, his eyes meeting hers for a brief instant. Mary gasped as she recognized White Messenger.

Msipessi nodded in greeting to them and the squaws turned in unison to watch them as they slipped past. In another instant, they were gone, hidden by the shadows along the eastern shore.

Mary stared after them, their canoes blending in seamlessly with their surrounding terrain, the war paint appearing now like nothing more than forestation along the riverbank.

It was dusk when they stopped. Mary had rowed until she thought her arms would fall away from her shoulders. She had fallen in tandem with the squaws at first but as the hours crept past with no relief, she found it more difficult to keep pace. Still, she knew she could not be viewed as weak or lazy, and she struggled to keep up. When at last they slowed, she found herself still moving reflexively until Msipessi nudged her.

She turned her face toward the shore as a massive corn field came into view. The stalks were tall and majestic and appeared to wave at them as they approached.

Then dozens of Indians appeared, running past the fields to the river. There were bare-breasted women in skirts of deer hide, necklaces of multi-colored beads, their black hair straight and gleaming in the remnants of light. Naked children cried out with glee upon seeing the large boat, excitedly playing with sticks and home-made balls. Older boys stood ramrod straight with spears by their sides.

There aren't many braves, Mary thought as they reached the shore. She was directed to get out and through hand signals, she realized they wanted her to help secure the boat.

Then she was led along a path toward a great village, much larger than the one they had left early that morning and obviously still occupied by a large contingent of Indians.

In the center of the village was a long, straight building made of wood and covered in bark. At each end were large entrances. She figured hundreds of people could fit inside that structure and wondered what it was used for.

She was led past rounded bark huts, the stares of squaws and children boring into her back. One young squaw raced up to her and slapped her across the face. Mary sidestepped her, keeping her eyes cast downward, and hurried after her group as the woman screamed after her.

At last, she was shown where she and the others in her group—now numbering six excluding her—would stay. Through signals and broken English, she learned she would be responsible for unloading all of their possessions from the boat and carrying it to this hut.

While the squaws reconnected with others they apparently already knew, Mary busied herself with the task at hand. It was a long, arduous process, her arms and shoulders still sore and throbbing from the long hours of rowing. Though she spotted Msipessi's eyes on her periodically, watching her intently, no one came to her aid.

She smelled the sweet aroma of meat cooking. As she repeatedly passed by the campfires, she watched as cornmeal cakes were slapped into large iron pots and saw corn cobs cooking, still inside the shucks. Some women cracked walnuts, sampling them as they worked while others gathered blueberries. She kept herself moving with the thought of a good supper and a sound night's sleep. When at last she was finished, she wandered around the hut until she spotted her captors. They had gathered for their meal and were now seated in a large circle amidst some thirty others.

Cautiously, she made her way toward them until she was close enough to Medicine Woman for the old squaw to notice her. The squaw nodded briefly, almost imperceptively. Mary silently sat behind her.

There were three white women in the circle, garbed in deerskins, their hair pulled into braids in the Indian fashion. There was even a man; Mary didn't know why, but she thought he might be French. He certainly did not look like the settlers she was accustomed to seeing.

An ancient woman with white hair and skin the texture of a redfish sat at the head of the circle nearest the food. One by one, each person passed their bowl to her. One by one, she filled it with food, lifted the bowl, said a few words, and passed it back down the line.

When it came Mary's turn, Medicine Woman did not look at her. The squaw on the other side of Mary sent her bowl down the line, and the service continued without interruption.

She did not know quite what to do. Looking about, she did not see any bowls other than the ones currently being used. Was she to wait until they were all finished and eat the scraps?

She glanced sideways at Medicine Woman and then at the others. The Frenchman appeared to understand her quandary but he did nothing.

The aroma surrounded her. The chewing of lean meat, the devouring of fresh corn. The mingled odors of ripened blueberries, hot corn meal cakes… She waited but no one moved to serve her or share their food with her.

When their meals were finished, they chatted excitedly for an hour or more. Sometimes they rose from the circle and made their way down to the river, where she could see their outlines as they washed out their bowls. Medicine Woman finished eating and gave her bowl to Mary. Her sharp words and gestures could not be mistaken: Mary was to wash her bowl.

She walked down to the river and rinsed it out. Not even a blueberry skin had been left inside. Her eyes searched the water for any leftover food but found none. She finally walked back to the circle, where Medicine Woman took the bowl from her.

She was then ordered to sing.

The Indians, even the one who had slapped her earlier, appeared to enjoy her voice. And while she was reluctant to sing as tired and famished as she was, she began to hope they would enjoy her voice so much that they would feed her.

So she sang. She sang soulful songs and heavenly songs and put all of her emotion into every verse.

Then at last the old woman silenced her. She was ready to return to their hut. Mary and the other squaws in their group followed a few steps behind.

Once inside, the squaws settled down to sleep, each with their deerskin and bowls.

Mary lay on the hard earthen floor, her stomach growling ferociously. Was she to starve to death because she'd lost her bowl? She wondered. She tried to sleep despite her swollen arms and shrunken belly but she slept fitfully, dreaming of her cabin home and nursery rhymes.

12

There was an order in the village that, over time, began to feel comforting to Mary. Though she knew that escape was impossible, she gradually warmed to the conclusion she would not be killed or tortured.

Far from behaving like the savages she'd heard so much about—and witnessed at Neely's Salt Lick—they appeared to have a complex society in which every man, woman and child played a part.

The voluminous structure in the center of the village was a communal gathering spot that reminded Mary of a social hall. It was not a hastily built hut erected by a primitive people, but a carefully constructed wooden building that rivaled structures built by the settlers. It even had openings in the roof to allow for venting smoke from the campfires made within.

Mary was often sent there to perform duties such as building or stoking fires in the huge center pits, delivering food collected throughout the village, or sitting quietly by while Medicine Woman socialized with other elder squaws.

Surrounding this communal building were smaller, family-sized huts. They were rounded and covered in bark, some large enough for four adults to sleep comfortably.

Mary shared a hut with Medicine Woman. The old woman slept soundly through the night but expected Mary to be awake long before her to prepare a breakfast of fruits and corn cakes.

After the elder woman ate breakfast, she sometimes sent Mary to the corn fields to gather the crops with other white captives and squaws. The corn was ripe now, ready to be picked and eaten, the stalks at their height of maturity.

The female children often joined them, but the male children spent their days throwing spears, hunting, and engaging in mock combat. There were a handful of elder chieftains in the village, the only adult males except a few Frenchmen who appeared to come and go as they pleased.

Mary joined the villagers at mealtimes, but only to serve Medicine Woman when the elder woman desired her. She was ashamed now of having left her bowl, a shame she felt mirrored in the faces of those who knew of her grievous mistake. She was never fed with the others. She learned if she were to keep from starving, she would have to scavenge for food. Sometimes, it was handfuls of berries while she was out gathering food for the others. Sometimes, it was leftover bits of cornmeal or hard kernels of corn. If she was lucky, she would find herself alone with the meats and would slip a few morsels in her mouth. She didn't know if the Indians would consider any of this stealing, but as the days passed on, she came to the realization they would have to know she was eating something; otherwise, she would have dropped from hunger by now.

The days were stifling. The heat was sometimes so unbearable that she longed for the shade; the air so still that she yearned for a breeze, however slight. Her arms, once pale and covered with barely perceptible white hairs, were now bronzing; her hands were now calloused, the nails broken. The soles of her feet, having been without shoes since leaving the abandoned village, had begun to harden with a thick crust.

She'd seen the young mother only once since arriving at this village. Her eyes had been distant and her face blank, as if her soul were far away. She sported bruises on her exposed arms and legs and from the painful way in which she walked Mary wondered if she'd been beaten across her back and spine. She longed to do something for her, but she was unable to even catch her eye to offer an encouraging smile.

Mary hunched over an open fire now near the center of the village, stirring a pot of water in which vegetables were boiling. She turned to put the hot sun behind her, almost bumping into Medicine Woman. The squaw had come up behind her as silently as a cat. It was a behavior that all the Indians appeared to possess and which Mary found disconcerting.

"Come," Medicine Woman said, beckoning to her.

Mary set her stirring stick on the ground a safe distance from the flames and followed the old woman to the northeast quadrant of the village. It was here that the Frenchmen congregated, and here where one of them operated a large trading post.

It was located close to the Spaylawitheepi River. Unlike the round structures of the Shawnees, this one was rectangular with a roof similar to those built by the settlers. Three sides were open, offering an unobstructed display of pelts, blankets, materials, whiskey, jewelry, and other assortments of goods.

A trail led from the building to the water's edge, leading Mary to believe Indians and traders frequented the post, often arriving by boat. A tall, thin Frenchman ran the establishment along with his Shawnee squaw.

Medicine Woman entered the building with Mary close on her heels. She pushed past the jewelry, appeared slightly disgusted at the presence of whiskey, and stopped only when she had reached a heap of pelts.

Medicine Woman spoke to the Frenchman but Mary did not understand her words. She gestured toward the pelts as she spoke, and the two rummaged through them until they located a heavy moose skin.

They appeared to bargain for it, the old woman almost leaving at one point, her chin high and proud. Then they must have settled, for she returned and nodded.

The Frenchman peered at Mary for a long moment. Then he turned to her and said in a heavily accented voice, "You are to make moccasins for Medicine Woman."

"You speak English?" Mary said, her voice barely above a whisper.

The Frenchman did not answer but pulled a tape measure off his bony shoulders and bent to measure Medicine Woman's feet. He clucked before standing and nodding to the old woman.

She turned to go and Mary started after her.

"Not you," the Frenchman called out. "You stay here with me."

Mary hesitated, but Medicine Woman continued to walk away without beckoning for her to follow. She turned back to the Frenchman and repeated, "You speak English?"

"*Oui.* A little."

He retrieved several small pelts. "You will make several pair of moccasins for Medicine Woman."

"I've never made moccasins before."

He gestured toward his squaw, who watched her intently from the corner of the trading post. "Brown Owl will show you how."

He shoved the skin into Mary's arms, followed by a spindle of strong brown sinew and a sharp but thin bone needle. She carried them to a chair beside Brown Owl, who waited patiently.

Brown Owl wordlessly motioned for her to sit beside her. She measured out two pieces, one smaller than the other, and marked them with a quill dipped in ink. Retrieving a small knife, she gestured for Mary to cut the pieces.

"Where am I?" Mary asked as she cut, peering upwards at Brown Owl.

The squaw did not answer but glanced at the Frenchman.

"Where is the Spaylawitheepi?" she said, turning slightly toward the Frenchman.

The Frenchman pointed to the water just beyond the trading post. "That is the Ohio River," he said.

"The Ohio?" Mary felt her emotions churn with the recognition of the name and the realization she was much further north than she had ever imagined. "And this place? What is it called?"

"Shawneetown," he answered. "And I am Pierre Pierpont. They call you Songbird. What is your English name?"

"Mary. Mary Neely."

"Where did you come from? Where were you captured?" He leaned toward her, his eyes narrowed.

"Neely's Salt Lick." When he didn't appear to recognize the name, she added, "Fort Nashborough."

He clucked and rubbed his pointed chin thoughtfully, displaying his bony profile with its large beak of a nose. "Ah, yes."

"You know the place?"

"I know of it. I have never been there."

"How far am I—?"

He shrugged. "I do not know. But it matters not."

She wanted to tell him that it did matter, that she would have to know in order to get back home. She wanted to ask him to help her—but instead she bit her lip and resisted the temptation until it threatened to turn her inside out. He was married to a squaw; he lived in this Shawnee village. The Indians trusted him. Therefore, she could not.

The squaw directed her to cut many pieces from the large skin, which was thicker than deerskin. She worked in silence for awhile and then asked, "What is to become of me?"

"You belong to Medicine Woman and her family. It is up to them to decide."

"Is this their home?"

He shook his head. "They are but travelers through here, as many are."

"Then where do they—?"

"North. That is all I know."

"Will they kill me?" she asked.

"Only if you deserve it."

She swallowed hard. When she had finished cutting the pieces, the squaw showed her how to sew two pieces together to form a slipper, the rough side out and the smooth side inward, against the skin. The skin was heavy and it was difficult to push the needle through it. Her fingers began to ache as she sewed one piece after another. Medicine Woman must be planning on doing a lot of walking, she thought warily.

It was late in the day when she finished and rose to leave.

"You will remember my name?" she said quietly to Monsieur Pierpont. "In case—in case anyone comes looking for me?"

He nodded but his eyes were veiled. "I will remember."

As she passed the merchandise, he stepped in front of her, blocking her way. He fingered a blanket close by. "Pretty, oui?"

"I have no money."

"Ah, but we could barter." He grinned, revealing long, yellowed teeth.

"Medicine Woman does not allow me to barter," she said, pushing past him.

"Ah, but she would not have to know…"

"She would know. Nothing escapes her."

"Not even you, *mon joli*," he said, cackling.

Mary stopped at the edge of the trading post. "Where are all the men? The warriors?"

He stopped laughing and glared at her for a long moment. "They will be back soon," he said. "And with plenty of white men's scalps. They are gathering for war against your people, even as we speak."

13

The waiting was always one of the worst things about war, Jim thought as he surveyed the village of Piqua through his telescope. But wasn't that what every army does: hurry up and wait. Forced marches through inhospitable land, covering distances in a span of time one would think is not humanly possible, and then wait through excruciatingly slow periods while the top ranks conferred.

It was the waiting he hated most. With the idle time, his mind always wandered to Susannah, her wide green eyes, and her golden curls. Oh, what he wouldn't give to hold her in his arms again, to profess his love for her, to marry her! And one day, when they had successfully defeated both the Indians and the British, he would bring her here, where they would build a cabin in full view of the water...

Reluctantly, he forced himself to turn his attention back to the present. Since leaving Chillicothe, they'd arrived at a prairie that left them too vulnerable to a surprise attack. To make matters worse, the cannon had become mired in mud so many times that more than one man could be heard swearing as if it were an uncooperative mule. Men were forced to dismount their horses and walk alongside them, lest they too sink shin-deep in mud. The gnats and horse flies were particularly aggressive, the flies leaving large red welts and circling the men's and animals' heads until the entire army appeared to be swatting at them.

Jim had long ago lost sight of the other two units as they separated outside Chillicothe to form the flanks. He'd ridden out ahead of Colonel Clark's unit, scouring the countryside for signs of Indians. Everywhere he went, he felt their eyes boring into him. Everywhere, he felt one prayer away from an arrow through his heart or a tomahawk in his skull.

He moved like an Indian himself, dismounting his horse at times to weave through the prairie en route to an area that rose above the others. Once there, he could survey the land, his expert eyes watching every movement, every blade of tall, wheat-colored grass as it swayed in the wind, every flapping of every bird that circled overhead. He watched Brandy race after butterflies, judging her behavior to help determine if there were Indians hiding in the tall grasses. She never ranged far from his horse, always circling back around to rejoin him.

The prairie itself was perhaps three miles long and one mile wide. It might have been a lake at one time; now it was dried up and the bottom vegetation had conquered it, making it appear as if it was land. But as the men and animals marched across it, it seemed destined to swallow them up in quagmires that couldn't be seen through the thick undergrowth until they were knee-deep and sinking fast.

The army was noisy enough to wake the dead, he thought wryly. But there was nothing to be done about it. Three hundred men made a lot of noise; there was just no getting around that. Add a few wagons and horses and that blasted cannon, and one could hear them approaching for miles around.

Now they converged upon Piqua, the units separating into companies and the companies into platoons. Here, they would mount a frontal assault against the Shawnees and their allies.

Through his telescope, he scoured the village of Piqua among the bluffs and followed the river as it snaked through the valley. Indians were stealthy, silent as a cloud. Unlike the Army, hundreds could move along the river and across this prairie with less noise than a field mouse.

"There's Colonel Logan," Tommy said, breaking his train of thought.

Jim shifted his telescope and watched them move with as much difficulty across the Mad River as Clark's unit had experienced moving across the prairie.

He turned toward the northwest, where the river disappeared into a forest thick enough to block out all light. Though he couldn't see them, he knew the third unit, under the command of Colonel Lynn, was converging along the wood line, waiting for the signal to attack.

Clark's unit still had a willow swamp left to cross, ending at a limestone cliff. Atop that cliff was the Shawnee village of Piqua, claimed by some to be the Shawnee capital. It was built after the fashion of a French village, not surprising since the French were often living amongst them. Rounded wigwams stretched for miles along the river as it wound high into the cliffs, the village separating into lower and upper sections, the lower section defended by a stockade fort not unlike those the settlers customarily built.

Some said the residents routinely numbered three hundred, but at times like these when battles are imminent, the message is carried on the wind and the ranks could swell to several thousand.

And when the sun set this evening, this village and all it represented would be conquered.

As Clark's unit neared, Jim spurred his horse onward, skirting the unit while he searched for ambushes and Indian spies. Not that they needed spies on the ground here, he surmised with a wary eye on Piqua. From the crown of the village, the Shawnees—and no doubt the British who would be there to help fight—could easily watch the Continental Army massing.

The cannon was at last stopped and set in place. The minutes ticked past. Jim squinted at the sun high overhead, bathing the earth in a sweltering heat; it was mid-afternoon.

The three units formed a U-shape around Piqua, with pack mules between them. The remaining side consisted of a rounded hill behind the village. Clark did not wait until the other units were completely in place before ordering the artillery bombardment to begin.

The six-pounder crashed into the limestone cliff, crumbling a piece in clouds of white dust that rose like powder.

Jim reached a good vantage point well out of range of any Indian defenses and pulled in the reins. Brandy whimpered beside him as Tommy pulled up alongside.

They both peered through their telescopes. Then after a long moment, Jim said under his breath, "Well, I'll be."

"What? What is it?" Tommy said excitedly.

"They're lining up like redcoats."

"Who? The savages?"

Jim rested his telescope on his knee. "Yep. Looks like ole Henry Bird's been busy training the Indians. Maybe he thinks he can turn 'em into Tories."

Behind him, he caught sight of a multitude of company flags being raised. He grinned. Clark was at it again. He'd used the same ploy on Hamilton in Vincennes, and to this day Hamilton was not the wiser for it: Clark had more company flags than he had companies. And he would use those flags to convince the enemy that his forces were three or four times what it really was. Even the mules had flags mounted to their packs.

It was impressive, Jim had to admit. Seeing all those flags flying at intervals that could easily be swollen with the ranks of three thousand, when they actually had a thousand. And that was more men than they'd ever had before. Barely one of five was an Army regular; the rest were settlers, called to arms to put down the Shawnees. And when they were successful—and he knew they would be—those settlers would go home to their families and their crops, while the Army would retire to fight another day.

But for now, the settlers were spread throughout the ranks of the regulars: men like Daniel Boone ready to fight side by side with frontiersmen defending their wives, their sisters, and their children—men like James Drake, George Spears and Sam Neely.

They lined up with the determination of men who knew if they were unsuccessful the Indians would perform unspeakable acts upon their families. Failure was not an option. They were ready to fight to the death with any weapon they owned. Many of them had bayonets, but every man Jim knew would rather be hit with black powder and shot than be run through with a bayonet.

Yet when they overran Piqua, it would be the bayonets they would have to fight with. It would be impossible once they got off that first round to reload in hand-to-hand combat.

He felt his blood begin to pump faster as he considered the inevitable hand-to-hand combat. He watched the cannon continue to fire, his horse pawing the ground with the same impatience Jim felt inside. Even Brandy's ears were pricked up now, her attention riveted on Piqua.

He was ready to be done with it. Yes, charge across that willow swamp and climb that blasted cliff and leap into Piqua with a longrifle in one hand and a pistol in the other and a knife at the ready.

Yes, waiting was one of the worst things about war. No doubt about it.

Colonel Lynn's men were the first to fire. They were lined up three ranks deep: like a well-oiled machine, the first line fired volleys in unison. When those stooped to reload, the next line would fire their volley, and then the third. Their efforts were met with return fire in exactly the same manner. Jim squinted through the telescope as if he could clear the air of the thick smoke that circled the village, marveling over the savages who lined up like British soldiers.

He wondered if Simon Girty would be amongst them and hoped he would be. He would like nothing better than to wrap his hands around that white savage's neck and provide him with a slow, painful death. Girty was legendary: once an Indian captive himself, he was now a leader amongst the Mingo Indians and rumored to be more ruthless and bloodthirsty than all the Indians put together. His savagery was directed not at the Indians, however, but toward his own kind, something Jim thought was unforgivable.

Now there were cries mingled with weapons fire: the shouts of white men directing the attack, the war cries of Indians, and the screams of both red and white men struck down.

And now the center unit had joined in the fire under Clark's command, followed very quickly by Logan's unit. They had completed the U-shape with a solid firing, squeezing the Indians against the rounded hilltop.

There was no cannon in Piqua, of that he was certain. Smoke and flames erupted from within the village, and when Jim studied the scene through his telescope, he saw people running—some in an attempt to put out the fires and others attempting to flee them.

The resulting steady stream of fire was having an effect: the Indians were retreating. Jim could see the far side of Piqua; against the rounded hill covered in trees, the Indians raced through the woods in an attempt to escape.

"So much for their bravery," Jim said as much to himself as to Tommy. "Get over to Colonel Logan," he said louder. "He'll want men to cut off their retreat."

Tommy spurred his horse, frantically racing toward Logan.

As the fire intensified, Jim watched the Indians cease fire and begin to run. He tried to see what path they were taking to escape the attack, but he lost them in the tall willows and reeds that grew in the open areas.

He turned his telescope on Tommy as he conferred Jim's message to the Colonel. Immediately, Logan dispatched two officers, who in turn sent the orders to bring up the reserve. They began the march toward Buck Creek, where they could cut off the retreat.

There would be no captives. Jim knew that once Logan's men had converged upon Buck Creek, they would massacre the Indians as they fled.

The hours stretched on. In a battle, one minute can seem like an eternity. An hour can resemble hell.

Jim had joined other scouts in fanning further away from the attacking army on their search for Indians regrouping and planning a counter offensive. But as they circled the miles surrounding Piqua, they saw only signs of escapees: a tattered piece of red cloth snagged on tree branches, a British pocket knife along a jagged path cut through the rocks, the blade of a tomahawk whose hafting eye was broken. He stopped his horse and peered at a ground smooth from the soles of hundreds of fleeing moccasins, from which a single silver tinkling cone poked out of the ground.

Colonel Logan's men were in pursuit in a desperate attempt to cut off the only means of escape. But as the hours wore on and Jim continued to stop periodically and peer through his telescope to the village, he wondered if there would be anyone left to stop. The small arms fire had dwindled now, and the cannon below was silenced.

He turned his horse to face the militia. They were regrouping for a final assault on Piqua.

14

The morning sun rose with the promise of another blistering day. The first rays of light found Piqua still smoldering from the previous day's fighting, though the firing had ceased by nightfall. The stench of gunpowder still hung in the air like some oppressive ghost.

Colonel Logan's troops had circled Piqua at Buck Creek but from Jim's assessment as he scouted the terrain, they might have arrived too late to stop the fleeing enemy.

He nodded now to the sentries as he made his way back to Colonel Clark's unit, which remained situated in their frontal position, though many of the troops had been pulled back to terrain safe from stray gunfire. His horse was in dire need of rest. Jim had ridden much of Piqua's perimeter in ever-increasing circles overnight, but there were no Indians to be found—just growing signs of a retreat.

Jim brushed his cheek with the back of his hand as he neared Clark's troops, barely noticing the stubble that was beginning to erupt. He stifled the urge to slump in the saddle; the adrenaline that had kept him going all night was almost spent.

"Colonel," he said as he reached Clark.

"What news have you?" Clark said as Jim dismounted.

Jim grabbed a stick and drew a circle in the dust. "Piqua," he said. He then drew a jagged line to the northeast of their present position. "It's a footpath; the only way to reach the village on this side. Cuts through the hills and that cliff yonder—" he pointed to an impenetrable-looking limestone cliff that showed no visible evidence of a footpath. "Single file, all the way."

"Passable?"

Jim nodded. "I put some men on it during the night. Checked with them just a short while ago. No sign of the enemy."

They turned and studied it. "They couldn't retreat in that direction," Clark said. "Once they reached the bottom, they'd have to pass through our lines to escape."

"Yes, sir."

"Can our horses make it?"

"They'll have to. Once we're up there, we might find we'll need 'em."

Clark's eyes didn't waver from the cliffs. "And Logan? How's he doing?"

"He deployed men to Buck Creek."

"Captives?"

Jim shook his head. "None. Looks like the Indians might have escaped during the night before he got his men in place." He drew another line in the sandy soil. "There's a creek back here; I think the Indians might have taken that route."

Clark swore under his breath. Then he said, "How many do you reckon are still at Piqua?"

Jim watched the smoke rise from the village. "Could be an ambush," he said thoughtfully. "But I don't think so. I think they've turned tail and run."

Clark signaled one of his aide-de-camps. "Get word to Colonels Lynn and Logan; my men are going up that cliff to Piqua. When we're clear, we'll raise the flag, as usual."

"Yes, sir," the man answered. "And their orders, sir?"

"Have Logan secure the outer perimeter. Shoot any who attempt to escape. Lynn's men are to remain in reserve."

"Yes, sir."

"Well, Lieutenant," Clark said as the aide hurried off, "you look like you're in mighty need of a rest."

"If it's all the same to you, sir, I'd like to go ahead of your troops up that cliff."

Clark nodded. "You have my permission." He turned to leave but then turned back to Jim. "Where's Lieutenant Buckingham?"

"Base of that cliff, sir. He's in charge of the men securing the footpath."

Clark nodded. He then sighed deeply, and Jim wondered what he might have been thinking as he surveyed the limestone cliff. As he strode to the officers waiting for his orders, Jim mounted his horse and trotted across the willow swamps, Brandy running just ahead of him. Sleep would have to wait.

Jim emerged from the footpath to find himself at the lower section of the village. As the first white man through, his blood was hot and his trigger finger ready; all the Indians or the British would have to do is wait just on the other side and pick them off one at a time as they rode through the narrow opening.

But there had been no ambush. No Indians ready to cut them off at the rear and trap them within the steep limestone walls; no stragglers still remaining to fight another day.

He stopped at a vantage point high above the surrounding terrain and peered down. A steady stream of men were converging at the base of the cliff, surrounded by sentries ready to protect their movements as they disappeared between the stone walls. Occasionally, he saw a head pop up as it rounded a bend; now and then, a hand steadying itself against the cliffs as they navigated the steep climb.

The second man through was Tommy and the third was Clark. They joined him in studying the ground below.

"This is a good position," Clark said. "If the tables had been turned, I would not have given this ground."

"But we know what the Shawnee are made of," Jim said. "They engage in surprise attacks on our women and children. They won't stand and fight like men."

As a flag-bearer entered the lower village, Clark directed him to raise the flag.

"But we haven't reached the upper village yet," Tommy protested to Jim.

"The others will know we've reached this point," Jim said. "Another flag will be raised when we reach the top."

As they wound their way through the lower village, Clark said, "Have the men search every structure here. I don't want a blade of grass unturned. No captives. Shoot anyone they find."

Jim nodded to Tommy.

"Yes, sir," Tommy said as he spurred his horse toward the others and repeated the orders before rejoining them.

"You men," Clark said, motioning toward a group of a dozen men, "come with me."

Jim caught a glimpse of Brandy devouring charred meat that had been cooking over a long-extinguished fire. As she dragged it into the tall grasses, he noted with a half-smile that it was about as big as she and he hoped their raids would serve to fatten her belly. Then he joined the group as they ascended to the upper village.

A few Indians lay strewn throughout the village, their bodies in pools of dark red blood, their eyes open but unseeing. Some of the men reached from their saddles and sliced their scalps in deft movements. Then without even dismounting, they slung the scalps over their saddles and continued the ascent.

Tommy started to protest but Jim interrupted him. "That won't be the last violation to which these bodies will be subjected," he said.

"But that just ain't right," Tommy said defiantly.

"The Shawnees believe when bodies are defiled, they'll spend eternity like that. Anybody wise to the Indians will take advantage of their superstitions."

"And do what?" he demanded.

"You really want to know?"

Tommy sat straight. "I do."

Jim swung his horse around and eased closer to the young greenhorn. "For starters, they'll chop off their legs and arms."

"That's disgusting!"

"Maybe even their heads. That way, a torso will go to the everafter not even knowing who he is."

"That ain't Christian," Tommy said, his chin jutting out.

"We're not dealing with Christians. And I'm pretty sure Christ wouldn't care for all the killing, either. But that's war."

Before Tommy could respond, Jim wheeled his horse around and joined the group as they reached the upper village. It was deserted. Many of the wigwams were burned or smoldering; bits and pieces of clay pots, British-made weapons and possessions were strewn helter-skelter.

A larger group followed them, fanning out to check every building. As bodies were encountered, they were rolled over or examined for signs of life. Jim noticed Tommy turning his head in disgust as many of the men continued to scalp the dead.

There was a knoll just ahead that would provide a good vantage point for overseeing the surrounding area. Jim strolled his horse toward it, the long hours without sleep beginning to catch up to him.

As he reached the knoll, the brush parted and a man rushed forward. As Jim reached instinctively for his longrifle, his brain registered the half-naked body smeared with war paint, the head shaved except for a single red topknot, and the grimy arms that reached in front of him as he stumbled forward.

"No!"

The voices were simultaneous: Jim's filled the air even as he recognized Clark's voice behind him. But they were both drowned out by a volley of gunfire.

The man bounced backward as if struck by a tree trunk, then stumbled forward before sinking to his knees. He knelt for only a second or two before crumpling to the ground.

Jim jumped from his horse, catching a glimpse of Tommy in his peripheral vision, his longrifle still raised and pointed at the man. Jim pushed the barrel toward the sky. "No more!" he exclaimed.

"He was gonna kill you!"

"He's white and he's unarmed!"

The blood drained out of Tommy's face as he turned back toward the man. Clark was racing toward him now and was the first to reach him.

Jim rushed to his side.

"Don't shoot," the man whispered. "I'm a white man!"

"Joe," Clark cried out, kneeling beside him and taking his head in his hands. "We've been looking for you!"

"Get the doctor!" Jim shouted at the men behind him. Then he pulled off his belt and knelt beside him. He wrapped the belt around Joseph Rogers' bicep and squeezed hard to stop the massive flow of blood from a gaping wound in his arm while Clark pushed his hands onto Joe's chest to stop the blood from rushing out every time his heart beat.

"Joe, you're safe now," Clark was saying. "You're safe. We're going to take you home."

"I—I knew you'd come," he said in a drawl that was barely audible.

"Hang on, Joe. The doctor's coming."

"You're not hurt that bad," Jim lied. "You'll be patched up in no time."

Joe stared at Clark, his light eyes glassy. "I knew you'd come," he whispered. The blood eased out of the corners of his mouth and his breath was raspy and then gone.

Clark bent his head over his cousin, a single tear falling on the war paint and smearing it across his face. Then another tear fell, followed by another.

Jim stepped back as the doctor reached them. He walked back to the men, his heart feeling as if the weight of the world was pressing upon him.

"I didn't know—" Tommy said weakly.

"You weren't the only one who shot him," Jim said. He pointed to the others. "Better get back to work," he said. "Get another flag up, and get back to checking those buildings."

He led his horse away but turned back when he was a decent distance from them. The doctor was walking away, shaking his head, while Clark's shoulders slumped, his hands still cradling his cousin.

15

Mary crouched at the water's edge under the glare of the scorching sun. She rubbed her hands together in the fast-moving water in a futile attempt to rid them of the grime that was ever-pervasive. Then she cupped her hands until they were filled with the cold river water and drank heartily. She allowed the water to run down her chin and neck, and she rubbed her wet palms across her face. She wondered what she must look like. She tried to run her fingers through her hair but it was too matted.

She hadn't seen the braves in several days and wondered, as she so often did, when they would return. She pondered which direction they might have traveled, wondering whether they had returned to the Cumberlands and if they might at this moment be engaged in battle with the settlers there.

She peered over her shoulder at the Shawnee village. There was the same monotonous routine as every other day: rising with the dawn, cooking meals, sewing moccasins and clothes, and preparing for the fall and winter while food was abundant. For the Indians, the evenings were filled with a hearty supper followed by hours of relaxation while the children played in the dusk and the captives cleaned the heavy pots and readied the cookware for the following day. Medicine Woman had given her plenty in which to fill her days but not enough to keep her mind from wandering to escape.

And escape she would.

She had not been physically abused, as she knew other captives had been. The worst she had feared in the comfort of her Cumberland home had happened, and she had survived. But she was an outcast, living on the periphery of the Indian civilization, balanced precariously between the white world she longed to return to and the red world in which she unwillingly found herself bound.

Medicine Woman did not allow her to take meals with the tribe so she was forced to eat alone. Though she knew logically that losing her bowl had been part of an event outside her control, she found herself fighting a rising guilt that was reinforced every day she was forced to scrounge around the village and outer perimeter searching for food. In the process, though, she began to keep mental notes of available food that would help her during her escape southward.

The Indians apparently were not concerned with her wandering, so long as she reappeared at intervals throughout the day. On one trek, she found wild grapes a short distance from the village. After getting her fill, she created a spot in which to lay them in the sun to dry. They were small enough and portable enough to travel with, hopefully providing energy for the long trip ahead. She returned every other day or so to check on them; once as dusk was settling, she found a raccoon amongst them. After scaring him away, she had to forage for more grapes to replace those lost.

She worked each day in the corn fields, helping harvest the sweet corn that was ripe for the picking. When her captors weren't looking, she managed to hide one small ear at a time. Later she would sneak from the village and hide the corn in the trunk of a decaying tree near her grapes. She would cover the small opening with hanging moss and leaves; from a distance, one would never be able to find it.

She once found a sweet potato, which she savored for hours. She ate it raw and it later made her sick to her stomach, but it was something in her belly when she needed it most. The experience taught her to forage deeply, turning over old leaves to get to the soil. She never found another one, but now the hope was there.

She learned the Shawnees were adept at drying and smoking meats. Though they were still in the long, hot days of summer, they appeared to be preparing for a long winter ahead. The meats they'd brought back from their journey were systematically skinned and the flesh quartered and further divided. Much of the meats were smoked for long periods of time in specially built huts. Then they were dried and cooked into jerky, a ten-pound slab reduced to a few ounces of tough meat that could wiggle teeth away from the gums.

As she helped Medicine Woman and the squaws in her immediate clan prepare for the winter, she kept an eye toward planning her own journey. She could escape with her grapes, jerky, and corn. She felt certain she would find additional food along the way.

The time was getting closer. She knew she had to leave before the braves returned; it was a simple matter of mathematics. With only the squaws and children and occasional male present, she ran less risk of being tracked down and returned to the village. Once the braves arrived, there would be double the number of inhabitants here. The braves were the ones who roamed far from home during their hunting expeditions. She had to leave while they were miles away and the hills around her deserted.

But she still did not know where the men had gone or which route they would take coming back. And she knew her journey would be over rough terrain, traveling in hostile country for hundreds of miles, and with every day that passed, she would run the risk of being recaptured—perhaps by a family that would be less civil to her.

She sighed heavily. The singsong voices of two squaws floated on the air. She longed for the sound of her own language. Now that White Messenger was gone, there was no one she could talk to except the Frenchman. Though nothing had happened out of the ordinary, there was something about him she couldn't quite put her finger on, something sinister, and she found herself keeping distance between them.

She washed her feet in the river, pulling her tattered skirt higher as she waded in. Her feet were cut and bruised and the soles were red and beefy. She knew they would pose a challenge in her long journey. She would have to have shoes, or at least moccasins.

She planned her movements carefully. The moon was becoming a thinner crescent each night. There would soon be a new moon unable to shed light on the ground below. And on that night, she would escape. She would do it when the rest of the tribe was busy eating their night meal; since she took her meals alone, they shouldn't miss her. They would assume she was foraging for her own food.

Her first goal was simply to reach the abandoned village up river. Entering the water but remaining close to shore, the countercurrent would help to pull her upstream to the abandoned village where she'd left her shoes. Once there, she would scavenge the village, locating anything else that could be of use to her in her long trip home.

Then leaving that village, she would travel at night and sleep during the day. She would use the river to navigate. She didn't know how she would cross the wide expanses but she was a strong swimmer and she would manage. She might even find a canoe that would help in her travels.

Mary didn't know if she would be able to reach Fort Nashborough by herself, but her goal was much simpler: to reach a white settlement. Once she was back with her own kind, finding her family and her way home would be easier.

The sun was beginning to set, and she waded back to shore and sat at the edge of the river. The sky was a brilliant red, heralding good weather ahead.

So her plan was set. When the moon was all but gone, she would make her escape.

16

Jim Hawkins watched as George Spears strolled through Piqua, stopping when he encountered each man and chatting for a brief moment. He'd seen it too many times before—men searching for a wife, a sister, or children. But this time it was more painful; this time, it had happened to someone he knew.

George's father, Old Man Spears, owned the farm adjacent to the Hawkins' land. He was a German immigrant fiercely loyal to the Colonists; when the war broke out, he became a wagon driver for the Virginia militia, helping to keep the supplies flowing to the troops. He and his wife Christeenah had ten children— five girls and five boys. The oldest was Elizabeth, who was almost twenty-five and the youngest, David, was born right about the time Jim left home three years ago. George was barely seventeen, the same age as Jim's younger brother, Teddy.

"Who's he looking for?"

The voice interrupted Jim's thoughts and he turned to face Colonel Clark, who was busy pulling a slab of bear meat off a spit.

"Young lady by the name of Mary Neely," Jim said. "She was captured at Neely's Salt Lick, near Mansker's Station and Fort Nashborough."

"You know this young man?" Clark asked curiously.

"Yes, sir," Jim said. "I reckon it shows?"

"There's a bit of melancholy about you... What happened?"

"George is a neighbor from back home," he said. "He tells me he went to Fort Nashborough with his older brother Jacob. They're in love with two sisters who used to live near us in Virginia. Their family moved west not more than a year ago. Anyways, the way George tells it, a group of men from Mansker's Station were hunting, and Mary and her pa came along with them to work at their salt lick.

"George said they begged them to return to Mansker's Station with them, but they wanted to finish the job they'd started and return the following day. When they didn't come back, they mounted a search party and went back to Neely's Salt Lick." Jim hesitated before continuing. It was still hard to believe William Neely was dead. His voice choked when he continued, and he cleared his throat as though it had only been a cough. "Mr. Neely was dead—shot through and scalped. Mary was missing."

"How long ago?"

"About ten days."

"They could be at Fort Detroit by now," Clark said, "If she's still alive."

Jim looked away.

Clark grunted and looked toward the north, the meat hanging precariously over the side of his tin plate. "We'll get there yet," he said, his blue eyes narrowed.

"That we will," Jim said with resolve. "We'll have those redcoats swimming back to England."

Clark took a hefty bite of the meat and wiped the corner of his mouth. "Any sign of 'em around here?"

"They've scattered. Some no doubt are heading back to Fort Detroit. The Shawnees are headed west, deeper into Indian country." Jim walked to the edge of the village a few paces from the campfire. He heard Clark behind him, chewing as he walked.

"And the dead and wounded?"

"Seventeen of our men were killed. God rest their souls."

Clark waited a moment before asking, "And the Indians? Brits?"

"About the same."

"Captives?"

"Squaws. Children. Possibly one or two warriors."

Clark nodded thoughtfully.

Jim thought it best not to ask about the women's and children's fate. He would find out, in due time. Whatever their fate was to be, it would not be the savage treatment the Shawnees directed upon the settlers' families.

They stood in silence. Below them stood most of Piqua. British and Indian possessions were strewn throughout the village; those the men did not choose to take with them were broken, burned, or smashed. Clark's instructions had been clear: when they left this village later today, they would not leave behind enough food to feed a bird nor sufficient shelter to harbor a rat. The village would be burned to the ground after destroying anything and everything they would not need themselves.

Further below them were cornfields bursting with sweet corn. It was a staple in the Indian diet. At this time of year, they harvested the corn and prepared it for the coming cold months in which food would be scarce and the winter would be harsh. Most of it would become cornmeal, which kept better than corn left on the cob; that, in turn, would become cakes they served at every meal.

But this year would be different.

Jim watched dozens of men harvesting the corn in one of the fields. The corn they picked would become the property of the Continental Army. This year, it would be used to feed white men.

And the fields that would not be harvested would be burned to the ground. The remaining corn would be too blackened for human—or animal—consumption.

As if reading his mind, Clark said, "Make a note of this date, my friend: as of August 9, 1780, Piqua is no longer a Shawnee village. It will stage no more assaults on our people."

"I imagine the Shawnees will be too busy this winter hunting and scrounging for food to bother with any more attacks."

"You know," Clark said thoughtfully, "the Shawnees have been driven from their ancestral homes in the east. Let this drive them from the west. We'll chase them—and the redcoats—all the way to Canada."

"Are we to follow them west, and drive them to the north?"

Clark sighed heavily. "I want nothing more." His sharp blue eyes followed the men working below. "But most of these men— as you know, Jim—will want to return to their families. Winter will soon be upon us, and they have their own crops to harvest and their own preparations to make."

"Then there's the matter of money," Jim said delicately.

"Yes. I must pay another visit to the Virginia legislature. They have not yet paid their bills, and my own money is now being spent on their debts."

A palomino made its way through the village below. At the sight of the two men standing above, the rider pulled off his hat and waved it.

"So how is Tommy Buckingham working out, Jim?" Clark said as the horse drew closer.

"He's a bit less green than he was yesterday."

"Hallo there," Tommy called out. He pulled in his reins and dismounted. "Been talking to some of the men. Did you know that John Morrison shot and loaded thirteen times yesterday?"

"Do tell," Clark said.

"It's true; there are witnesses. He got shot in the ear, too, but kept right on a'shooting."

"Well, that is a feat. Indeed it is. John is a brave man. A good man."

They stood for a moment watching the men harvesting the corn, reining in the horses left behind by the enemy, ransacking the village, and carrying out anything the Army might need.

"Your orders, Sir?" Jim asked.

"Tell the other colonels to dismiss the settlers tomorrow; they are free to return to their own homes and families. Those who wish to remain with us will begin our march back to Chillicothe." He chewed another piece of meat. "Ask the colonels to meet me here within the hour. We'll begin planning our attack on Fort Detroit."

17

Mary watched a thin trail of smoke waft above the huts and vanish in the treetops, the only remnant of a campfire that had supplied the Indians with their latest meal. It had rained earlier in the day; a cooling, steady mist that had eventually saturated the ground and drenched the village, leaving the paths between the structures channels of mud. Still, it had been a much appreciated respite from the scorching summer sun. And now as the coolness of the water merged with the summer heat, a thick fog developed that cloaked the village in an ethereal blue haze.

Night was descending. The air was thick with the sounds of crickets and frogs and the occasional hoot owl. The sun had long since shrunk behind the gray-blue clouds but the moon did not rise.

It was time.

Mary glanced behind her at the hut she shared with Medicine Woman. The old squaw's blankets and deerskin were piled neatly on one side while Mary's single deerskin, the only thing that had served to cushion her sore bones against the bare ground, lay folded on the opposite side. She had decided earlier in the day not to take it with her; it might alert Medicine Woman prematurely of her departure. By leaving it behind, perhaps she would assume her captive was about the village and would return shortly. By the time she realized she was not coming back, Mary hoped to be well on her journey to freedom.

Her eyes fell briefly on the pile of moccasins she'd made for Medicine Woman. She had yearned to make a pair of them for herself, but the squaw had watched the fabric like a hawk. Her feet were much shorter than Mary's and she knew if she stole a pair now, they would not serve her.

As she crept past the huts, she heard the occasional soft murmur of the squaws' voices. They wafted through the air from the direction of the communal building, where they might remain for hours huddled together in a circle, even if no one spoke. It had become a part of their nightly ritual.

The children were playing a game near the center of the village, their small bodies difficult to see in the darkness, their happy voices carried on the winds. They would soon retire to their respective beds and sleep until dawn found them.

The Frenchman's trading post was at the north end of the village, well away from her escape route. As she threaded her way past the huts, she tried to stop the rapid thumping in her chest and quiet her labored breathing lest her own body give away her intentions.

Her feet eventually found the path leading down to the water's edge. She followed it cautiously, the mud rising between her toes and causing her to slide at unexpected moments. She had almost reached the edge of the woods nearest the water when she thought she heard a twig break.

She instantly froze. Had the squaws detected her escape already, when she had barely made it outside the village?

A long, agonizing moment passed. She knew these squaws could sneak up silently upon her and she might never know they were there until her throat was slit or her scalp sliced open. She forced herself to keep her head rigid and still while she peered about. The fog was thicker now and each tree began to morph into the apparitions of Shawnee warriors.

Another twig cracked.

She fought to keep her chest from heaving with her sudden shortness of breath. Slowly, painfully, she turned her head over her shoulder to her left. She fought to quiet her breathing. Faintly, almost imperceptibly, she heard the footsteps; they were muffled and laborious as though the person was dragging their feet or perhaps dragging something heavy behind them.

Mary thought briefly of turning around and returning to the village. No one would question her if she was coming into the village, she reasoned, only if she were retreating from it. She could always say she had simply wanted to go to the river's edge; the Frenchman could interpret her excuses.

And then what? Wait for another new moon? By that time, the braves might have returned and her chance would be forever gone.

No; she had to leave tonight. She had no choice.

Her eyes strained through the murky woods, trying to make out the slim shape that wove its way hesitantly through the trees. When it appeared out of the fog, she almost gasped; it was almost upon her. The ghostly shape loomed out of the darkness, the arms almost straight out, the hands groping as if the eyes were unseeing, the feet dragging as though they were carrying a heavy weight.

As the apparition passed within inches of her, she recognized the frail facial features of the young mother. Her eyes were unblinking, seemingly focused straight ahead as she continued her movement toward the water.

Then Mary saw a leather strap tied to her ankles, keeping them only inches apart. And in the middle of the strap a stone the size of a man's head was bound securely.

The young mother continued past Mary, breaking through the woods and moving gradually, painstakingly toward the water.

Mary almost cried out. She could have reached out and grabbed her, pulled her into the woods, and talked her into going with her. But as quickly as the thought entered her mind, she realized neither of them would be able to escape if they were together. The young woman was only a shell, an emaciated remnant of a human being, too feeble for the long journey ahead. Mary had nothing with which to cut the leather strap and free her of the stone. And the whole village might be pressed into the search if two captives were discovered to be gone.

With a heavy heart, she watched as the young mother dragged her feet to the river's edge. Then with a great deal of difficulty, she waded into the water, the stone seeming to take on weight as she walked. She stumbled as the current caught her, sucking her under. Her head bobbed above the water once before Mary fought back stinging tears and forced herself to turn away.

She wandered to her special tree where she pulled the moss and leaves from the hole in the trunk, revealing the corn and wizened grapes and berries she had squirreled away. Reaching deep into the trunk, she pulled out the precious jerky she had risked punishment for stealing. And there at the base of the tree, hidden under mounds of leaves and dirt, was a bag sewn from deerskin scraps she'd kept from making Medicine Woman's moccasins. It was small and her food barely fit inside, but it would have to do. It was all she had.

She then made her way through the woods to the water's edge some distance from where the young woman had entered. She glanced briefly downstream but she saw no sign of the wretched creature. She offered a brief prayer and consoled herself with the thought that the poor woman's suffering was over.

Gingerly, she moved into the crosscurrent. Once there, she stumbled onto rocks as she labored south, holding her precious bag of food above the water.

Should I return? She thought more than once as the minutes wore on and her world melted into the mist. She hadn't been tortured; she hadn't been kept tied and encumbered as the young mother had. Medicine Woman had not been good to her but she had not abused her, either. But that would change if she was found to have escaped; the penalty could be more horrid than she wanted to admit.

More than once she thought of turning around and going back. She could say that she'd followed the young woman to the river and watched her wade in. She could say she tried to save her. She could even sound the alarm at the water's edge, bringing the squaws to her and attempting a mock rescue.

She thought of these things as she put one foot in front of the other, the rocks cutting her bare soles, making her progress more painful with every step. She began to shiver uncontrollably in the night air as the cool water soaked her clothes. She prayed that she had not somehow crossed into the center of the river in the confusion brought by the darkness, where she would be pulled back to the north and deposited once again at the village.

Hour after agonizing hour passed. She heard the hoot of owls and the howls of wolves. Sometimes she heard rapid footsteps racing away from her, and in the darkness she couldn't tell if it was something as docile as a deer or as threatening as a bear. She tried not to think of the wild animals who might even now be watching her struggling against the current, but filled her mind with thoughts of George, Ma, Sam and Elizabeth. She could no longer see the faces of her other siblings, could no longer remember the details. She would have to work on her memories, she thought; work on them each day lest she forget…

At times, she tried to float upon the current, no longer caring whether her food was soaked, but she often was pulled toward the center where her course was reversed. She attempted to swim at times; then those periods were followed by longer ones in which she remained at the river's edge, her feet still underwater, still trying to tread south.

Above all else, she had to remain in the water. If the Indians found her footprints, they would track her—even if it was tens of miles. Her only hope was to remain in the river where she would leave no signs of her passage.

The dawn crept upon her, the horizon a deep ruby red. She had no idea where she was or how far she had been able to get from the village. In the darkness, she would not have seen the Cumberland emptying into the Ohio, even if she'd been just yards away from its mouth. But the river was wide here, so wide that in daylight she could scarcely see the other side. She had no choice but to keep moving south.

By this time, Medicine Woman would be awake and her breakfast would not be before her, as was her custom. She would see the deerskin against the wall of the hut and she would realize Mary had escaped. She would soon be sounding the alarm, if she hadn't already.

How far was she from the village? She wondered. Her calves ached with the exertion of struggling against the currents all night; her legs felt like wooden weights tethered to her hips. Surely, she would be a good distance away by now?

The sun rose hotter than it had all summer, its merciless orb taunting her. The air was thick and she found herself stopping often to drink the river water, but now it tasted warm and heavy and it did not refresh her.

When the sun was high overhead, she finally climbed out of the water and stopped along the river's edge, where she opened her bag. Her food was soggy. She reached inside and grabbed a handful of hard corn kernels. She had nothing with which to start a fire and even if she did, she could not risk detection.

She sank to the ground and ate the corn raw. When the handful had been eaten, she slowly and painfully rose to her feet. She would not eat more. A heavy stomach could slow her progress and, she thought with a sickening lurch, she had far to go. She didn't know when she might find sufficient food again.

The sun had long descended when Mary detected the abandoned village around a bend in the river. The moon had risen but it was barely a thin crescent in the night sky, barely illuminating the earth below. But as she neared the village, the buildings became clearer and more distinct.

She almost held her breath as she approached the clearing where they had stopped only a few days—and a lifetime—ago. She climbed out of the water and stopped to survey the wooden structure she had helped build to keep the meats from scavengers. Her knees were shaking and for the first time, she realized she had caught a chill. She reached to her legs and felt the goose bumps forming along the skin, the texture as scaly and dry as a fish.

She rested for what could have been a few minutes or an hour or more; she supposed she might have dozed but she did so fitfully. With every sound, no matter how minute, she jerked awake, her heart beating so rapidly that her chest ached.

Finally, she turned over and came to her knees in the dirt, her palms stretched across the barren ground. She forced herself to rise. Then she strained as she placed one foot in front of the other until she had retreated down the footpath to the abandoned village. It seemed as if an eternity had passed before she reached the hut she had shared with Medicine Woman.

When she stepped inside, she was astounded by the familiarity she felt. It was almost as if she had come home. She didn't understand this feeling, and she hesitated for a moment, wondering about it. As her eyes adjusted to the darkness, she caught sight of her shoes, still resting where she had left them.

Her legs wobbled and she sank to her knees and crawled to them. She dusted the mud and dirt off her feet and slipped on each shoe. They felt cumbersome and heavy and she almost removed them, but then decided otherwise. They would not come off her feet again. She would need them to get her safely home.

She found her bowl in the darkness and she knelt her head over it and sobbed. Then she clutched it in her hands and lay back upon the earth and fell fast asleep.

18

ary bolted upright as a wicked crack of thunder erupted in the night. Her heart pounded as a simultaneous lightning flash sliced through the shadows.

The next instant she was plunged into a darkness as black as pitch. Unable to see her hands in front of her face, she groped behind her until she located the back wall, and then settled against it. Outside the storm raged, the water pounding against the roof and walls with such fervor that she grew concerned the aging structure would not hold.

As another flash of lightning lit up the interior, she spotted a rivulet encroaching into the hut. She backed further into the opposite corner and drew her legs under her.

Every muscle in her body ached. Her feet, still crammed into her shoes, felt swollen and cramped, the soles bruised and cut from countless brambles and rocks. Each leg and arm had grown heavy, causing every movement to become excruciating.

She tried to stretch but even her back, neck and shoulders were filled with sharp pains. As she cautiously extended her legs one at a time, she bumped something in the darkness.

Groping near her feet, her fingers closed around the rim of her bowl. She gently held it to her chest, her heart heavy. Who would have known that something so small, something seemingly so insignificant, would come to mean so much?

As the storm raged, Mary's eyes instinctively gravitated to the open doorway, where the sheets of rain howled as if trying to enter. Forked lightning illuminated the sky as a simultaneous crack of thunder seemed to shake the ground.

With the next burst of light, a figure appeared in the doorway of the hut, filling the entrance.

Mary gasped. Her body was paralyzed while her mind raced. Every hair on her small frame stood completely erect.

There was no way out. The figure blocked her only exit.

The next flash revealed the form still in the doorway as if he hadn't moved a single muscle. For the briefest of moments, she caught sight of an almost naked body, the chest, arms, legs and face painted with black and red stripes, the hair plucked to the scalp except for one shiny black patch on top, from which a single long tail extended.

She realized her nails were pressing hard into the sides of her bowl. Yet she was unable to let go. Somewhere in the back of her mind, she saw herself sitting completely still, her bowl clutched in her fingers with the intensity of a mother protecting her child.

When the next burst came, he was standing over her.

"Msipessi!" she cried out as she recognized the Indian who had slain her father.

The storm raged outside, the briefest of flashes lighting up the room—he was standing; then he was kneeling; then he was staring into her face from inches away. She never felt his presence, never smelled his breath, and yet he was there like a speechless apparition.

He was peering at her face; then with the next flash, his eyes were focused on her hands. The next one found him leaning forward, studying her shoes and then her bowl.

My God, she thought. Help me!

As the thunder rolled across the sky, she lifted her bowl toward him. She forced herself to smile, hoping beyond hope that she did not look forced or contrived. As the next flash raced through the small hut, she forced herself to cry out again, "Msipessi!"

Then there was a great laughter emanating deep from within him.

And when lightning raced across the sky again, faces appeared behind him—faces that were equally as painted, scalps that were equally as plucked, bodies that moved with the silence and agility of ghosts.

He was laughing and now he was pointing. And as she realized he was pointing out her bowl to the others, she raised it higher and smiled broader, gesturing toward her bowl.

God help me, please, she thought again and again. God help me!

He was reaching for her foot, and she stifled the impulse to yank it away from him. In the shifting light, she could see him bending her ankle this way and that, studying her shoes and her feet. His face grew serious, his smile still there but seemingly frozen, his eyes questioning.

She managed to free one hand from her bowl and she pointed to her feet. "Shoes!" she said.

He laughed again. He rose and turned to the others and said something she did not understand. The others moved forward, peering at her face, the bowl, and her shoes as the storm continued to beat against the small hut.

And then one figure dropped to his haunches, his face expressionless. It was White Messenger.

19

Even to Mary's untrained eye, she knew the flatboat they traveled in was not of Indian origin. She tried to remember if she had ever seen a boat like it at Fort Nashborough or any of the settlements she'd passed through on their way west, but she could not place it. As the minutes wore on and they moved further from the abandoned village and closer to Shawneetown, she struggled with her thoughts and emotions. She tried not to think about the white settlers who might have used this boat and who might have been overcome by savage Indians and died at their hands.

She was surprised they did not punish her or at least tie her up. Though she was free to move about the boat, she sat silently with her bowl clutched in her lap, trying to focus on the water ahead and not on the shores she'd traversed with such difficulty. She was afraid if she looked toward the shore, she would burst into tears or fling herself overboard in a desperate attempt to escape. And she knew, at least for the present, that escape was no longer an option.

She wondered if they would have found her if she had not been inside the hut. But how could she have known that the braves were there? She would make a mental note of this mistake. She could not afford to slip up again.

She stole a sideways glance at Msipessi. As he looked her way, she forced herself to smile and raise her bowl. "Bowl!" she said with what she hoped was the same enthusiasm as a small child on Christmas morning.

"Bowl!" Msipessi answered as the other braves laughed.

Only White Messenger did not laugh as he stood near the front of the flatboat. He didn't watch the river ahead but seemed to be studying her intently, his face immobile and his eyes veiled.

He knows the truth, she thought, as she lowered her eyes to her lap.

The storm had long since passed when they spotted Shawneetown ahead. As the village came into view, women and children began running from their huts, waving and shouting as they raced to the shore.

Several of the squaws leaped into the boat and hugged the braves fiercely. They all seemed to be talking at once.

Mary remained seated, still clutching her bowl.

She heard a woman's voice cry out. Surprised, she looked up to see Medicine Woman standing on the shore, pointing at her. As the others stopped chattering and stared at her, Mary forced herself to raise her bowl. "Bowl!" she exclaimed.

Msipessi stepped forward and spoke to Medicine Woman. The old squaw leaned forward and looked first at the bowl and then at Mary's swollen feet protruding from her shoes like biscuit dough in a too-small container.

White Messenger grasped her arm and pulled her to her feet. "Go to her," he said curtly.

As Mary stepped forward, she almost tripped on her grotesquely swollen feet, but White Messenger caught her. His eyes widened as he looked into her face, no doubt seeing her poorly concealed grimace, before his face again became immobile.

Mary slid more than stepped toward the edge of the boat, where Msipessi grabbed her around her waist and set her on the shore near the old woman.

Medicine Woman began to speak rapidly, her arms gesturing in all directions. She pointed at the village, then at Mary and at the water.

They will kill me now, Mary thought. I will never see my home again. I will never see Ma or Sam or George—

Then White Messenger spoke. He had moved behind her as silently as the wind. "Medicine Woman says they thought you were dead."

Mary turned to look at him but she didn't respond.

"Medicine Woman says Black Cloud drowned here in the river. Her body washed up on shore."

For a moment, Mary didn't understand. Then the memory of the young mother wading into the water returned. Instinctively, she turned to face the river.

"They thought you might have drowned with her."

Mary realized she was still clutching her bowl. "I wanted my bowl," she said, keeping her eyes downcast. "I could not eat with the rest of the village. I had to eat like a wild dog." She paused while he spoke to the group that had crowded around them. Then she continued, "I thought if I had my bowl, I could eat with everyone again."

White Messenger spoke again. The Frenchman had joined them and was watching her curiously.

Medicine Woman pointed to her feet and spoke.

"Medicine Woman wants to know why you wear the white man's shoes when they do not fit."

Mary looked at her feet. "They were my shoes. But my feet…" her voice trailed off.

Medicine Woman stepped forward and grasped her hand. "Come," she said in English. "Come."

Mary was led along the trail to the hut she'd shared with Medicine Woman. The others followed. When they reached the hut, the old woman led her inside and motioned for her to lie down. Once Mary complied, she gently but firmly took her bowl and laid it down beside her. She said something Mary did not understand but she smiled when she said it, revealing teeth that had been ground close to the gums.

Then Medicine Woman began pulling off Mary's right shoe, causing her to cry out in pain. The old woman stopped briefly and said something to the others who had gathered in the doorway. Two young squaws left and Medicine Woman turned her attention to Mary. She untied the shoes and pulled the tongue away from her foot, causing her to cry out again. Her foot was covered in dried blood that had adhered itself to the shoe like glue. As Medicine Woman removed the shoe, Mary could feel the skin pulling away with it.

Mary wanted to cry then; she wanted to sob as if her whole chest was filled with the tears of centuries of pain, but she dared not. She dug her nails into her skin as Medicine Woman continued to force the leather away from her foot.

The squaws returned with a bowl of warm water. Medicine Woman dipped a rag made from the skin of an animal into the water, wrung it out, and washed Mary's foot, clucking as she removed the blood and inspecting the appendage. Then she spoke to the others again, and again they disappeared.

While they were gone, she started work on the second shoe, which was adhered to Mary's foot even more strongly than the first one. She prayed she would faint, but she didn't. She stared at the ceiling of the hut, at the wood bent to form a circular roof, and at the skins laid across the wood. If she could only concentrate on the skins, she wouldn't feel the pain, she told herself again and again.

At last her feet were cleaned and the others had returned. They provided Medicine Woman with a smaller bowl and several plants that appeared to have been freshly harvested. Then the others left and Medicine Woman busied herself just outside the hut with the bowl and herbs.

Mary dozed off. Occasionally she would begin to awaken but was pulled back into an abyss where she was surrounded by Indian faces streaked with red and black and blue stripes. She knew on some faint level that Medicine Woman had returned and was wrapping her feet in a poultice that stung briefly but left her toes feeling warm and gooey as if bathed in mud. She knew her feet were being wrapped in some sort of material and tied tightly around her ankles.

And as she succumbed to sleep, she remembered White Messenger's words: "My people will often heal a warrior," he had said, "sometimes even before they are led to their death."

20

It was late afternoon when Jim spotted the remnants of a massacre alongside the Ohio River. He directed his men to steer the flatboat toward shore while Tommy and two Cherokee Indians kept their eyes on the surrounding area, on the sharp lookout for roaming Shawnee.

The Colonists had long ago made peace with the Cherokees, and many of them were trusted partners, serving as spies, traders, trackers, and often as soldiers. Now Jim traveled with a small band of scouts that included two of them as expert trackers as they journeyed a safe distance ahead of the main army.

They'd left Piqua two days earlier, traveling back to Chillicothe, where the men had completed the harvesting of the remaining corn crops before setting the fields ablaze. While they plundered anything left in the village, Jim and his men had tracked the fleeing Shawnees and their allies until it was obvious the enemy did not intend to turn and fight. Instead, they appeared to be escaping to the relative safety of British-controlled Fort Detroit, traveling overland from Piqua to the Maumee River, where they would no doubt commandeer boats that would take them right into the fort.

Jim and his men had then returned to Chillicothe and made their report. But instead of pursuing the Indians and preparing for battle at Fort Detroit, Colonel Clark had made the reluctant decision to return the militia to Fort Jefferson, located in the opposite direction—instead of moving due north, they would travel southwest.

Though Clark didn't state his reasons, Jim knew all too well the uphill battle he faced in marching on Fort Detroit. Now that nothing was left of Chillicothe and Piqua but burned embers, most of the thousand-strong men who had made this campaign successful were returning to their wives and their families. They had their own crops to harvest before the winter set in, and they had their own families to protect. None of them wanted to remain with the militia for a march that would take them hundreds of miles away from their homes and settlements, and leaving their own families vulnerable to Indian attacks. Even George Spears had reluctantly decided to return home to Virginia while the man George had once thought of as his future brother-in-law, Sam Neely, returned to Fort Nashborough.

The skeleton army of just over one hundred and fifty men who remained was exhausted and malnourished. So they would return to the safety of Fort Jefferson near the Mississippi River, just south of the Ohio and Cumberland Rivers, where they would most likely spend the winter resting and preparing for a spring offensive.

The scouts had left Chillicothe first, fanning out on horseback and on the river, clearing the way for the main forces to follow.

Now as their flatboat came alongside the shore, Jim and Tommy leapt off and secured it along the banks. The remains of a massacre were evident. The Cherokee squatted beside each body and read the surrounding moccasin prints the way one would read a book. There were a dozen bodies in all—eight men and four women, all white settlers—lying in grotesque positions, scattered beside the shoreline and in the nearby woods, no doubt struck down in their attempts to escape. From the looks of things, there had been some struggles but since no dead Indians were found amongst them, they concluded they'd been the victims of a surprise attack.

Jim knelt beside one of the women. Her head was bloodied from a huge chunk missing from her scalp. There were stray pieces of long blond hair scattered around her; curled, shiny hair that obviously had been well cared for. A deep hatred welled up inside Jim. And now the blond tresses would be worn proudly from some Indian's waist, who would no doubt brag of his exploits in battle against an unarmed woman. He wished they'd traveled faster, perhaps left Piqua earlier; he might have come upon them before the savages had done their grisly deed; he might have saved this young woman's life…

There had been no horse or wheel tracks, leading them to believe the settlers had traveled down the Ohio River by boat. As he listened to the Cherokees' assessment, he felt his blood grow hotter with a renewed desire to capture Simon Girty. It had been Girty who taught the Shawnees how to persuade the settlers to leave the relative safety of the river and come close enough to shore for the Indians to capture, kill and scalp them. They used other white captives to run alongside the shoreline, calling out to the inhabitants of the boats to rescue them from pursuing Indians. Many times the boats would turn toward shore, intending to sweep up the captives and be on their way. But once they were close enough to land, the Shawnees hiding in the underbrush nearby would rush the boat, kill or capture the settlers, and seize all of their goods.

Though they couldn't be certain this ruse had occurred here, the absence of horse or Indian tracks leading away from the site forced them to conclude the Indians had taken to the water by boat.

Jim crouched beside the river and untied the bandana from around his neck, dipping it in the cool water. He then squeezed the cloth across the back of his neck, letting the cool droplets run down his naked back to his buckskin breeches. It was a humid day. A heavy rain had come through just the night before, seeming to spawn hundreds of mosquitoes and biting flies that had emerged once the storm blew over, hounding them on their trek downriver. It would be hot and miserable digging graves, their only saving grace the possibility of soft earth from the heavy rains.

He wiped his face with the bandana, then cleaned the cloth in the river and replaced it around his neck, the wet material serving to cool him off a bit.

After a few moments, he rose to his feet and studied the terrain. "Over there," he said to Tommy.

As the younger man peered toward the woods, Jim directed the others to begin digging the graves for the settlers whose journey westward had ended here.

The sun was setting when they reached the Cumberland River. Jim ordered the men to halt, allowing the boat to drift in the current still strong from the heavy rains. He pulled out his telescope.

"Shawneetown is just north of us," he said to Tommy.

"How far?"

He peered through the telescope at the silent, still woods along the shoreline. "Few hours." He turned to face the south. "There's an abandoned Shawnee village just around that bend," he said, pointing. "It's called Savannah Old Settlement... hasn't been occupied in 50, 60 years."

"So do we go north?" Tommy asked excitedly. "Scout out Shawneetown and get word back to Colonel Clark?"

Jim hesitated. He would like nothing better than to pursue the Indians who had killed and scalped those settlers along the Ohio. And he had no doubt they were probably en route to Shawneetown at this moment. He sighed heavily. "Those aren't our orders," he said to a disappointed Tommy.

Jim's voice rose as he spoke to the others. "We head south," he said. "We anchor the boat before we reach that bend. We travel on foot into Savannah Old Settlement. Make sure everything is clear. The army will have to move right past that village to return to Fort Jefferson."

With that, the men steered the flatboat back into the center of the river. As their journey continued south, the sun disappeared behind the trees.

21

Mary's fever raged, her skin damp with perspiration and her breathing labored and hoarse. The fever was followed by chills and a wet, clammy skin as Mary's entire body convulsed with tremors. She was suspended between a dream state and wakefulness, sometimes understanding that Medicine Woman was pressing something against her lips and urging her to drink; other times, she was surrounded by her family in their house near Fort Nashborough, smelling the sweet aroma of wild turkey and all the trimmings while Sam, Elizabeth and the others babbled on, their joyous voices filling their home.

Pa was preparing to carve the turkey and dole out the tender meat while Ma passed around some sweet apple cider.

Then Pa turned to Mary and smiled, but his eyes betrayed a deep, dark sadness.

Mary breathed in the musky deerskin bedding and the pungent odors inside the hut, her feet still covered in the herbal poultice that radiated more warmth on this hot, still August day.

The sound of laughter reached her ears, the high-pitched, soft voices of Shawnee squaws gathering outside her hut.

She yearned to return to the warmth and serenity of the table and her family, to shut out the growing chorus. She wanted to ask Pa why he looked at her with such sadness.

Then he removed his hat and his scalp was gone, leaving only bone covered in a labyrinth of bloody veins.

The sound of the voices grew louder and now she struggled to awaken herself. She had groggily opened one eye when she was roused from bed by an array of hands and arms that seemed to descend upon her all at once.

When she was unceremoniously tugged to her feet, she realized she was surrounded by four of the squaws, members of the original tribe that had attacked Neely's Salt Lick. One of the squaws appeared very young, perhaps in her late teens, as Mary was. Perhaps they had been born in the same year but worlds apart.

Two of the women appeared to be about ten years older, their skin already beginning to turn leathery and tough from hours in the harsh elements.

The fourth woman was much heavier, her substantial breasts sagging as if from the weight of having fed too many children, though Mary had not seen anyone younger than herself in this family.

Now the heavyset woman yanked her forward by both elbows, pushing her out of the dark hut and into the bright sunshine.

As Mary struggled to adjust to the bright orb directly overhead, she wondered how long she had slept, how many days she had been suspended in a feverish sleep. The squaws were circling her now like wolves moving in on their prey, as they pulled her further from the hut and toward the river bank.

As she stumbled along the path, she became aware of the others in the village gathering and following them, smiling broadly as they nodded and chattered their approval.

Once they reached the riverbank, the heavyset squaw pushed Mary to her knees on the ground. Then at once, all four began pulling at her head, snatching huge clumps of hair with each attack. Mary screamed out and clutched her head, covering it in a futile attempt to protect herself.

But four sets of hands continued pulling and yanking and jerking, and try as she might, she was unable to keep them away from her. They came at her like angry bees swarming from a nest. Their fingers locked around her long strands so close to her scalp that when they came away with a fistful of her precious hair she was convinced part of her scalp was still attached.

She tried to come to her feet in an effort to flee, but she was pushed back to the ground. She swung her arms in all directions, calling out for them to stop, but she was answered only by laughter that seemed to emanate from both the attackers and the onlookers.

She saw her hair landing on the ground at her feet – matted, dirty, stringy hair that didn't look like her hair at all. Through the tears that stung her eyes, she felt as though she was looking at the hair of a nomad, wandering in a wilderness without comb or brush. Her heart sank as she realized that was precisely what she had become.

Now the braves were surrounding them, spurring them on with shouts and calls. Some were beginning to tap the blunt end of their spears on the ground while chanting. Even the children raced in from the cornfields and gathered with the others, their high-pitched voices joining in the mayhem.

She screamed out as she clawed at them. She struck the youngest squaw squarely on the jaw, but to Mary's astonishment the young woman didn't even flinch. Her resistance simply seemed to goad her on with a vengeance as she attempted to pull out every last hair on her head.

She swung in a circle, her fists punching in every direction as she tried valiantly to hold them off, but it was useless. There were too many of them and they seemed to be everywhere at once.

When the pile of hair had grown to a tangled mass, they began to pull her into the river as the villagers watched and shouted encouragement.

My God, she thought. They are going to drown me! They want me to join Black Cloud!

They pushed and prodded her into deeper water until the warm liquid rose to her chest. The two squaws that appeared to be about ten years her senior took their positions on each side of her, unceremoniously pulling each of her arms straight out at her sides. Though she struggled, she was unable to move them more than an inch in any direction.

While her arms were pulled taut, others began rubbing her skin.

The harder she fought against them, the louder the laughter became.

They gathered silt from the river bottom and rubbed her from her fingertips to her elbows, across every inch of her skin to her shoulders. Once at her neckline, they ripped her clothing from her, leaving her naked in the river water.

She was acutely aware of the other Indians on the river bank, watching and laughing from the shore as if they were attending a play. Even the French trader had emerged. She spotted White Messenger sitting tall atop a mottled mare, watching her with an immobile expression.

She cried out to him to help her, but her cries were answered by the squaws plunging her downward into the water then quickly raising her back up. While she sputtered and coughed out water, they rubbed her bald and sore head with their leathery hands.

She screamed again and tried to fight with a renewed vigor, but the two who still had her arms held on tightly. Then they were dragging her back toward shallower water, where her breasts and back were pummeled with the same intensity and ferocity.

"Help me!" she cried out to White Messenger. "Help me!"

Some of the braves laughed and looked at White Messenger as though they shared a comical secret.

Then she was pushed back under water, and now her stomach and her legs were being pummeled.

"God, let me die quickly!" She called out. "Drown me quickly!"

White Messenger broke away from the rest of the group. He rode slowly into the river while the squaws wrestled with her. As he drew near, she called out, "Kill me or rescue me, but don't let me die slowly! Please, I beg of you!"

He stopped his horse just feet from them.

"Stop struggling," he called out to her. "They are only trying to wash you."

Her knees gave way beneath her but as she plunged under water, she was caught and pulled back up.

Stunned, she stopped her struggle. As the warm water continued to cascade over her and the squaws continued their efforts, she remained as still as she could, though her entire body was quivering in terror and pain.

Finally, the ordeal was slowing. She was led naked from the river, but they released their hold on her arms now, freeing her to shield her body as best she could from the prying eyes on the shore.

Medicine Woman was walking down the path toward her, carefully carrying a dressed skin as if she were transporting a valuable object. The squaws led her to the old woman.

Medicine Woman held the skin above her head and softly spoke words that Mary did not understand. Then she pulled it over Mary's head while the squaws pulled her arms through the holes, allowing it to drape her as a long overblouse.

The skin irritated her flesh, now reddened and raw. Every inch of her body had been scrubbed. As she instinctively reached to her forearm, she realized they had rubbed her so vigorously that the fine hairs on her body had been sloughed away.

The crowd parted as she was led up the path from the river to the community building at the center of the village. There, others from the village joined them.

The original group that had captured her gathered in a semi-circle in front of her. Eagle Feathers stood in the center, directly across from her. Medicine Woman stood on one side of the old brave while Msipessi stood on his opposite side.

Eagle Feathers spoke in a clear, strong voice. The villagers moved to the sides as White Messenger strode into the building. He spoke to Eagle Feathers before turning to Mary. Then with a surefooted grace, he stepped to her side and faced the others.

Eagle Feathers spoke for a long time, his arms gesturing first to the left and then to the right, his voice rising and falling in an eloquent singsong cadence. The villagers nodded and some murmured.

Mary was still shaking as White Messenger turned to her.

"Eagle Feathers says you are no longer a white woman. Your white blood has been cleansed from you, and all that was before is gone.

"You are now a Shawnee. You are now of our tribe."

He reached to her forearm and held it up for all to see. The skin glowed with a red intensity from the vigorous scrubbing. "Your blood is now Shawnee blood.

"From this day forward, you will be known as Songbird, for it was your voice that saved you."

After a pause, Eagle Feathers again began to speak, again his voice rising and falling in cadence. He pointed to Medicine Woman and spoke for a long time. Then he turned to Msipessi and spoke for an equal length of time. He finally turned to Mary and seemed to be speaking directly to her.

White Messenger again turned toward her.

"Medicine Woman wishes for you to serve her. You would live as her servant and serve her needs however she wishes. You are a good worker, a hard worker. You make good moccasins for Medicine Woman and you serve her needs well. You would be well cared for."

Mary opened her mouth to respond, but White Messenger stopped her.

"Msipessi," he said, the syllables coming out slowly and deliberately, "professes his love for you. He also loves your voice. He thinks that you are a brave woman and a good woman. Msipessi wishes for you to become his squaw. You would live with him as the wife of a strong warrior. You would give him many children who would grow to become strong warriors. They would have the spirit and the goodness of you and him."

Mary gasped. She felt the blood drain from her face.

"It is your choice," White Messenger continued, his eyes not wavering from hers. "You may serve Medicine Woman or become one with Msipessi."

Mary looked at the faces around her. The squaws who had just washed her beamed as though she was a new infant brought into the world. Medicine Woman watched her intently, her face an expressionless mask but her eyes inquisitive. Then her eyes fell on Msipessi, whose wide eyes seemed to beseech her. At this moment, he did not look like the warrior who had tossed a part of her father's scalp at her feet. Instead, he looked like a lovesick schoolboy.

She drew herself up to her full height. "If it is my choice," she said in a clear voice that carried through the hall, "then I wish to return to my people. Set me free so that I might be reunited with my family." She turned to look at White Messenger.

His eyes flashed in conflicting emotions. He seemed to be relieved, but there also appeared to be a flash of anger. He appeared to be weighing his words.

"Tell them what I said," she urged.

She watched as his eyes wandered over the audience, stopping at the French trader. Mary realized they both understood her words, and she wished she knew what they seemed to be silently saying to one another across the crowded room.

When White Messenger spoke, it was not to Mary but to Eagle Feathers. His head was high and noble, his words sounding melodious in the quieted room. He waved toward Medicine Woman.

Msipessi's face grew dark and he turned suddenly and made his way through the crowd to the doorway. Medicine Woman nodded approvingly.

The Frenchman nodded once, almost imperceptibly.

The youngest squaw gently coaxed Mary toward Medicine Woman.

She took two steps and then stopped. She turned back toward White Messenger. "What did you tell them?"

There was a moment of silence before he answered.

"I told them you chose to serve Medicine Woman."

"How could you do that?" she said, realizing her voice had become shrill. The others were turned toward them, listening curiously to a conversation they could not understand, their eyes searching their expressions for clues.

"You had but two choices: become Msipessi's squaw or serve Medicine Woman. Had I told them you wanted to return to the white man, you would have been killed."

The room was silent. Her heart beat so rapidly inside her chest that she was certain the others could see it.

"You are now Songbird," he said. "You now serve Medicine Woman."

The young squaw gently but firmly pulled at Mary's arm. As she approached Medicine Woman, a refrain began in her head: I am a slave. I am a slave.

She stopped again as she reached the door of the community building and turned back to White Messenger. She again drew herself up to her full height and felt her square jaw jut forward.

"Songbirds," she said in a clear, strong voice, "are free."

22

The boats began to arrive shortly after daybreak. It started quietly with two braves who appeared as if from nowhere, their canoes gliding silently beneath the thick tree branches that hung over the river's edge on the far shore until they were almost even with the village. The village dogs barked incessantly, causing the Indians to emerge from their huts and to put down their tasks.

Then as though they were acting as one giant being, the entire village swarmed to the shore at once, surrounding the braves. The village elders, Eagle Feathers among them, seemed to be questioning the men. When the visitors answered, a hush fell on the crowd. As they spoke, the villagers occasionally looked at the river in the direction from whence they came, a soft murmur rising and falling as if in tandem.

When they were done, Eagle Feathers and another elder spoke, frequently gesturing toward specific villagers or toward the fields and huts. After each sentence or two, one or two would break away from the crowd and race toward the fields or the village. As Mary watched, they appeared to be preparing for a great feast.

The soft murmur and quiet activity grew in intensity as the day wore on, reaching a crescendo that Mary had not witnessed with the Indians before.

The young squaw from her adopted family, Shooting Star, soon pulled Mary into frenzied activities. She was sent to the fields to gather more corn and then to the storehouse to gather great amounts of jerky—jerky that Mary knew instinctively should have been set aside to feed them through the winter.

But now they were laying the jerky out on large wooden tables in the community building, piling them so high that some would teeter to the ground, only to be picked up and placed back on the pile more gently.

As Mary raced through the village with her chores, more boats soon arrived in growing numbers. Where the initial canoes carried one or two braves, those that followed were frequently overloaded and twice Mary saw flatboats mooring. Wishing fervently to know what was happening, she was kept so busy that she could only glance occasionally in the direction of the river or at the scores of muscular, young and nearly naked men descending upon them.

When she was so tired from hauling food that she wanted only to drop to her knees and rest, she was put to work cooking huge bats of cornmeal and whole slabs of meat. As Mary slaved over the rising heat, she marveled at the amount of food—more than she had ever before seen in one place.

This must be for hundreds, she thought as she pulled ear after ear of corn from the huge vats and placed them on large serving platters that young squaws and their slaves carried to the community building.

At mid-day, she was sent to the trading post with two bowls of food. Having never brought food to the Frenchman and his squaw before, she found her curiosity and excitement growing. But when she turned the corner past the last huts and came into full view of the trading post, she wanted to drop the bowls on the ground, turn and run.

There were dozens of braves surrounding the Frenchman's trading post—so many that they stood three and four deep. The Frenchman and his squaw were kept racing to and from the far ends of the long counters while braves fondled muskets, shot, knives and trinkets. Occasionally, one would fire into the air and the Frenchman would say something to them in the Shawnee language, only to be completely ignored.

Mary slowed to a walk. Though she was dressed in buckskin that draped over her shoulders and fell to her knees and her shoes had been replaced with soft leather moccasins, it would be obvious she was not a Shawnee woman. Her hair had only begun to pop out in soft stubble, and her light skin and her green eyes would betray her. She kept her head down as she walked, not wishing to look in any of the savage's eyes as they pushed past her to reach the trading post. She found herself reciting the Lord's Prayer as she tried valiantly to calm her pounding heart.

Beyond the trading post were boats lining the river's edge two-deep and counting. Braves and squaws alike were busy packing and unpacking them, as though they were deciding what to keep and what to trade and where to place their newly acquired possessions.

She reached the trading post and slipped behind the counter. Neither the Frenchman nor his squaw acknowledged her. She quietly placed the bowls on a table near the back of the lean-to. She sensed that she should return immediately to her chores but instead she sat in a wooden chair in the shadows and silently watched the activity.

It was astonishing that only a short time ago these braves would have killed her in less time than it took for her to catch her breath. But here she was, sitting just a few feet away from them, and she was completely ignored in their frenzy to purchase or trade items.

During a lull in the activity, the Frenchman turned around. His eyes widened as he spotted her.

"I brought you food, Monsieur Pierpont," she said.

"Ah, merci, merci," he said, stepping toward the bowl. With his bare hands, he grabbed a slab of meat and took a bite out of it.

"What is happening?" she asked.

"Your people," he said, brushing sweat from his brow, "have attacked two very large Shawnee villages to our east—Chillicothe and Piqua."

Mary looked down at her lap, shielding her eyes from view. "Were many killed?"

The Frenchman waited until she looked up at him before answering. "Accounts differ. Some say seventeen, some as many as forty."

"And the settlers—?"

He shrugged. "No one knows. No one cares, until they wish to display the scalps and brag of their exploits." He reached to the plate and grabbed a piece of cornmeal, which he stuffed into his mouth as he spoke. "Their villages have been torched—burned to the ground. The food the Indians counted on for the winter is gone."

"All of it?"

He studied her reaction. "What they didn't burn, they took themselves. They left them nothing." He spat out the last sentence as specks of cornmeal flew from his mouth. He wiped his lips with the back of his forearm.

"Are they coming here?"

"Who—your people?" He shrugged. "We do not know. But the Indians—they will not wait."

"What do you mean?" Mary asked, her eyes wandering from the Frenchman to a brave purchasing black powder from the trader's squaw.

"They are preparing for an attack. Tomorrow, they march on Fort Jefferson."

"Fort Jefferson?"

"On the Mississippi. A day's journey from here. And they plan to get their revenge for the attacks on their villages. For every one of their people who were killed at Chillicothe or Piqua or any of the smaller villages, they will seek ten scalps and ten slaves."

The Frenchman bit off another mouthful of venison. He pointed toward a pile of blankets the Indians had ignored in their haste to purchase weapons. "You will need a blanket."

Mary almost laughed. It was a sweltering August day, almost too hot for the garment she now wore.

Monsieur Pierpont stepped toward her. His eyes were small blue orbs ringed in black under thin, straight brows. "You will be going north," he said. "It is not safe here for the women."

"It is not safe?" she said, waving her arm toward the village. "With all of these men here?"

"You are not listening to me," he said, moving close. "The braves head south tomorrow to attack Fort Jefferson. The children and the squaws will head north, deep into Indian territory, where the only white men you will encounter are likely to be redcoats and Canadians."

"Canadians!" she almost shrieked. Then she leaned back in her chair, the word hanging in the air. Canadians. At least twice as far from home as she was at this moment.

"You will need the blanket," he whispered, his lips close to her ear. "Winter will begin in mere weeks. You are nothing but a slave; the Shawnees will not provide for you."

"Are you willing to give me a blanket?" she asked. "I have nothing to trade you in return."

"Ah, but you do," he said, his lips now brushing her ear.

She leapt to her feet, almost knocking him over. So intent was she in their conversation, she hadn't seen White Messenger standing just feet from them, calmly studying them from the other side of the counter.

She grabbed the bowl and slid past the table. "I will return to get the other bowl later," she said loudly. As she passed White Messenger, she glanced up at him, expecting to find an expression belying his displeasure with her. Instead, she found him looking at Monsieur Pierpont with a fixed and chilling glare.

23

The first shot rang out, startling Mary awake. Her heart pounding, she bolted upright on her deerskin, her ears straining for the sound of settlers attacking the village. After a minute or two, she heard another shot and then another. But they were not constant, as she supposed they would be in the heat of battle. They seemed instead to be random.

She eased out of her bed and slid her buckskin dress over her head. Her hut was her own now; after her initiation into the tribe, Medicine Woman had begun to share one with Eagle Feathers. For the first time, she wished she wasn't completely alone as she mentally calculated the distance between her hut and the others in her tribe.

She felt her way in the darkness to the flap and pushed it aside. The moon was full and high overhead. She turned back to her hut, now swathed in a gentle purple light. She returned to the side of her bed, slipped on her moccasins and grabbed her bowl and the black shoes that now appeared clunky and inflexible.

There were shouts now. A drum began beating incessantly, gaining in intensity and beating at a faster and more frenzied rhythm. But there were no sounds of settlers, no white voices; only the occasional musket shot and war whoops.

She eased out of the hut and pulled the flap down behind her. She quietly crept around the hut to face the center of the village.

Near the community building was a bonfire larger than any she had seen before, the sparks flying so high that she marveled the nearby roofs had not caught the embers and burst into flames. In a circle around the bonfire were scores of almost naked braves, their faces and bodies painted in gruesome multicolored patterns. At least a half dozen of them wore masks that effectively hid their faces and part of their torsos—hideous masquerades that looked like something out of hell itself. They danced in the flickering light, raising their feet high as they moved, their torsos bent and their sinewy arms waving spears and muskets. Their voices rang out through the village in sinister sounds that made Mary tremble.

She remained in the shadows, her eyes riveted on the activities before her.

Their heads were almost completely shaven but for a single rectangle on top. Some wore the remaining hair in fat braids that reached down their backs, while others had dyed theirs in varying colors of reds and purples. Some wore feathers high atop their heads, held on by bands around their foreheads or fixed to their braids in back. And all had scalps of various colors and lengths hanging from their hips.

The braves sporadically slowed their dancing and whooping just long enough to take mighty swigs from liquor jugs. This was often followed by more shouts and gunfire into the air above them.

A movement caught Mary's eyes and she turned toward the edge of the village, which would have been bathed in shadows had it not been for the bright moon overhead. She caught a glimpse of fleeing Shawnee squaws as they pushed and hurried the younger children into the fields toward the woods beyond. Their movements were frenzied, frightening Mary almost as much as the braves.

She turned and abruptly ran into a muscled chest smeared in a blood-red design resembling a ram.

She instinctively cried out, but the brave's hand covered her mouth so quickly that only a faint sound escaped her. She looked upward but his face was hidden in the darkness, the full moon now obscured by the tall feathers that sprang from the tuft of hair on top of his head.

"Songbird," he whispered.

She instantly recognized his voice and nodded. He removed his hand and turned toward the center of the village. The moon caught his profile, revealing broad red and black strokes across his nose and cheeks. It was difficult to recognize White Messenger under all the war paint and feathers. Even his shaved head was striped in red.

He pointed toward the path that led to the river. "Go," he said, "join the others. Do not make any noise. Stay in the shadows. Go to the far side of the river, where you will be safe."

"Are you coming with me?"

He turned to face her, his eyes wide with surprise. "No," he said after a brief moment. "We leave tomorrow. I will find you in the weeks ahead."

"But how?" she asked. "How can you find me in this wilderness?"

He rested his hand on her shoulder and squeezed it gently. "I will find you," he said firmly. "Now go."

She grasped her bowl and her shoes as she moved toward the path.

"Quickly!" he called in a hoarse whisper.

She broke into a run. She headed for the woods beside the path where the trees would hopefully obscure her movements. In her peripheral vision, she saw others moving through the trees to the safety of the river.

When she reached the river's edge, she was startled to see a half dozen canoes waiting, half-filled with squaws and children. She found Medicine Woman and Shooting Star, and with a slight nod from the old woman, she slid the canoe deeper into the water and climbed inside, grabbing a paddle to push her further away. As White Messenger had directed, they moved toward the opposite shore, fighting the strong current in a frantic attempt to reach the other side.

When they reached the middle of the river, the moon bore down on them as if it intentionally sought to expose them. She redoubled her efforts, rowing like a madwoman as she kept her eyes focused on the far shore, afraid to look back, terrified that she would see the drunken braves coming after them.

When at last they reached the far shore, she came shakily to her feet. She grabbed a tree branch that hung heavily over the riverbank and sought to steady the canoe in the swirling water. All three turned to look back upon the village.

Now dozens of braves were shooting pistols and muskets into the air. Many of them were staggering, and fights were breaking out. They could hear the sounds of crockery breaking as some flung the liquor jugs into the bonfire. Some of the containers were not empty and the alcohol only intensified the flames.

A dozen Indians had gathered at the trading post where they tore through the small structure, stealing trinkets and food and even more black powder. Some were rolling barrels of homemade brew from the building toward the others. The Frenchman and his squaw were nowhere in sight.

My God, she thought as the flames caught the side of the community building, they will kill each other.

She felt a tug on her lower leg and turned to look at Medicine Woman. The old woman directed her in broken English to move northward. She reluctantly pried her attention away from the village, returned to her seat and dipped the paddle into the fast-moving water. As she settled into rowing against the strong current, she glanced back at Shooting Star just in time to see a single tear roll down her cheek.

When they reached a bend, she turned one last time to look at the village, now bathed in the bonfire's glare. No one followed them, and she wondered briefly where all the other squaws had gone before turning her attention to putting more distance between them.

24

Jim leaned back in his chair and propped his feet on the table that served as his desk. It had been a lazy afternoon, one filled with the kind of summer heat that saps men's strength. The minutes ticked by so slowly it was worth succumbing to a long nap with the prospect of awakening when the sun was lower and the heat less intense. His eyelids sagged as he began to read the letter he had labored over for the past hour.

Then he crumbled it, tossing it into the waste bin. He held his head in his hands, his fingers slowly caressing the sun-bleached locks that fell across his brow.

He was being overly sentimental, he told himself. He'd been gone for more than two years; it had not been realistic for Susannah to wait for his return. And though his letter begged her not to marry another, implored with her to wait for his imminent return, and spoke of his plans with her and their offspring in this new land, he knew he could never dispatch it. He could not allow a letter to speak the words he knew he had to utter in person. But would it be too late, he wondered? Would he return home, only to find her with another? Had he lost her forever?

He thought of young George Spears searching for the woman he loved, turning over the bodies of those who had died, dreading the possibility but understanding he had to know if his beloved was dead at the hands of savages. Jim could not bring his adored Susannah to this wilderness, not yet. He could not risk losing her to Indians; better that he forfeit her to another white man, if he were to lose her at all…

He sat for a long time in the shadows of the small room before beginning a second letter.

August 17, 1780

Dear Mother and Father,

It has been many months since I have written to you and you no doubt have wondered if the savages have made off with my scalp by now, but rest assured that I am fine.

I am now at Fort Jefferson, the one Colonel Clark constructed about seven months ago. It is a pretty site, near the mouth of the Ohio.

It is peaceful here now. We arrived about a week ago. We soundly thrashed the Indians at Chillicothe and Piqua and sent them retreating toward Canada with their tails between their legs like misbehaving hounds. We suspect we will have a quiet, peaceful winter.

Colonel Clark has left for Williamsburg. The Virginia legislature has not paid its bills and it is getting harder to keep good men. Many, including myself, have not been paid for many weeks now. The Colonel has done what he can to pay for things himself but his money is low, from what I hear.

I wish I could have gone with him, for I miss seeing you and would like to have spent Thanksgiving or Christmas beside the fire and eaten of Mother's good food. But I was ordered to Fort Jefferson with some of the men, to bide out the winter here.

Since we expect it to be quiet, we plan to do a lot of hunting for the animals are plentiful in these parts. Their meat should help to tide us over the winter. We are low on powder so I suspect we will have to devise other ways of taking them. We have a corn field that is bursting with corn, and some of the men's families are out there now gathering it. Some of the wives are adept at canning berries, of which there are many, but none of them are as good at it as Mother.

He stopped and gazed across the small room. He'd made his chair and table himself; chopped down the trees and peeled the bark, and used an aging axe and his sheath knife to build the legs and notch them together. It wasn't his best work but given the scarcity of tools and time, it was a decent effort.

Now he ran his hand across the tabletop, a single piece of wood barely two feet wide. This was his office: a chair, a table, and a two-shelf bookcase upon which yellowed maps were piled.

It was stifling in the room now, but soon it would be winter and the fireplace he'd helped to build in the corner would come in mighty handy. And as long as the venison and the vegetables held out through the winter months, they could make it through until Clark returned.

He sighed heavily and turned back to his letter and continued:

Please give my love to all and tell them there's no need to worry. I might be a long ways from home but I'm as safe as if I was sitting on your front porch whittling wood.

I hope to get back home sometime soon, even if it's just for a short visit.

Love to you all,
Jim

He folded the note and wrote on the back of it:

John and Permelia Hawkins
Augusta County, Virginia

Then he turned his desk candle sideways until a sufficient amount of wax had dripped onto the paper at the fold, sealing it.

He set it at the edge of his desk. He should have written it in the days before Clark left for Virginia. One of the men could have delivered it to a postal office, one of many that had sprung up in the east.

Now that they'd left without it, it would sit here on his desk until someone else was dispatched to the east, or until such time as a traveler came through that was headed toward Virginia. It might not reach his family for months.

He considered tearing it up and throwing it away, but thought better of it. Even if they didn't get it for some time, any word from him would be better than none. They'd probably worried too much about him anyway.

The sound of dogs barking reached his ears. He recognized Brandy's distinctive baying and cocked his head to listen. Then sound of gunfire ripped through the air, causing him to instantly bolt upright. More shots followed amidst a rising torrent of shouts.

The air had changed. There was an excitement now, the sounds of mayhem and a myriad of activity.

He was up and at the door when Tommy burst in.

"Indians," Tommy shouted breathlessly. "They're attacking the fort!"

25

Mary wiped the perspiration from her brow and paused in her rowing. Her hands were covered in blisters brought by the hours of grasping the rough-hewed wood that served as her paddle. She picked at a splinter with dirt-encrusted nails before taking up the paddle again.

The days since leaving Shawneetown had crept past. Unlike the early days of her captivity when her captors had hurried northward, the squaws seemed to be intentionally traveling slowly, almost as if they did not want to get too far ahead of the braves.

The other three squaws in their party had joined them during the waning hours of that first night. Over the course of the ensuing days, Mary would learn the heavy squaw was called Buffalo Woman, while the two younger squaws were Little Fawn and Silent Tree. The names seemed to fit, as Buffalo Woman appeared as strong as the animal for which she was named, while Little Fawn was timid and she had yet to hear Silent Tree utter a sound.

They traveled in two canoes and remained close, one usually right behind the other. Mary frequently caught them looking over their shoulders, as if expecting someone to appear behind them.

Mary had no idea where Fort Jefferson was or how many hours or days it would take for the braves to reach the fort. She wished she had some way to warn the settlers there and perhaps to prevent the bloodshed that now seemed inevitable. She could only hope and pray the fort was well-guarded and well-prepared to fend off an Indian attack.

Perhaps the squaws also wondered where the braves were at this moment, and whether their Great Spirit would protect them.

Mary found herself trying to fit each one of the party into a neat little pigeonhole. She'd already known that Medicine Woman was Eagle Feather's squaw and that White Messenger considered himself to be their son. While in the village, she'd observed Buffalo Woman, Little Fawn and Silent Tree appeared to live in separate huts, each with a brave as though they were man and wife.

And Shooting Star, who she frequently found wiping away a tear, appeared to be in love with Msipessi, the only one in their little tribe who insisted on retaining his Shawnee name. For his part, though, Msipessi seemed to be more interested in Mary than in Shooting Star, a situation that Mary was loath to accept.

Perhaps now, as each squaw in turn kept one eye on the river behind them, they were looking for their men. They had not seen any of them since they'd left Shawneetown in the middle of that first long night.

In the days that passed, they eased into a routine. They awakened each morning as dawn broke and foraged for food. The mornings were filled with an almost leisurely rowing northward. The woods were thick on both banks, easily shielding anyone who ventured by land, so they stayed near the center of the river where it was the safest for women traveling alone.

They usually stopped when the sun was high, pulling the canoes to the riverbank and hiding them from others traveling by water, while they again foraged for food. They knew which plants were edible, which tasted fair or even good, and which ones were sour, ill-tasting or harmful. Mary tried to watch and learn, realizing that someday—perhaps someday soon—knowing which plants to eat could mean the difference between life and death.

After their meal, they took long naps to avoid the heat of the day.

Sometimes Medicine Woman gave her a sprig or two and directed her into the woods to find more of the plants, which she would place in one of her many buckskin pouches.

Then they returned to their rowing until nightfall, when they would camp for the night near the banks of the river but obscured by the thick woods.

They slept on the ground with no blankets to cover them or soften the earth, with only the tree branches overhead as their roof, and the sounds of coyotes and wolves howling in the distance. A good campfire, stoked through the night hours, would have been efficient at keeping the animals at bay, but Medicine Woman did not want them to start a fire, and the others obeyed her without question. Mary wondered if they were afraid white men would see the smoke and the six women alone would be vulnerable to attack.

Now Medicine Woman tugged at her shoulder, and Mary turned to look at her. The old woman grunted and pointed toward the shore. Mary and the squaws turned in the direction the old woman pointed, pulling the canoes onto the banks and into some underbrush.

The sun was beginning to set and the squaws, as was their habit, began to forage for food. They instinctively moved outward in a semi-circle, each one attending to their own little area while staying in close proximity to the others.

Mary and Buffalo Woman converged upon a small clearing almost at the same time. She could hear the others on both sides of her, even if she couldn't see them for the thick woods. Buffalo Woman was stooping to pick some berries when she abruptly froze, her hand in mid-air.

Mary stopped, listening for anything out of the ordinary. She heard nothing—not even the other squaws. It was as if everyone except her were responding to a silent alarm.

Then Shooting Star was pushed into the clearing by a white man holding her by a fist knotted into her hair.

Mary and Buffalo Woman both stood at the same time, their eyes riveted on the man. Mary was dumbfounded to see a white man. He appeared to be in his late thirties, and he was amazingly tall—at least six feet, which made him tower over the squaws.

He had large black eyes set into a huge head. He wore buckskin in the Indian manner, his torso naked, the breechcloth barely covering his loins. His arms and legs were sinewy and appeared to be rock-hard.

Though his face was tanned as leather and the jagged scar across his cheek made him appear even more sinister, his nose was patrician, his jaw line that of a European, and his hair was light brown with reddish streaks.

Mary thought if she'd ever see a white man again, she would rush to him and beg his help in rescuing her. But there was something about the viciousness in which he led Shooting Star forward, grabbing her hair so fiercely that she cried out in pain that made Mary want to rush to her aid instead.

The man saw the two others and halted in the middle of the clearing. A sheath knife hung from his breechcloth and glinted in the remaining sunlight.

"Ah," he said, eyeing Mary's body with such scrutiny that she instinctively covered her bosom with her arms, even though she was fully clothed in the deerskin. "And who might you be?" he asked in clear English.

Her mouth was as dry as cotton.

His tongue moved slowly over his cracked and peeling lower lip. "A captive, eh?"

As he released Shooting Star and moved slowly toward her, Mary thought quickly. None of the braves in the village had bothered her—none of them. Only the Frenchman had approached her, and he might not have done so, if he'd thought she belonged to an Indian brave.

"I am Songbird," she said, her voice sounding clear and strong, much stronger than she felt. She hoped his eyes would remain fixed on her face as they were now, so he wouldn't see her knees beginning to quiver. "I am the daughter of a great chief."

He stopped a mere three feet from her and eyed her head, now covered in downy soft hair that was so short it simply stood on end.

"Are you now?" he cackled. "And who might that be?"

Beyond him, Mary spied Medicine Woman as she silently moved into the clearing behind the man. She raised her finger and pointed behind him. "I am the daughter of Chief Eagle Feathers and Medicine Woman."

He half-turned, his eyes widening as he spotted Medicine Woman. He spoke to her in a language Mary did not understand. As he spoke, Medicine Woman's eyes widened and she looked from the man to Mary and back again.

Then Medicine Woman came to stand beside Mary, her chin lifted high. "Ah!" she said, the single syllable sounding deep and broad. "Ah!" she repeated, followed by other words. Mary caught the words "thee-me-tha White Messenger."

The man turned to Mary. "So White Messenger is your brother," he said, his eyes narrowing. "Lucky you."

"Oh? And why is that?"

He smiled, displaying long yellow teeth. "Because today you will be left unharmed."

She felt her skin turn instantly to ice, although the hot, humid summer air swirled about her.

Two Indian braves entered the clearing pushing Little Fawn and Silent Tree in front of them.

The man spoke to them and they released their grips on the squaws. Then he turned to Medicine Woman and said a few words.

She nodded and spoke to the other women.

Then he turned back to Mary. "You are to join us for our evening meal," he said. "We are having squirrel."

"Who are you?" Mary asked, her chin still held high.

"The Indians call me Katepacomen," he said, his black eyes fixed on her so strongly that she struggled with the desire to flee from him. "The British and the Colonists know me under a different name."

He turned and crossed the clearing to join the other braves.

"Oh?" Mary said, her voice carrying across the clearing. "And what name is that?"

"Girty," he said over his shoulder. Then he stopped and peered back at her, his thin lips curling. "Simon Girty."

26

The sun had disappeared from the horizon, leaving only the remnants of a red sky to warm the tops of the trees. The shadows had lengthened and widened in the vanishing light as the campfire that once danced and flickered began to burn down. Above the fire, a kettle hung on sturdy wooden poles, the battered pot half-filled with a watery mixture of squirrel meat, wild onions, and corn.

The squaws had eaten little, though Mary was certain they were every bit as ravenous as she. The men had watched them with the eyes of hawks as they worked, first to start the nearly smokeless fire, then to boil the squirrel and peel its meat off the bones, and finally as they added the onions and corn the men carried in a type of haversack. When it was done, the men ate first, leaving nothing but scraps in the kettle for the women to divide amongst themselves.

Under Medicine Woman's direction, Buffalo Woman had been painstakingly fair in providing each squaw with the same amount, but it still amounted to little more than a handful of food swimming in a soup of flavored water.

One by one, they went to the riverbank and washed their bowls under the men's attentive eyes.

Now the women sat on cushions of pine needles several yards from the men, their bodies still as statues. Only their eyes betrayed a hint of life, as the narrowed slits followed the men as they rose from their campfire. Without turning their heads, they followed them to the horses the men had led into the clearing earlier and tied to trees with strapping hemp. Their unblinking eyes watched them go through their haversacks until they had wrapped their fingers securely around earthenware jugs.

Their drinking continued for such a long time that Mary wanted nothing more than to be gone from this place and away from these men who appeared fiercer than any of the savages she'd seen at Shawneetown. Fearing she'd bring unwanted attention to herself, she remained as still as the other women, though her legs were beginning to cramp.

They spoke in a tongue Mary could not understand but as she observed the other women appearing to listen intently, she came to the conclusion they must be using the Shawnee language. There were certain words they used that caused the women to quickly glance in each other's direction as though they were able to communicate without words and from their stiffening postures, Mary did not like what she was seeing.

Girty occasionally rose and stretched and stumbled into the bushes for a minute or two, then returned to drink still more while the braves followed in turn.

The braves were not young, Mary decided as she watched them. They were probably the age of her father when he'd been struck down. Their limbs were long and lean and somewhat muscular but they lacked the litheness of the younger braves she'd observed in the village. One of them appeared to have back problems; upon rising, he remained stooped just a bit longer than he should and he groaned as he straightened.

As the hours stretched on and the moon rose high over their heads, the brave without the back problem rose unsteadily. He teetered just a bit as he peered in their direction, at one moment almost looking as if he would fall face-first into the kettle.

Then he spoke, his voice low and guttural.

Girty laughed and waved his hand toward the women.

The brave staggered as he approached them, his dark eyes fixed upon Shooting Star. She cast her eyes downward and did not move, even when he spoke to her and gestured for her to join him. He became increasingly louder and more belligerent, finally reaching out to grab the young squaw. Mary moved to stop him but Medicine Woman blocked her arm and her movement went unnoticed.

Puzzled, Mary watched as he pulled Shooting Star to her feet and manhandled her back toward the fire and the others. Mary turned to look into the other women's eyes, noticing an alarm she hadn't witnessed since the night they left Shawneetown. But in the next instant, their eyes were dark, veiled and unreadable.

Mary watched from the edge of the clearing as the men passed the young squaw back and forth between them, laughing and belching as they felt of her young body. Shooting Star fixed her eyes on a distant object and refused to look at the men, her face as impassive as stone though Mary could only imagine the horror she must be feeling. She didn't know what was worse: being the victim or being forced to watch. She wondered why the women didn't run or try to fight these drunken monsters, but then she reasoned they would be no match for the two braves and the strange white savage.

Then their eyes were on the remaining squaws as Girty called out to them, waving his hand in the direction of the horses.

Silent Tree started to rise but Medicine Woman directed her to remain seated and the old woman herself stood and made her way to the nearest horse. She groped in the haversack, finally finding a flask. She hesitated, her back to the men, the moonlight illuminating her profile to the squaws. She quickly pulled the cap off the flask and reached for the pouch she kept suspended from her waist. Deftly, she dropped some of the herbs into the bottle.

Girty bellowed out to her in a drunken stupor, angrily slinging an empty jug into the fire, causing the flames to soar. The old woman turned as though she had only just pulled the stopper from the flask and hurried wordlessly to his side. He grabbed the container from her and took a long, hard swallow, his Adam's apple bobbing in the light of the flames as he drank.

One of the braves murmured something as he tugged at his forearm. Girty reluctantly handed the jug to him, wiping his mouth on an unclean arm and watching covetously as the brave indulged in the liquid. Then the bottle was passed onto the third.

Medicine Woman backed away from the light of the fire, returning to the women. As she approached, she briefly glanced at Mary and her head seemed to nod in a barely perceptible movement.

Shooting Star remained at the campfire, held to the ground now by one of the tottering braves. The men resumed their drinking, their laughter and their boisterous bantering filling the night air.

She had been passed around briefly but now she appeared to be the possession of one brave in particular, whose stupor was growing at such a rate that it appeared he would soon pass out.

The other women were ignored, much to Mary's relief.

Then as the seconds passed, the brave with the bad back held his forehead in his hands as if it were a child's top spiraling out of control. For the briefest moment, Girty peered in their direction, the fire emphasizing the jagged scar that ran across his cheek toward his jaw line. He opened his mouth as if to speak but fell forward, his hair barely missing the campfire.

The second brave rapidly came to his feet, his hand on the knife that dangled from his breechcloth, but his knees slipped from under him and he hit the ground, his torso falling forward onto Shooting Star.

As the young woman rolled him off her, the brave who had been holding his head fell sideways.

Everything happened at once; Medicine Woman grunted and issued directives to the other squaws, who came to their feet instantly and fled toward the riverbank.

"Ha-le!" Medicine Woman shouted at Mary, pointing in the direction of the river. Her heart pounded as she rose and hurried to catch up with the others. She glanced back when she was almost out of sight, just in time to see Medicine Woman slit the throat of the brave with the bad back. Stunned, Mary stopped in her tracks. Medicine Woman tossed the knife to Shooting Star, and the slender young woman straddled the man who had lain across her, his head face-down. She tilted his head upward, and slit his throat with one clean movement.

"Ha-le! Ha-le!"

Buffalo Woman grabbed Mary's arm and shoved her forward, pointing toward the boats. "Ha-le!"

Mary turned back toward the river and ran as swiftly as her feet could carry her.

They worked in tandem to pull off the underbrush that hid the boats from view. They worked rapidly, skillfully, their hands in unison as they lugged the canoes to the river and cast them off even as they climbed into them.

They stopped a few feet from shore, waiting wordlessly until Shooting Star and Medicine Woman appeared. Then as they waded into the water and climbed into Mary's boat, they pushed off.

They rowed as one, their paddles pumping the water with a simultaneous current, hurrying northward as if their very lives depended upon it.

27

The first sharp rays of sunlight found Jim dozing on the ground with his back propped against the stockade fence, his head lolled forward on his chest, and his longrifle still grasped firmly by both hands across his lap. The warmth caused him to stir, his tongue instinctively brushing across his chapped lips. The summer sun was harsh and as he awakened, it served to remind him of the lack of water.

Fort Jefferson was situated on a hill overlooking the Mississippi River, ironic that so much water was within their sight but unattainable now that the Indians had them completely surrounded.

He opened his eyes and then quickly narrowed them against the blazing sunlight. His lean, handsome face was streaked with black powder smoke from firing his weapon countless times. He tried to uncoil his fingers but they were stiff and unyielding.

It had been four days since the Indians first attacked. Four days of relentless assault and siege. Four days of five hundred settlers and their families and militia desperately fighting to hold onto the only fort along the western front. Four days of women rushing from man to man, post to post, providing shot they carried in their aprons, of children screaming and crying and huddling in the close confines of the vegetable cellars. Of men screaming from wounds and litters crowding the church. Of relentless Indian and British gun fire and of their own return fire which by necessity was more measured and sure as they found their shot and powder diminishing.

It had been four days since he'd dozed more than a few minutes here or there. The nights were as horrific as the days; when darkness descended, the Indians shot arrows tipped with fire, illuminating the fort as though it were day. Every man, woman and child old enough to lend a hand were forced to fight valiantly to extinguish the flames before they lit the entire fort afire. They were constantly plugging holes—the areas scarcely manned—which the Indians were adept at finding as they attempted repeatedly to climb the hill and walls and penetrate the fort.

Four days and their food, their water, and their powder were almost gone. The surprise attack had even left their livestock outside the fort's walls and with them, their milk, eggs, and meat.

Surrender was not an option. The fort was conceived by the Virginia legislature—some said by Patrick Henry, but Jim suspected Colonel Clark had more to do with it. It was the Continental Army's westernmost presence and their only opportunity to protect the western settlers from the Indians and the British. Nearby Clarksville consisted entirely of civilians who would no doubt leave if the fort fell. For all Jim knew, Clarksville was itself under attack at this very moment, since none of the settlers there had come to their assistance. And if the militia and the settlers left, the land would be forfeited to the British. Jim believed as Clark did; if they could not secure this land now, their descendents would forever be fighting the enemy at their back doors.

His eyes scanned his surroundings. Captain Edward Worthington's men had been invaluable. It was clear from their well-coordinated efforts they'd been together for a time—more than two years now. Originally formed from farmers wanting to protect their families, livestock and land, the unit was a hodgepodge of Frenchmen, Ohio Valley longhunters and Colonists who had fought the Indians consistently over the past months.

It wasn't the first time Jim had fought alongside them; they'd been at Vincennes when Clark seized the cannon that had come in so handy at Piqua. They'd been at Piqua itself and Chillicothe too, hardened from a springtime of fighting at St. Louis and Cahokia.

Now their blue and white uniforms were covered in dust and grime and many of their white hats were long gone or turned varied shades of brown.

During this lull in the fighting, he watched the men attend to their various needs—some inspecting their weapons and melting lead into shot for the next onslaught; others were going in search of food or water, and still others inquiring as to the condition of wounded comrades.

They could not get word to Clark, who was days from Fort Jefferson and perhaps approaching the Cumberland Gap by now. They'd discussed the night before of slipping a man out of the fort in an attempt to get reinforcements, but careful consideration of the vast number of Indians and British who had them surrounded had made that plan appear suicidal.

Jim rose and tried to stretch out the stiffness that permeated his limbs. He watched as a few women meandered past the men, handing out hard tack biscuits that had been stored for the winter months. The fact they were using them now was not lost on him.

Through the dust, Jim spotted Tommy trudging toward him. He carried a single battered tin cup, which he passed to Jim as he reached him. "Coffee," he said. "It's weak but it's something."

Jim offered his thanks and took a sip of the tepid liquid, allowing the moisture to roll over his parched lips. It tasted more like rainwater than coffee.

Tommy sidled up to the fence and peered through a gun hole.

"Chickasaw," Jim said without looking.

"There's a few Shawnee and Wyandot," Tommy said.

Jim raised one eyebrow. The tone in the young man's voice sounded like a seasoned fighter. "I reckon there are."

"Wonder if Girty is out there?"

"I would love to get my hands around his neck," Jim said, taking another sip before reluctantly handing the cup back to

Tommy. "But no, from what I hear, he stays with the Miami. Haven't seen any of them out there. Not yet, anyways."

Jim angled up beside Tommy and peered through a neighboring gun hole. The sound of gunfire reached them, but it sounded more muffled than the past few days. He swore under his breath.

"What is it?"

"They're killing the livestock."

They watched helplessly as the horses were spurred out of their corral, the Indians' war whoop causing them to bolt and run. But the few cattle they had were apparently too slow for the savages or perhaps they simply wanted the settlers to suffer as they watched the precious meat and milk cows slaughtered. Most of the chickens were gathered up and emptied into sacks on the horses while still struggling to escape, no doubt intended to be the source of food for the Indians.

"They're burning the crops," Jim said.

"No."

"Yep." He watched as the Indians lit the fields on fire, the corn that would help them survive through the winter going up in smoke. "Payback for Piqua and Chillicothe," he said more to himself than to Tommy.

Others were gathering as the smoke drifted high over their heads, peering through holes in the fences and swearing. One young girl burst into tears before an older woman relieved her of handing out biscuits and ordered her to the makeshift hospital on the other side of the fort.

The Indians were using the flames now to light the ends of their arrows before shooting them around the perimeter of the fort.

"What are they doing?" Tommy said, his voice rising. "They aim to burn us alive!"

"Or smoke us out," Jim said, watching. He raised his longrifle and shot one Indian as he prepared to shoot an arrow. The man fell from his horse and rolled over the flames, screaming in agony. "Wait," he said, "they're covering their retreat. They're leaving!"

Word spread rapidly. With the Indians moving out of range of the militia's weapons, they could only stand at the walls to their fort and watch them ride or trot away, their movements eventually obscured by thick black smoke.

28

Mary thought she'd never before seen a sky this large. She lay flat on her back on a bed of dry leaves and evergreen straw and stared upwards at the vastness of it all, the midnight blue hues and the hundreds of stars twinkling. Gone were the mountains and treetops that often obscured parts of the sky. In contrast, if she stood at the edge of the woods, she could see the horizon, as flat as this land was.

She wondered if George or Ma or any of her family were looking at this same sky, seeing the same stars blinking, at the same full moon as it illuminated the earth. When she got back home, she'd tell them how much larger the sky was out here, how many more stars one could count, and how much larger the moon appeared.

She'd lost track of the days now. Instinctively, she ran her hand across the top of her head and felt the strands of hair that grew each day. She realized as they became long enough to lie flat, as they were beginning to do now, it signaled the passage of time.

It had only been in the last few days that her thoughts had caught up with her. And with her thoughts came the raw emotions associated with her ordeal. Now she saw George's face whenever she closed her eyes, and was only now beginning to realize the future she'd planned with him might never take place. The courtship, the wedding, the marriage, the children—her life had changed in the blink of an eye.

Somewhere behind her on an Indian trail was the only part of her father she'd managed to bury, a pitiful strand of hair and piece of scalp. It wasn't right for someone to be cut down in his prime when he'd done so much good and had so many plans ahead of him.

She wondered where Ma was and her sisters and brothers, whether they'd managed to escape or if they'd been captured by another Indian family and were out there somewhere like she was, still plotting her escape and waiting until the time was right.

Her stomach growled ferociously, a reminder that she'd eaten nothing for two days now.

The journey here had lasted too many days to count. They'd traveled along the Ohio River. Then one morning as the sun broke through the darkness, the river wasn't as wide. And as the days passed by, they could see the river bottom as they looked down while they rowed; it was as white as anything she'd ever seen before.

The squaws called this river the Wabashike, a four-syllable word they pronounced as Wa-ba-she-keh and they seemed to know exactly where they were, as though they had traveled this way many times before. And instead of remaining near the center of the river, as they'd done on the Ohio, they stayed closer to the shoreline. This river ran from north to south and as they traveled northward, they tried to remain in the countercurrent. Still, Mary thought as she rubbed her aching shoulders, it had been a physical ordeal.

When they finally stopped at this nondescript clearing, she welcomed the break. But as the days crept by, she wondered why they continued to remain here. Unlike the abandoned village, there was no shelter here. Unlike Shawneetown, there was no food. And they had not seen any others—white or red—since leaving Girty and his men.

And she had to assume those men were dead. Watching Medicine Woman and the gentle Shooting Star slit the throats of the braves so easily and so readily, rekindled her fear of them. Though she had not witnessed them attack Girty, she could not assume they had left him alive to track them down and take vengeance upon them.

Now they were living in a simple clearing in the bend of the river. It was surrounded by thick trees and undergrowth, but they could easily maneuver around at various points.

They'd dragged the two canoes, their continued seaworthiness questionable, deeper into the woods. They buried them under piles of leaves and cypress straw, spending the better part of the morning obscuring them. With every armload of leaves she dumped on top of the overturned vessels, she knew she would never be able to dig one out and escape undetected.

In fact, Medicine Woman did not want any of them to venture far, which meant the precious few wild berries they found were gone quickly. They had no corn, no cornmeal, no jerky, and no other form of food.

She rolled onto her stomach and peered through the trees at the bend in the river. Each morning on their journey the sun rose in their faces; it had been difficult at times due to the sun's brilliance reflecting off the top of the water and into their eyes. At night, the sun had set behind them.

So they had traveled northward and eastward, she thought wearily.

Mary Neely is my name,
At the Salt Lick when they came;
North on the Cumberland past the Fort,
Joined at the Red River by additional escort.
North on the Spaylawitheepi,
"Ohio" we call it, white women like me.
Remained for a time at Shawneetown
Until more braves came down.
We fled northeastward on the Wabashike…

She repeated the new verses until she had them memorized, though she knew she could never return home by retracing her path. It had been too far and most of it by water; she would never be able to remember every turn they'd taken along the way.

But as she watched the river rolling gently by in the moonlight, she realized that to the east was civilization. Though they'd seen no one else since they'd left Girty, she knew if she continued her eastward trek, she would eventually end up on the other side of the Cumberland Gap in a more populous region of Virginia.

Her heart began beating faster as a plan formed.

She would head due east. She could follow the movements of the sun to make sure it rose every morning in her face and set every evening behind her. Ultimately, if she traveled far enough, she could even wind up at the ocean's edge. And the farther east she traveled, the fewer Indians there would be. Her chances of encountering white men would improve—and with them, her chances of sooner or later getting back to her home and her family.

She heard Buffalo Woman rise and head into the woods, only to return a few minutes later. She would have to wait until the others were asleep. Then she would arise and wander into the woods as if to relieve herself, only she would keep going. It would be dawn before they would find her gone and by then, she would be far from here.

She tried to doze but sleep would not come. With her newly formed plan, she was afraid she would not awaken until the others were rising for the new day. That thought alone was enough to keep her continuously opening her eyes and peering about, waiting for the right time.

The moon was high when she rolled onto her knees. She watched the others breathing rhythmically. Then slowly she came to her feet and strolled through the clearing toward the east, as if she were simply planning to relieve herself. But once she began traveling through the woods away from the others, she did not stop.

Her heart pounded in her ears as she planned her next move. With the bend in the river, it meant she must cross to the other side in order to continue moving eastward. She walked for a short time along the edge of the woods, surveying the water in the moonlight, calculating the best place to attempt to swim across. She wasn't the strongest swimmer and she would have to use every ounce of strength to get to the other shore; failure meant the current would take her right back around the bend and within sight of the others.

She took a deep breath. Once she stepped away from the woods, she would be in full view. And when that occurred, she must move swiftly.

She tried to quiet her heart and steady her breathing. God would be with her, she reminded herself. She was wasting precious time here. She would take three more deep breaths and then she would make her move.

She closed her eyes and took one long, deep breath and exhaled. She shrugged her shoulders in an effort to loosen them for the swim ahead.

She inhaled deeply and held her breath for a few seconds before exhaling once again. This time she bent at the waist and tried to stretch and loosen her spine.

She stood up, her eyes still closed. This was it. One more deep breath; then it would be time to go.

A man's voice floated across the water to her.

Her eyes flew open.

No one was there.

Had she imagined it? She thought wildly. She cocked her head and listened.

There it was again: the distinct sound of a man's voice. She strained to hear him, trying to determine his location in the darkness.

Another man answered him.

Their voices had a strange accent and their words were difficult to decipher. But they were white men, not Indians.

She gasped.

They were British.

She rested her hand on a nearby tree trunk and stretched her neck beyond the tree line just as a boat came into view. It was traveling from the same direction the squaws had come and was rounding the same bend that had been in sight of their camp.

As she watched, the front of the boat appeared: it was a flatboat and was manned not just by two white men but by dozens of Indians as well. These Indians did not dress as Medicine Woman, Msipessi and the others dressed. They wore deerskin breeches but white fabrics over their shoulders. One had a bright red fabric that reached from his left shoulder to his right hip, where it was held in place by a brightly colored belt. Another had a number of tall feathers protruding from a crown of long black hair, his face proud and head held high as he cruised upriver like the Egyptian Pharaohs Mary had often read about in the Old Testament.

The white men wore red uniforms; confirmation, she thought, that they were indeed British.

She heard a twig snap behind her and she jerked her head.

Medicine Woman stood behind her, her black eyes intently watching her.

Mary felt the blood drain from her face. She had only one option.

She held her finger to her lips and pointed to the river.

Medicine Woman did not immediately draw her eyes away from Mary. But as the sounds of more men reached both their ears, the old squaw turned her head slightly and peered through the trees to the river beyond.

The flatboat came into full view, followed by another.

She felt her heart stop as she realized had she not taken the time to catch three deep breaths, she would be out there in the middle of the river right this minute, in the direct path of the oncoming boats. They were white men, yes—but British. And they were friends with these Indians they freely traveled with.

Would that have made her a captive once again?

The man with the tall feathers came into clearer view as the boat came even with them. Afraid to move a single muscle, she could only look across the water and wonder if they would have treated her badly—perhaps raping, torturing, or even killing her.

But she would never know.

When it had passed and she thought it safe again to move, she rushed back to Medicine Woman like a child who had wandered unintentionally too far from her mother.

She would escape. Someday, but not tonight. But soon—very soon, her time would come.

29

The boats continued to arrive; increasing as the darkness gave way to the sun's piercing rays. By mid-afternoon, Mary had counted at least four flatboats and a dozen canoes.

Each time a vessel approached the bend, the squaws would remain perfectly still in the shadows, their bodies almost blending in with the vegetation. She could feel their growing anxiety as they studied each one, no doubt looking for their men. There had been times when Pa and Sam had joined other settlers in fighting back the Indians and Mary had stood with Ma and the other women and children as the men rode back home. But unlike the settlers, the squaws did not flag down the incoming vessels and ask for news of their loved ones.

At times, Mary wondered whether she should rush from the woods as a boat drew near in an effort to flag down white men who could possibly help her. But her fear of the British kept her from following through. She tried to remember the snippets of conversation she caught as Pa conversed with others about the War for Independence; nothing they said about the British was complimentary, even though their own ancestors had come from England, Ireland and Scotland.

And Medicine Woman had not hurt her. Neither had the others, really, if she didn't count the overzealous way Buffalo Woman tried to wash the white blood from her. And there were too many Europeans willing to cohort with the Indians, like Pierre Pierpont and Simon Girty. How would she know if she were leaping from the frying pan into the fire?

The sun was high overhead when Little Fawn began to point excitedly toward three approaching canoes. The others joined her at the edge of the woods, standing tip-toed as if the extra height would allow them to see the men more clearly.

Then Medicine Woman said, "See-la! See-la!"

At this, the women rushed from the woods to stand on the river's edge. Not wanting to be left out of the excitement, Mary ran after them, stopping just behind them to peer downriver. She had to shade her eyes from the sun's harsh rays and even then she was unable to see clearly from the glare that reflected off the surface of the water.

But when the man in the first canoe rose and held his hand up in greeting, Mary knew why they had remained in this spot for so many days. It was Eagle Feathers.

The women raced into the river as the canoes came near and for the first time, Mary witnessed smiles and laughter as they greeted one another. Eagle Feathers was the first to step out of the canoe, placing his arm around Medicine Woman as the old woman spoke rapidly. Buffalo Woman almost turned the second canoe over as she reached a brave in that vessel and literally pulled him into the water with her.

As Msipessi stepped into the water, Shooting Star rushed to him, throwing her arms around him. He stood awkwardly before gently resting his arms about her shoulders, glancing at Mary as he did so. She thought she detected the color rising in his cheeks, but she quickly looked away only to find White Messenger casting a fleeting look at her as he guided the boats to shore.

Even Silent Tree was whispering in one of the brave's ears as they walked hand in hand to the water's edge.

Only Little Fawn stood alone. Mary followed her eyes as they darted from one to another before coming to rest on the third canoe. When she began to wail, the rest of the group stopped cold and turned toward her.

The third canoe had arrived at the riverbank, guided by a lone Indian whose eyes remained downcast. Eagle Feathers left Medicine Woman's side to stand beside Little Fawn. When he began to speak, the others listened attentively, all except Little Fawn, who sobbed quietly at first and then rushed to the canoe and tried to plunge herself into it. From his gestures and head held high, Mary imagined he spoke of their heroism as he paid tribute to them.

Mary hung back, watching the braves as they lifted two wrapped bodies from the depths of the vessel. They carried them reverently to the edge of the woods, where they laid them in the relative coolness of the shade. Little Fawn dropped to her knees and wailed; her voice carried on the wind like a chorus.

There were six braves now, where once there had been nine. Six braves, five squaws, and Mary.

They buried them just before nightfall on the shore that wrapped around the bend in the river. They were placed a few feet away from the tree line facing east where the morning sun would warm the burial mounds. The evergreens on the north side of the mounds would stop the cold winter winds and the absence of trees to the south would allow the sun to penetrate even in the bleakest of winter. Their possessions had been laid gently beside them while Eagle Feathers spoke in a sing-song tone.

When the ceremony was over, Little Fawn lay across one of the mounds, her body wracked with sobs. Mary remained a short distance away, caught between the feeling that she should pray for his soul and the satisfaction that came from knowing there were two less Indians to kill and capture the settlers. She didn't realize Msipessi had come to stand beside her until he spoke.

"Hel-lo," he said haltingly.

Mary looked at him in astonishment. "Hello."

"I learn language," he said, adding an extra syllable to the last word.

She nodded and turned her attention back to Little Fawn.

"Why you no sing?"

"What?"

"Nuc-kum-mo," he said, gesturing with his hand in front of his mouth. "Sing."

"I am too sad to sing," Mary answered. "You killed my father."

He looked at Little Fawn as she cried inconsolably. "Had I known," he said slowly, as if grasping for the right words, "he was your fath-her, I would not have killed him."

Mary watched Little Fawn for a moment and then she walked quietly to the mounds. Once there, she knelt and began softly singing. The others stopped what they were doing and gathered nearby, watching and listening. Even Little Fawn stopped her wailing and eventually her sobs were quieted.

Mary closed her eyes and continued to sing verse after verse. She choked back the tears that stung her eyes, her voice rising in the waning light, floating softly over the waters. Only she knew her song was for Pa. Somewhere to the south and west, she could only hope he was buried now in a proper site. And as the words flowed gently from her, she vowed that someday she would sing this song while she bowed over his grave.

30

They left shortly after dawn. For the first time in days, Mary had a breakfast of venison jerky, bear fat, and cornmeal. Eagle Feathers served each person as they sat in a tight circle and passed their bowls down to him, one by one. Each time he received a bowl he filled it and lifted it to the heavens while he chanted. Then the bowl was passed back down to the proper person. Mary thought she detected a gleam in his eyes as she passed hers down, and she noted that he also gave her an amount that equaled the others' servings. She was being treated as a member of the family, someone who belonged with them, though she was coming to the conclusion that she now was the only person there who realized her stay with them would be short-lived.

They did not dally after breakfast. Mary was enlisted along with Silent Tree and Shooting Star to uncover the canoes they'd hidden a few days earlier. Then they gathered their meager possessions and assembled at the edge of the river. They had five canoes amongst them; Mary was placed in one with White Messenger and Little Fawn and to her relief, White Messenger rowed.

Unlike the boats they'd witnessed over the past two days, they did not round the bend and head toward the south. Instead, they crossed the river to the northeast.

Once they'd reached the opposite shore, they banked the canoes and collected their possessions. It took some time for Mary to realize the next leg of their journey would take place on foot. The women carried most of the possessions by tying the bundles onto their backs with woven hemp. When they loaded a large bundle onto Mary's back, she thought she would certainly sink to her knees under its weight. She stood for a time trying to steady her legs while the men lifted the canoes and turned them upside down. Then with one brave carrying each vessel, they began a trek along a narrow trail. Only Eagle Feathers did not carry a canoe or a bundle.

As Mary was directed to fall in behind Buffalo Woman, she realized the squaw carried two bundles at least as large as her own strapped to her back. As Mary struggled to remain on her feet, she concentrated on the larger woman in an effort to focus on her strength.

The walk was slow and arduous. As the sun rose, biting flies and sweat bees came out in full force, encircling Mary's head. Thankfully, her hands were free and as she walked through the woods, she tried to fend them off. But as the day wore on, the woods grew deeper and the path narrower and she found herself pushing vines and branches out of her way as she trudged onward.

When the sun was high overhead and they encountered a suitable clearing, they stopped. The canoes were laid down and the packages removed from their backs. Mary thought her spine would never be the same and she marveled at the ability of women smaller than she managing such burdens.

Instead of resting, the squaws went in search of food, eventually stumbling upon some dark purple grapes, which created quite a stir. When they returned, they started a fire, cooked some cornmeal cakes, and ate more jerky, cornmeal, berries, and grapes. They had no water so Mary savored each grape, sucking the juice out of it before chewing.

They spent the hottest part of the day resting and chatting. Mary picked up the word "Katepacomen" several times as Medicine Woman spoke to Eagle Feathers, and she concluded the old woman was telling the chieftain of their narrow escape from Simon Girty. The old man's brows creased and his face grew dark as she spoke. Several of the younger braves, including Msipessi, stood and spoke loudly, seeming to posture as if ready to fight. In contrast, White Messenger remained seated and silent. The old man issued several guttural directives that had the hot-headed men returning reluctantly to their seated positions.

By mid-afternoon, they were on the move again, carrying the same loads as before and following a foot trail that led them northeast through a heavily wooded area with increasingly mushy earth. At times they encountered swamps and had to detour around them while giant mosquitoes emerged and harrassed them unmercifully.

They stopped at dusk. Some of the men left, presumably to hunt for the evening meal. Silent Tree and Buffalo Woman embarked on a quest to find more wild grapes or berries, though they had all packed as many of the grapes from lunch as they could, not knowing what they would find ahead of them. Little Fawn sat silently, her back to the others, who appeared to respect her mourning. Medicine Woman directed Mary to start a fire.

Mary had never started one for the Indians before, but she had helped both Pa and her brothers many times. The Indians prepared their fires differently, though, which created far less smoke. Mary was eager to learn how they accomplished this; she never knew when the knowledge would come in handy.

She assembled dry leaves and grasses and old bark in one pile, small twigs and sticks in another, and a few larger pieces of old wood in a third pile.

She found a solid piece of bark with a slight indentation in it, perfect for taking a stone and another stick and rubbing together until a flicker began. This was easier said than done, however, and as she labored over the job, she detected movement beside her. White Messenger had returned and was leaning back on his haunches only two or three feet from her, watching her efforts.

When the flicker began, she blew on it, adding dried leaves as she did, until a flame burst forth. Then she continued to add the leaves and grasses, followed by the twigs and finally, the larger sticks.

When the fire was well underway, she leaned back to survey her work.

"Do not let the flames die down," White Messenger admonished.

As she complied, she asked, "What does that do?"

"When the flame is high, there is less smoke. And in the coming winter months, smoke means your fire is cold and it will not warm you."

Mary digested this information as she added increasingly larger pieces of wood. As she began to add another piece, he grabbed her wrist.

"Do you see the moss on the side of that wood?" he asked.

She studied it. There was the slightest bit of green on one side, so minute that she was surprised he'd seen it.

"That wood will not burn well. It will create more smoke and your fire will lessen."

"Thank you," she said, tossing it into the woods in favor of another piece. When it was going well, she leaned back and admired her first effort at a relatively smokeless fire.

"You taught Msipessi to speak English," Mary said at last.

"Some. It is time all of my family learn to speak the white man's tongue," he said.

"Why is that?"

He waited a long moment before answering, his hazel eyes reflecting the growing flames. "The Shawnees once lived far from here," he said at last. "For many, many fathers before Eagle Feathers, they were born in the same land. They drew strength from their fathers before them. They knew where to hunt, where to find water, how to grow food. They knew the passing of seasons. And when the old men and women passed on to the Great Spirit, their own spirits visited those lands and provided much wisdom."

He stopped as a noise akin to a puppy yelping sounded overhead. They both looked up to see an eagle soaring above them, calling out its strange vocalizations. He studied it for a time before continuing, "Things are not the same. The Shawnees were driven from the lands of their fathers. Then they were forced from their new lands. Now they are pushed from each place they inhabit." He waved his hand toward Eagle Feathers, who sat in a corner of the clearing with his eyes closed. "They wander. They sleep under the trees where once they had homes. They search for medicines when once they knew where all the herbs grew. They go for days—or weeks—without food, sometimes without water. And each time they find a place where perhaps the spirits there would help them and provide them strength, they are driven from it."

"Perhaps," Mary said quietly, "they should make peace with the white man."

White Messenger drew his attention away from the flames. "And which white man would that be?" he asked. "The ones in the red coats, who drove us from the land of our fathers? Who sold the land that was not theirs to sell? Or the men who fight the red coats now, who have forced us from our new homes, claiming their rights are above ours? Or perhaps the French, who do not take our lands, who trade with us but cheat us and lie to us? Which of these white men will return the land of our fathers to us?

"And how can we make peace with the white man when they can not make peace among themselves?"

Mary's voice was barely above a whisper. "But you were born white," she said hesitantly. "Yet you speak as though you are one of them."

He tossed a small log onto the fire. "I do not remember my white family," he said. "I remember Medicine Woman cradling my head when I was sick. I remember Eagle Feathers teaching me how to live and thrive by hunting and fishing. I remember playing with my red brothers, laughing with my sisters. They are my family. And I am theirs."

They grew quiet.

"Why does your family have names I can understand, except Msipessi?"

"Msipessi."

His eyes became veiled and she wondered if she should tell him she felt no attraction toward Msipessi.

"His name means 'Big Cat'," he said before she could speak. "But he wishes to be known as a great Shawnee warrior. He wants someday to lead our people back to the land of our fathers. And when we arrive, he wishes proudly to wear the name he was given—Msipessi, not Big Cat."

"So where do we go now?" Mary asked. "Are we being driven away again?"

He turned toward the north. "We go to Fort Detroit," he said, "where we will get provisions. Then we head north into Canada."

31

Jim watched as the man rode through the gates on a
golden-colored horse that gleamed in the bright sunlight.
The man who sat rigidly in the saddle was a curiosity to the
men at Fort Jefferson; he was dressed in a uniform that might
once have been blue, but was now covered in a thick layer of
dust. Under the heavy jacket was a yellowed vest with just a hint
of a lace shirt at the neckline and wrists. He wore yellowed
breeches that were probably white when new, which kissed the
tops of his dusty black boots.

Behind him rode two more men who were clad in the same
type of uniform but without the lace shirt. One horse was a
stippled gray and the other brown, both of which appeared drab
next to the golden stallion.

As the horses trotted toward Jim, the man in front removed
his tricorn hat and bowed in the saddle. "Lieutenant Hawkins, I
presume?"

"Jacques Danton?" Jim returned, extending his hand.

The Frenchman halted the horse and shook Jim's hand. "It
has been a long journey."

Jim waited until the riders had dismounted. "I assumed you
would be hungry when I received your dispatch. I've taken the
liberty of ordering some food brought to my cabin." He waved
at two privates nearby. "Take the horses to the livery."

"Mine enjoys carrots," Danton said as he handed over the reins.

The private stole a sideways glance at Jim.

"I'm afraid we don't have any carrots," Jim said as he strolled toward his cabin. "Things are dire here."

"Yes, I heard," Danton said. He said something in French to his men and they fell in behind the privates.

"I have food in my cabin for them as well," Jim said.

"No need. They will eat with your men. Ours is a private conversation."

"As you wish, though they will find less than a hearty meal with my men. The Chickasaw burned roughly forty, forty-five acres of crops we'd expected to get us through the winter. They also stole or killed all the livestock outside the stockade—except one pig, which the men have been fattening up."

"Chickasaw, you say?"

Jim nodded. "Some Shawnee, maybe some Miami. Mostly Chickasaw."

Danton hesitated and Jim stopped to follow his gaze. "Those savages," the Frenchman said, motioning toward a group of Indians loading provisions, "why are they here?"

"They're Kaskaskia Indians. They're intent on revenge."

"Revenge their own kind?"

"They don't see the other tribes as 'their own kind', any more than we see the redcoats as ours."

"And what will they do?"

"They plan to ride out tonight in search of the Chickasaw."

"And when they find them?"

"They will kill them, of course." Jim began walking again toward his cabin. Before he reached the door, the distinct odor of freshly cooked venison tickled his nose. Until provisions came in from the east, they were living only on the wild animals they could shoot within an easy distance of the fort.

Danton strolled to a sideboard where a large bowl was filled with tepid water, in which he washed his hands. As he was drying them on a worn cotton towel, he said, "I may as well tell you why I am here."

Jim nodded. "Please do."

"Augustin de La Balme is very much enthused about the victories at Chillicothe and Piqua."

"Chillicothe was abandoned before we got there."

"Ah, but Piqua had not." He pulled out a chair and seated himself at the head of the table. "You whipped the savages."

Jim quietly sat opposite the Frenchman, his foot brushing Brandy, who lay curled beneath the table. "Meat is all we have at the moment. Please," he motioned toward the platter.

Danton piled the meat high atop his plate, taking a portion that might equal those required to feed three men within a few short months.

"You have inspired us by your victories," Danton continued, "Therefore, we plan to march on Fort Detroit."

Jim almost gagged. "You what?"

"We are marching on Fort Detroit. And we are told you can provide us with valuable information."

Jim slid a piece of fat to Brandy, who wolfed it down before he answered, "And whose decision is this?"

"General Washington has ordered de La Balme to capture the fort." His head nodded with a slight tremor that made him appear arrogant.

Jim continued chewing. Colonel Clark had argued before the Virginia legislature and General Washington himself for men to overtake the fort, traveling back and forth to Williamsburg several times over the past four years. Each time, the legislature had endorsed his efforts but they had supplied no men. The fact was they had none to spare. The war was raging in the northeast; very few outside of the legislature even saw the need to secure the western borders. But Clark had been persuasive and had finally been able to muster all of one hundred and fifty men. The rest of their army had been comprised of settlers who served only for the length of time it took to rid their own back yards of the marauding Indians and redcoats.

"How many men do you have?" Jim asked.

"We will recruit Frenchman sympathetic to your cause en route to Fort Detroit."

Jim stifled a grin. "And where will you find them?"

Danton shrugged. "Kaskaskia is not far from here—"

"To our west. Through Indian Territory."

"We will begin there. Then travel to Vincennes and Cahokia."

"And what makes you believe the residents will join your men and march on Detroit?"

Danton cackled. "They are only waiting for us to arrive, to join our ranks."

"I see."

Both men concentrated on their food for a pensive moment. "Then what?" Jim asked.

"I am told you know an overland passage that will take us very close to the fort."

Jim wiped his mouth with a cotton handkerchief that had seen better days. Then he rose and crossed to the other side of the one-room cabin, where he pulled out a map. Returning to the table, he pushed the platter away from the center and unrolled the document across the table, anchoring it on both sides with their mugs.

"If Vincennes is your last stop for recruits, you can pick up the Wabash River here—" he traced the route with his finger "—but to reach Detroit, you must leave the river here." He pointed to a curve where the river began to wind southward.

"Ah, yes. That is why I am here. I understand we must travel overland for a short piece before reaching the Maumee River."

"That 'short piece', as you call it, is treacherous. It is a thick wetland forest, in some places nothing but a black swamp. Your men can be mired in it. Your equipment and your horses will be sucked down by it. And those who survive the swamp are prone to fevers."

"Save me the theatrics," Danton said. "I am told of a safer passage. And I am told that you know it."

Jim returned to his seat and stabbed a piece of the venison before answering. "There is a portage between the Wabash and the Maumee Rivers. It is controlled by Chief Little Turtle of the Miami tribe. The Miami call it their 'sacred gate' and they believe it is their mission to protect it at all costs."

"And yet," Danton said, leaning back in his chair and dabbing at the corner of his mouth with a handkerchief, "it is heavily traveled."

Jim nodded. "Other Indian tribes—those friendly with the Miami. Fur traders traveling from French Quebec to New Orleans. But an army such as you suggest—"

"We have nothing to fear from the Miami. You perhaps forget our excellent relations with them."

Jim viewed the Frenchman thoughtfully. "You perhaps forget the Indians change their allegiance rather frequently."

"Nonetheless, I only require your services to guide me across the Portage. That is all."

"I presume you refer to my showing you the route on a map. I can not leave Fort Jefferson."

Danton raised his chin defiantly. "And why not?"

"Monsieur Danton, there are sixty-five Kaskaskia Indians who will leave the fort tonight under Colonel Montgomery in search of the tribes who laid siege to Fort Jefferson. I can spare only eight men to go with them.

"Since the siege, it has taken all my powers of persuasion to prevent the settlers from abandoning the fort altogether. And yet our circumstances are dismal. We have insufficient food to get us through the winter. We haven't enough powder to withstand another assault. There are families here—women and children—who may not survive a harsh winter.

"And you, sir, wish for me to leave my post to accompany you hundreds of miles along a dangerous route that can be seen only as suicidal? I think not."

They sat across the table from one another, their eyes narrowed and jaws firm. Then Danton spoke.

"If you will not accompany us to sure victory, perhaps you will indulge me by showing me the exact route on your map."

"That, Monsieur Danton, *that* I can do."

32

The days dragged on in an unmerciful heat that grew even more oppressive as the number of trees multiplied, blocking out the sun and the free flow of air. The heat was there in the morning when Mary awakened and it was still there at night when she fell fitfully asleep—a formidable inferno like nothing she had ever experienced before.

They had become hindered by swampland with thick, black quagmires. As they wandered deeper into the swamp forest, the mosquitoes grew in size and ferocity and were no longer confined to the dusk.

Mary could not help but wonder if they were lost. Surely this must be what the children of Israel experienced when they wandered in the wilderness for forty days and forty nights, she thought. How would they know if they were going in circles? She could no longer see the sunrises for the thick canopy of trees.

In the blackness of the forest, there were all manner of insects and creatures Mary had never seen before. There were lizards that reached a foot or more in length and that blended in so well, she wouldn't know it was a live creature until she touched it. Colonies of ants zipping along the tree trunks could swarm over a misplaced hand in seconds, inflicting dozens of bites before they were shaken loose.

There were frogs so large and fat the braves caught them with the same eagerness with which they hunted big game. This was of particular interest to Mary. She watched as they located branches that could be fashioned into prongs, using their knives to sharpen them. They waited until nightfall, when the frogs would croak loudly. The braves used their pitchforks like spears; they could remain so still and quiet, they looked like statues until the very moment they gigged the frogs. She had become accustomed to the Indians eating every piece of an animal—organs and entrails as well as the meat—but with the frogs, they only ate the hind legs. She wondered why, when they needed to gig so many to make a meal.

With every step she took, her bare feet became heavier with the muck that encased them. Their breaks increased by the necessity of breaking away the hardened mud with sticks lest they become so heavy they were unable to continue moving.

Days into their trek, they encountered an area in which they were unable to locate a dry place in which to sleep or eat. They took to eating while they walked, passing back venison jerky and occasionally peeling strange-looking fruits off vines that grew unfettered in this wilderness.

To sleep, they were forced to climb the sycamore trees where they could nestle against the trunks while seated in their strong branches. Floating high above the swamps, Mary slept fitfully, only dozing off when she could no longer bear to keep her eyes open, afraid at any moment she would fall headfirst into the mud.

When at last the terrain began to rise and they found themselves overlooking a river to their east, she saw in the faces of the Indians the same gratitude and relief she felt in her own heart. Though it took another two days to actually reach the water, she knew then there was an end in sight. She also knew that no matter what happened, she could never return to her family through that black and unforgiving wilderness.

By the time they reached the river's edge, they'd been forced to abandon all but two of the canoes and those that were left now looked pitifully unseaworthy. They rested for a time along the shoreline while the braves carefully inspected the vessels.

Then the women packed them with the possessions they had so dutifully carried through the swamps, and they climbed in. It was miserably tight, and Mary hoped they would not be forced to venture far.

It was two more grueling days before they encountered a trading post along the river. Eagle Feathers and Silent Tree had become ill, sometimes vomiting over the side of the canoe into the fast-moving current. Though the days had remained hot and the sun relentless, they both had begun to shiver uncontrollably even as their foreheads were drenched in perspiration.

Thankful to be among other people once again and cramping from her ordeal, Mary stretched her legs while the braves bartered with the two white traders. She found it curious they were not French and came to the conclusion they must be British. Her freedom was short-lived when Medicine Woman beckoned to her, calling out "nip-pee", the Shawnee word for water. She used Medicine Woman's buckskin pouch to get water from the river, then hurried to where the women had laid Eagle Feathers and Silent Tree upon the ground. Mary held their heads and dribbled the water into their mouths, hoping whatever they were inflicted with was not contagious and wondering if they all had eaten a frog or fruit that would prove to be poisonous.

When at last they were summoned to resume their journey, Mary found the braves had obtained five canoes, allowing for more room. She was also relieved to find these were not taking on water as their old ones, which had been left behind, had begun to do.

They rowed until dusk and then resumed their journey the next morning. By mid-day Mary noticed the river had become wider. By mid-afternoon, it was continuing to widen as they were caught up in rapids that swept them along amidst the excited whoops of the braves.

When at last the rapids subsided, they found themselves floating gently along a placid river the Indians called Myaamia.

They stopped after dark and made camp along the shoreline. They were all too tired to do more than nibble on the last of the jerky and lay down with their own thoughts—all but Medicine

Woman, who was still tending to Eagle Feathers and Silent Tree when Mary drifted off to sleep.

33

For the first time since Mary had been captured, she awakened with a film of morning dew on her skin and clothes. Her nose was cold and the unmistakable scent of autumn was in the air. As she wiggled into her own arms for additional warmth, she realized a cool breeze was penetrating her limbs, stiff from a night of hard sleep.

She reluctantly opened one eye. Startled, the other eye flew open and she came to a seated position in a fraction of a second.

Before her lay a vast body of water like she had never seen before. The sun was rising on what should have been the opposite shore but there was no land in sight. Instead, she beheld a pristine wonderland bathed in the reflection of the rising sun. Against this backdrop, dozens of birds sailed effortlessly on puffs of air, their cries unlike any sound she'd ever heard. Surely this was the most beautiful place on earth.

"What is it?" White Messenger whispered.

Mary pulled her eyes away from the water to look at him, seated just a few feet away. From his easy posture and thoughtful gaze, it appeared as though he'd been awake for some time soaking in this wondrous sight. "It's the ocean," she said in awe. "We've reached the ocean!"

He laughed softly. He rested on his haunches as effortlessly as she used to sit in a chair.

"Aren't you excited?" she said. "Have you ever seen the ocean before?"

"It is not the ocean," he said gently. "The white man calls this Lake Erie."

She wrapped her arms around her knees and watched the sun as it rose ever higher. "How do you know so much about the white man, if you can not remember your white family?"

He hesitated and she wondered if the mask she had seen envelop his face would return. Instead, he focused his eyes on the scene before them and answered quietly, "Eagle Feathers had a dream. And in this dream, he saw a white buffalo who spoke to him in the Shawnee language. And this buffalo told him he would soon have a white son, and this white son would be a messenger between the white man and the Shawnee Nation."

"That is why your name—"

"Yes."

"Do you remember what your name once was? Before you were captured?"

He shook his head. "I do not know. I do not care to know." He came to his feet. "The others are rising. It is time we eat."

The others had indeed begun to rise, the murmurings now reaching Mary's ears. As the camp stirred and came to life, she heard Medicine Woman cry out.

Buffalo Woman and Shooting Star rushed to her side, where she knelt beside Silent Tree. They spoke rapidly in hushed tones. The braves gathered silently behind them, their heads downcast. Mary did not have to understand their language or see Silent Tree to know what they were saying: she had died in the night.

It was mid-morning before they launched their canoes from the shores of Lake Erie. As Mary looked behind her, she saw the tiny mound along the tree line where they'd buried Silent Tree. Eagle Feathers had been too ill to say words over her grave as he had Little Fawn's husband, so White Messenger had officiated. Mary did not know what he said, only that his voice sounded melodious in the cool breeze. Afterward, they chanted "Nuc-kum-mo, nuc-kum-mo", pushing Mary ever closer to Silent

Tree's grave. Mary complied with a soulful song, which seemed to please the Indians.

As they cast off, White Messenger assumed the lead canoe. The others now looked to him for guidance. Medicine Woman was in the second vessel with Eagle Feathers prone in the canoe, occasionally rearing his head to heave over the side.

Now Little Fawn was feeling faint and could not bear to see Eagle Feathers' suffering. She had not eaten breakfast, preferring to stay away from the food altogether, and Mary wondered if she might be next to fall victim to this strange illness.

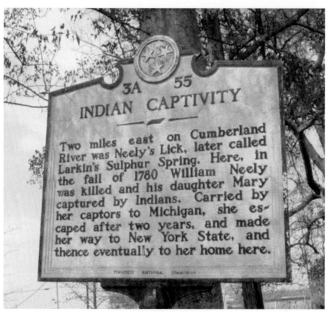

Two miles from Neely's Salt Lick is a Tennessee Historical Marker.
It is located on busy Gallatin Pike near Nashville, Tennessee.

The Cumberland River in the vicinity of Mary's capture.
Signs marking Neely's Salt Lick and Larkin's Spring have
been replaced by urban growth.

When Mary and William did not return as expected, settlers
from nearby Mansker's Station mounted a search party.
They found William dead and scalped and Mary was missing.

MANSKER'S FIRST FORT

Here on west bank of the creek that
he discovered in 1772, Kasper Mansker and other first settlers built
a log fort in 1779. John Donelson's
family fled here in 1780 for safety
from Indians. Mansker abandoned the
fort in 1781 and moved to Fort Nashborough. He returned in 1783, built
a stronger stockade on east bank of
the creek a half mile upstream, and
lived there until he died in 1820.

Today, Mansker's Station Historic Site is operated and
maintained by the City of Goodlettsville, Tennessee.

William and Margaret Patterson Neely and their ten children migrated west to Fort Nashborough less than a year before William was killed in the Indian attack at Neely's Salt Lick.

At the time of Mary's capture, Shawneetown was a bustling Shawnee village with a population around 2,200. Today, it is known as Old Shawneetown. The 2000 census lists a population of 100 households, 99.64% white and only 0.36% Native American.

William Neely's family settled in middle Tennessee.
The home above is located at Historic Collinsville near
Clarksville, TN. Proprietor JoAnn Weakley provided a wealth
of information on pioneer life for this book.

The author, p.m.terrell, with father
John William Neelley, Sr. at Fort Nashborough in 2007.
John discovered Mary Neely's story while
researching the Neely/Neelley family geneology.

34

It was late afternoon when they arrived at Fort Detroit. It had been an interesting trip, as they'd been joined by numerous other vessels of all sizes and types, and had encountered as many moving south. They were filled with more white men than Mary was accustomed to seeing, even at Fort Nashborough; but these were not settlers, but British, Frenchmen, and some with red hair and strange accents that she concluded were Scots. There were also Indians in a variety of clothing; White Messenger told her they were Wyandot, Ottawas, Ojibwas, and Chickasaw as well as Shawnee. It was mind-boggling, after so many weeks alone with her small Indian family, to see so many people bustling here and there.

In their journey there, they had remained relatively close to shore where the current wasn't as strong and they were able to stay out of the way of the larger, faster-moving vessels. The skies had become cloudy and the winds picked up as the day wore on. The Indians hurried northward as though they knew a strong storm was brewing and they were intent on reaching their destination before it struck.

It had been early afternoon when they left the wide expanse of Lake Erie, and Mary felt a pang of disappointment. She missed the serenity of the lake. She knew that morning's sunrise would always be emblazoned on her mind, and though she knew in her mind it was not an ocean, her heart felt the same excitement as if she'd seen the Atlantic.

She'd looked behind her reluctantly as the lake narrowed into a tributary. The terrain and her line of sight lessened considerably now that she was able to see the opposite shoreline and as the traffic tapered, the Indians found themselves within shouting distance of many of the vessels.

Mary's spirits were buoyed when she saw so many white men. They could not rescue her while she was in the canoe—they didn't even look as though it occurred to them—but now that she was amongst her own kind, even if they were European, there was considerable hope she would be taken away from the Shawnee and returned to her family.

They passed an island filled with cattle grazing lazily. There was a house there, too, and a chicken yard behind it, as well as a few horses. Mary's heart leapt when she saw a white woman scattering chicken feed. They came so close she could see the square neckline of her bodice, the elbow-length sleeves and the full skirt. She looked up as they passed and to Mary's astonishment, she did not seem at all concerned at the scores of Indians passing right under her nose. Self-consciously, Mary felt the top of her head, where her hair was now so long it was flopping about on her head like yarn on a rag doll. Surely, she would see she was a captive and call for the men to help her!

She heard the sounds of Fort Detroit even before she saw it: the shouts and laughter of so many people, she couldn't fathom how many must live there. And when she saw the fort, it was vaster than Fort Nashborough—in fact, far larger than anything she had ever laid eyes upon.

They steered the canoes toward a shoreline guarded by at least two batteries. The area was bustling with activity: men carrying sacks of food over each shoulder, British soldiers milling about, women buying fish and fruits and vegetables from vendors who called out their wares to the passersby. There were saloons and inns and public eating establishments. And they were in real buildings—wood buildings with real windows and real doors. And even street signs!

White Messenger ordered the squaws to gather their possessions from the canoes. Msipessi began speaking with a Frenchman; from what Mary could determine by their gestures and the Frenchman's careful inspection of their vessels, they were discussing their sale. She wondered if they intended to remain here in this large town, to live side by side with white people, people she could converse with—people who could help her get back home.

While White Messenger disappeared in the crowd, the other braves helped a fragile Eagle Feathers out of the canoe. He was barely on his feet before he collapsed, causing the others to rush to his side and catch him just before he hit the dirt. Medicine Woman began speaking rapidly to the Frenchman, who beckoned to someone nearby. Within minutes, they brought her a flask. She seated Eagle Feathers on a worn split-rail fence that appeared to be more of a divider of property than a means of keeping animals or people in or out. Then she carefully poured the liquid into the ailing chief, clucking as part of it ran out the corners of his mouth.

Little Fawn assisted in removing their possessions from the vessels, never complaining although her face was turning ashen. She even hauled a heavy load onto her back in preparation for carrying it like a human mule.

While Mary's back was loaded, she took the opportunity to absorb as much of her surroundings as possible. There were so many hiding places here, she thought excitedly. If she could manage to get out of their sight, she had a good chance of escaping. Perhaps one of the families who lived here would take her in until she managed to prepare passage back to her people.

White Messenger returned as they were finishing. He spoke to Msipessi and nodded approvingly as he saw the items he'd traded in return for the canoes: trinkets that had seen far better days and a bolt of cloth. He then bent in front of Eagle Feathers and spoke to him in a quiet tone. The old man nodded his consent and White Messenger ordered the family to follow him.

Two of the braves tried to assist Eagle Feathers but he proudly waved them off, determined to walk on his own two feet. Just a short distance from the piers, he faltered and eventually gave in to assistance from one of them, whom he leaned heavily upon as they continued their trek.

Not far from the river, they encountered a stockade. Mary could see several gates on the eastern side. They made their way down a wide dirt road to the closest gate, where they were stopped by British soldiers.

"State your business," one of the soldiers said, ogling Mary impertinently.

"We have scalps and a prisoner," White Messenger said, stepping in front of her.

A prisoner! So that is what they call me, Mary thought. Perhaps I am to be handed over to the British as a prisoner. Then they will surely set me free!

Her mind began racing as the two men conversed in lower tones. She could not stand idly by, hoping she would simply be turned over to the British. She must take matters into her own hands.

The soldiers stepped aside and waved them on. As Mary passed by, she bumped into one of the soldiers, who turned to scowl at her.

"I am a captive," she whispered hoarsely. "Please help me!"

35

hey were led into a courtyard and instructed to stand in a ragged line that stretched for more than twenty yards. Mary was stunned by the inaction of the soldiers at the gate and now, as she moved into her place in line, she felt as if she'd descended into hell.

Before her were scores of Indian warriors, each grasping handfuls of scalps. Some were white-haired, some gray, and some were tiny scalps of short, fine hair that could only have come from the smallest of victims. One was braided and almost three feet in length; as Mary stared at the silver hair, she envisioned a grandmother of sixty or seventy struck down by these heathens. By the way the Indian held it aloft, he was clearly proud of it.

The Indians laughed and talked while they gestured and postured. Mary was sickened. It was unmistakable they were bragging about their feats and how they obtained the scalps, no doubt embellishing along the way.

Amongst these savages, some of whom still sported their war paint, were white women and children. Some stared in wide-eyed terror and others were visibly shaking, and some appeared to be in total shock. They were all dirty, some with their clothes hanging in tatters, and some bloodied. A few even had bruises and scars that were easily seen, even from a distance.

There were small children who appeared totally alone even in the midst of such a great crowd and Mary yearned to run to them and take them in her arms. She wanted to ease their suffering, to mother them and protect them from these brutal savages.

Then there were the children who stared vacantly, their eyes not seeming to focus on anything in particular. They were skinny as rails and filthy and stood like small statues, their arms hanging limp by their sides. When the line moved, they were unceremoniously pushed forward; they moved like little wooden nutcrackers that had no feeling. It was not unlike Black Cloud, the woman Mary had watched as she drowned herself in the river, a woman whom she realized she would never know her Christian name.

The adult women kept their eyes downcast, never looking in their captors' faces, shuffling along like the condemned being led to the gallows.

White Messenger muttered something to Medicine Woman. In response, the old squaw took Buffalo Woman, Shooting Star, Little Fawn and Eagle Feathers and moved out of the line. Mary started to follow them, but White Messenger gently but firmly stopped her. "Stay here," he said curtly.

Mary watched as the others found a bench across the courtyard, where they placed the old chief and went about tending to his needs. Now Mary was left with only the five braves in her Indian family. With each step forward, they also began bragging of their exploits, raising the scalps high and gesturing. She stifled the impulse to spit in their faces as her own father's scalp was hoisted like a trophy for the others to admire.

There were savages all around her now, but she was determined she would not look down at her feet like a scolded dog. She would raise her chin high and look them squarely in the eyes. When one brave listened to her Indian family's tales and looked in her eyes with an icy cold glare, she defiantly returned his stare.

The Indian said something and the others turned toward her. His face was darkening now, a scowl covering his features. She noticed a scar running from his forehead almost to his chin, as though his entire face had been laid open by a scythe. He spat something louder, and Mary realized he was demanding she look away but she neither acknowledged his command nor diverted her eyes.

Finally, the brave lunged toward her, his hand reaching to his breechcloth where a large sheath knife hung.

Instantly, White Messenger and Msipessi stepped forward. Msipessi's arm flew in front of Mary, shielding her from the Indian. He began a heated exchange; his nostrils flaring, feet spread wide, his hand instantly raising his own knife.

White Messenger stepped between the two braves, his moderate tone causing both to eventually and reluctantly step back from one another.

The line began to move again. The others who had accompanied the brave with the scar prodded him forward and grudgingly he complied. As Mary also moved forward with Msipessi and White Messenger, she whispered, "Thank you."

"Do not shame us again," White Messenger said quietly, his eyes focused straight ahead.

The rest of their wait was uneventful until they reached a position in which Mary could see inside a small building. There were British soldiers seated at the end of the darkened room. One sat behind a table and to his side was none other than Simon Girty.

Mary stifled a gasp and considered telling White Messenger but one glance at his no-nonsense expression and she decided to remain quiet. Her heart was beginning to quicken and her breath became labored.

Each brave was brought forward. He spoke for a moment, proudly displaying his scalps. Then a British soldier who stood by a roaring fire withdrew a branding iron and branded the inside of each scalp, making sure to cover every inch. The stench of burned flesh reached her nostrils and she instinctively covered her nose. The Indians who surrounded her appeared not to notice the odor but continued to wait their turn.

Another soldier counted the scalps, wrote something on a piece of paper and gave it to the brave, who took both the paper and the scalps and exited a door on the other side of the room.

Then a brave approached with a white man whose ankles were tied with hemp rope, preventing him from taking steps larger than a half-stride. His arms were pulled behind him, where both his upper arms and wrists were bound. His clothes were simple, as though he'd been a farmer, but now they were soiled and tattered, the back of his shirt hanging as though the fabric had been ripped. His feet were bare and every inch of flesh that could be seen showed signs of scarring and festering wounds. He did not look up as he was led in front of the men, but kept his gaze downward.

Mary could not hear their conversation but followed the gestures of the brave who led him by a rope tied about his neck. Then Simon Girty stepped forward, placed his hand under the man's chin, and raised his face to peer at him. He dropped his hand and stepped back, then raised an accusing finger toward him. All of the others appeared to be listening to Girty, and Mary tried fervently to hear them but she was too far away.

The man nearest the fire reached his hand into the cooled ashes that had fallen just outside the fireplace, and with the black ashes he made the mark of an "x" across the man's forehead. With that, the man began to scream, "No! No! He lies! He is lying!" as he was led away.

Now Mary felt her whole body begin to quiver. She was near White Messenger's elbow, and she tapped it gently but the brave did not respond; his eyes fixed straight ahead. "That man," she whispered. "That is one of the men who wanted to rape Shooting Star. I thought Medicine Woman had killed him."

White Messenger's expression did not change but she could see the faintest of color rise in his cheeks. As they stepped forward in line, he said, "Do not say one word, do you hear me? Not one word."

She nodded even as her trembling increased.

The captive was led to a stake in the center of the courtyard, where he was tied so tightly that he could not move more than an inch in any direction. He continued to shout, "I am not a traitor! I am only a farmer! I have not fought against you! Long live the King!"

The brave who had brought him there spat on him before leaving, his expression sour.

At last, Mary was brought forward with the five braves in her Indian family. She kept her head down but couldn't stifle the impulse to glance at Simon Girty. He stood near the seated soldier's elbow, sneering at her. A kerchief was tied around his neck.

She quickly looked away.

White Messenger spoke of their journey to rich hunting grounds along the Spaylawitheepi and Warioto Rivers. He told of fighting white men who had raised their arms against the Crown. At various times, the braves displayed certain scalps, which were taken from them and branded.

When he spoke of Chillicothe, the seated man leaned forward.

"Were you there?" he asked.

"We were going to our brothers' aid," he said, looking pointedly at Girty. "But we encountered them on the Me-ah-me. They told us Chillicothe had been burned."

"Where did you go from there?" the man asked.

"To Piqua. We fought them there while our brothers—" again he looked pointedly at Girty "—escaped to safety." He spoke to the others in the Shawnee language and they produced a few more scalps.

"These are from the Colonists you fought at Piqua?" the man asked.

White Messenger nodded. "They are."

The man held up a scalp that was smaller than the others. The hair was barely an inch long and very thin and fine. Mary fought back a wave of nausea as she realized even a blind man could see this was a baby's scalp.

"And this one, this is from a settler?" the man prodded.

Again, White Messenger nodded. "My brother, Me-tho-tho Wis-sa-cut-tawie—Strength of an Ox—fought bravely."

The man nodded though he appeared unconvinced.

"We joined our brothers again at Fort Jefferson where the great rivers Missi Sepe and Spaylawitheepi meet," White Messenger continued.

The man questioned him at length, but White Messenger was unable to tell him how many settlers or military personnel were stationed at the fort. The man appeared pleased when he was told all of their crops were burned and what livestock they could not take with them, they destroyed.

One of the men had been counting the scalps as White Messenger spoke. Now he interjected, "Sixty-seven."

"Good job," the man said. "You are returning to help your brothers?"

"We go now to Michilimackinac for the winter."

The man laughed. "Not me. I would be heading south."

White Messenger only nodded and did not join in his mirth.

"How many in your family was lost in the fighting?"

"Three."

"You will receive a bonus."

He nodded.

"And her?" he said, turning his attention toward Mary. "She is your only captive?"

"See-la," he said. "Yes."

Simon Girty leaned forward. "She has been here before," he said. "We have paid for her already."

Mary felt White Messenger stiffen beside her. "That is not true."

"Then let us look at her back."

"What would her back tell you that I can not?"

"If she is not branded, then I admit my mistake," Girty said, his eyes blazing. "And we shall brand her now so she is not paid for again."

Mary shifted from one foot to another. She could feel the perplexity of the other braves, who questioned White Messenger in their native tongue.

"When did you begin branding the prisoners?" White Messenger asked calmly, though Mary could see a vein beginning to bulge angrily in his neck.

Girty leaned across the table. "Since you began to cheat us by parading the same captives in here time after time. Why do you think we brand your scalps now?"

White Messenger's hand flew to his weapon and the soldiers stepped forward.

"There will be none of that," the seated man said. "Show us her back."

He hesitated before slowly moving his hand away from his weapon. Without a word to her, he grabbed her by both shoulders and spun her around so her back was to the men. Her deerskin was raised, displaying her naked back. She knew they could see her shaking violently, but she didn't care. She only wanted to be out of here. She was biting her lower lip so hard to keep from screaming out that she now tasted the blood that was beginning to flow. It was only her fear of what White Messenger would do to her if she spoke that kept her silent. More than anything else, she did not want to be handed over to these men—though they were white, they were surely more barbaric than her current captors!

As she prayed he would drop her clothing back in place and they be allowed to leave this hell, she felt a searing pain in the middle of her back. Against her will, she screamed. The last thing she saw were the faces of the braves rushing around her as she fell, their bodies blurring like ghosts in the candlelight as darkness surrounded her.

36

The hours turned to days and the days into weeks. They moved into several small huts at the edge of Fort Detroit, where a myriad of Indian tribes moved in and out, sometimes peacefully and sometimes not. Sanitation became an enormous issue with so many people, and their quarters became increasingly cramped.

Mary could see much of the city from their new home. It was furnished with neat rows of wood houses, many of them with gardens that were now dying back in the crisp autumn air. They were filled with hundreds, if not thousands, of families: white women and children who went about their business as though no Indians or captives were within a hundred miles of their homes. At night, the horizon was filled with the smoke from scores of chimneys. The smell of hardwoods burning and the sounds of laughter and English tongues were enough to pull at Mary's heart and bring tears to her eyes, particularly on Sunday mornings when the sound of singing swept from the churches over the landscape.

On the southwest side of the town stockade was a triangle-shaped fort the Indians and their captives referred to as the Citadel. It was there that Mary had been taken to be paid for, she thought, like a sack of rotten potatoes: something they'd agreed to buy but which they didn't want to keep.

She was separated from this white civilization by an invisible line—the last row of frame houses. On this side—the Indian side—life was as different as black from white. This side was filled with Indians and their captives; masters and slaves. Many of the Indian braves spent the evenings drinking until they collapsed in a stupor or ended in fights to the death while other Indians and captives huddled inside their tiny huts, hoping to remain out of harm's way until the morning sun signaled the beginning of a new day.

It became obvious to Mary that her Shawnee family had no intention of remaining in this place any longer than was absolutely necessary. She was put to work making moccasins for each member of the family—not just one pair but a dozen per person. The sheer volume told her they would not be taking the waterways but would begin the next leg of their journey on foot. She hoped and prayed they did not intend to go back through that great black swamp.

In addition to the moccasins, she was expected to sew clothes for each of them: long-sleeved buckskin dresses that reached to the squaws' knees with breeches underneath, while the braves would receive a shorter version, reaching to their hips, with similar breeches. The skins were thick and tough and she labored over each stitch until her fingers were calloused and bleeding.

The piece of paper White Messenger had been given entitled them to purchase provisions. They also traded in the bolt of cloth they'd received for the canoes. They used their note to purchase the skins from which Mary sewed as well as cornmeal, plenty of jerky, and other provisions, including a new blanket for every member except Mary. She was given an old blanket pockmarked with holes that she was afraid would fall short of providing any warmth at all. They kept the trinkets they'd also received for the canoes wrapped in one of the blankets, presumably for future trading, and all of their provisions were packed securely and compactly for the day they would move onward.

White Messenger had asked her what one item she would like to have. She had thought long and hard on it, considering shoes, clothing, a new blanket like the others had, or even extra food. In the end, she decided on a Bible. To her amazement, he returned with a worn yellowed Bible that she thereafter carried with her wherever she went. She was not a good reader or even a fair one, but she stumbled through the passages and pondered on them each day, taking special pleasure in reading how the slaves had escaped from Egypt and how God had cursed their captors.

And though she had asked for nothing else, White Messenger had brought her another item: a comb. Now each morning and each evening, she ran the comb through her growing hair, marveling at how special she felt now that she owned this simple tool. It made her homesick, though, for Ma and her sisters, and she frequently wondered if they, too, were combing their hair at that very moment and wondering what had happened to their Mary.

Eagle Feathers was still suffering from his strange illness. He remained in the hut he shared with Medicine Woman, who faithfully lingered at his side. He was feverish and perspired heavily, though he trembled constantly and repeatedly wrapped himself in his arms as if he were chilled. Medicine Woman wrung her hands in despair as she rummaged through her herbs until it became apparent to all that she had no clue how to cure his illness.

During her waking hours, the only times Mary was allowed away from her sewing was during mealtimes and when she was ordered down to the river to retrieve water. Sometimes the water would be used to bathe and cool Eagle Feathers; other times, it would serve for cooking and cleaning. When at the river, she would have the briefest of moments with other captives, whom she discovered spoke a variety of languages. Some appeared to be Dutch and some French or German, and the others spoke an assortment of English dialects. Each time she would encounter one, she would tell them her Christian name and ask for theirs, and if they had the time and no one was peering over their shoulders like wardens in a prison, they compared stories and learned more about this strange city to which they found themselves adjacent.

Mary learned it was the lucky ones who were allowed to leave the Citadel; those less fortunate were imprisoned or executed, especially if they were male captives of fighting age. Sometimes in the middle of the night, she was awakened by hideous screams and she would bury herself deeper under her buckskin with her hands pressed against her ears, wishing the moans and shrieks would cease. Now she learned those were male prisoners who were tortured before being put to death. Again and again, she heard rumors of Simon Girty's involvement; he was reported to have personally supervised many of the interrogations.

As she met each person for a few minutes here and there, she pieced together their reports like an experienced old woman assembling a quilt. Now she knew beyond a doubt that her own capture was not happenstance, as she had believed all along. Eagle Feathers and his family had not been acting alone. It hadn't been a chance encounter but one small part in a broad plan.

Like figures in a game of chess, the Indians were being dispatched by the British to travel southwest into the very territory the Neelys had settled. Once there, they were expected to kill as many settlers as possible, taking their scalps as proof of their exploits. They were also encouraged to capture as many women and children as they wished, bringing them to Fort Detroit—to the office in the Citadel—for payment.

An old Scot woman had lived in the Indian huts since early August with her own captors, a Wyandot family of twelve.

"The Brits were keepin' us," she whispered to Mary one day as they dipped their buckets in the river. "But there were too many brought in, ya see. They couldn't a' feed us or clothe us an'more. So they turned to payin' them fer us, but givin' us back to our Indian masters…"

"The Injuns were paradin' the same folks back an' fort," said an almost toothless woman with broken English, "so they took to brandin' us so's they wouldn't pay for us twiced…"

"We've got to get out of here and warn our families," Mary said.

"And how're expectin' to do that, Missy? Just a'walkin' outta here and all the way back home? Do ye even know where yer home is?"

Mary lay awake at night and contemplated her escape. She was surrounded by hundreds—maybe even thousands—of people. But was there one, just one, who might be in a position to help her?

She was almost always within sight of Indians, if not her own family then others who would be quick to sound an alarm. The other captives could not help her; many of them were treated far worse than she ever was and they couldn't even manage to help themselves.

She ventured a couple of times further downstream under the pretext of looking for cleaner, clearer water. If she came within shouting distance of one of the people living in the town, they hurried away as if she were a savage herself, intent on doing them harm. She was unaccustomed to people—some of them women who appeared to be her own age—looking at her with wide eyes and open mouth, scurrying away with backward glances, rushing to put distance between them. Did they think she had turned to the Indians' barbaric ways? That she would yearn for blood-letting and scalp-hunting? How could she, when she was a Colonist and it was the Brits themselves who were encouraging and paying the Indians to be so despicable?

Her Shawnee family had been horrified when they observed the brand on the small of her back. It had stung furiously for the first few days, keeping Mary awake at night and torturing her throughout the day when her clothing rubbed against it. But each night, Medicine Woman placed a salve on it that helped the swelling and the rawness subside, until it eventually began to scab over. She could not see it, as she had no mirror, but the constant clucking of the squaws when they had occasion to tend to it made her think it was large and unsightly. She told herself she should be thankful they had not branded her forehead or some limb that would likely be visible, but it was difficult not to feel hatred for the soldier who inflicted such pain—and for Simon Girty.

Little Fawn was not sick with the same illness as Eagle Feathers. Instead, as the weeks passed by, her stomach became rounded and more pronounced until it was obvious that she was with child. She spent her days attending to chores—mostly cooking—and sitting very still, holding her stomach and staring from the high vantage point of the fort toward the river below.

She saw the two little girls who had huddled together in a canoe in those early days on the Cumberland River. They were now dressed in full Indian garb, their heads mere fuzz as if they, too, had been inducted into their Indian family. No longer wide-eyed and frightened, they played with round gourds that they batted around with sturdy sticks, their laughter sounding exactly as it would if they were at home with their white families.

She did not see any of the other captives and wondered if they were now living amongst the Indians as she was, or if they had met the same fate as Black Cloud or, even worse, been tortured and killed.

Her family told others of her beautiful voice and she was encouraged to sing as she worked. She sang every church hymn she knew and then took to singing the verses in the Book of Psalms to any melody that took her fancy. The Indians were pleased and some of the captives appeared amused at the verses foretelling of the downfall of thine enemies. It was their own little secret—and her way of continuing to focus on her most important goal: escape.

One day after she sang around the campfire and was preparing to retire to the hut she now shared with Shooting Star, Msipessi approached her.

Sheepishly, he looked at his feet as he said, "I enjoined your singing."

"Thank you."

"I have gift for you."

As he started to reach inside a buckskin pouch, Mary placed her hand over his. "No," she said firmly. "There is no need." Afraid she would offend him by her rejection, she smiled reassuringly.

"You want this one," he said haltingly. Then he pulled her father's scalp from the pouch, opened her hand and placed it in her palm.

She gasped and held the scalp as though it were sacred. She turned it over. It was not branded.

"You—you did not show this to the soldiers," she said.

"No. I do not wish to have your father's hair scarred."

She looked again at the scalp and the shiny black hair. What a strange, strange group of people these were, she thought, who can kill and scalp a man and then protect the scalp from being scarred. When she finally looked up, Msipessi was disappearing behind another hut, his knife swinging at his side in the moonlight.

37

Mary was awakened in the predawn hours by the sounds of people shouting. She sat bolt upright and stared through the semi-darkness, her heart beating so strongly that her chest was heaving with the effort. Under the flap that covered the doorway to their little hut, she could see feet running past them in the moonlight. Shooting Star stirred and Mary glanced at her as she sat up. The young squaw's eyes mirrored her own confusion and fear.

The flap was pushed abruptly aside as Buffalo Woman burst into the hut, grabbing Mary by her wrist. She was propelled out of the hut and into the open, where a full moon fought to illuminate the Indian village through thick clouds. Eagle Feathers had emerged from his hut and was circling it now while he emitted a steady barrage of shouts. He kept his arms rigid and straight up in the air, as if he were beseeching the gods, a multitude of bracelets of every description rolling backward toward his elbows as he moved.

Indians and captives alike were emerging from their homes and were crowding around him, sometimes having to step out of his way as he continued to circle. From their wide-eyed, open-mouthed expressions, Mary knew his ranting was ominous. Many of the braves were approaching with muskets and knives, ready to fight but finding no foe.

The normally unflappable White Messenger had his hands full with his attempts to calm the old man. He circled with him, staying with his face close to his, talking softly in words no one else could hear but the old man ignored his pleading. At various times, White Messenger shouted into the growing crowd, his tone less ominous than his father's. Any other time, he would have sounded reassuring but the crowd was only becoming more agitated.

Buffalo Woman pushed Mary toward White Messenger, herself too frightened to venture any closer. When the brave saw her, he stepped away from the old man and pulled her to him. "Get a doctor," he whispered in her ear.

"A—a white doctor?" she stammered.

"Yes. Go to the corner house and tell them you need a doctor."

Mary hesitated like a child who had been repeatedly warned against touching hot embers, only to be instructed to embrace them now.

"You are white. They will not harm you."

"But you—you know where to go—"

"I can not leave my father. Now go! Go! I am depending upon you, Songbird. Do not fail us."

She raced as though her feet had wings. The huts became a blur as she dashed past them, the Indians and captives parting to allow her passage. She half expected a bolt of lightning to strike her down as she crossed the invisible line between the Indian's encampment and the white families' homes. But she flew to the house on the corner, just as White Messenger had directed her, and pounded on the door.

"Who goes there?" came an immediate, gruff voice.

"Mary," she answered breathlessly. "Mary Neely."

"Go away!" the man's voice bellowed. "Go back to your own!"

Stunned, she stepped away from the door. Go back to my own? She thought. In all the excitement, she hadn't realized this could be her chance—perhaps her only real chance at freedom. Then she redoubled her pounding. "Tell me where a doctor lives! I need a doctor!"

"Get away from that door or I'll shoot you!"

She dashed into the street and looked at the houses as their windows came to life amidst the flickering of candle lanterns. She could run for her life—or she could save Eagle Feathers.

She raced down the street and turned the corner. Seeing a house lit up with activity, she rushed to the door and pounded on it.

A small man opened the door a mere crack. "What do ye want?" he asked in a heavy Scottish brogue.

"A doctor!" she said. "I need a doctor!"

"There ain't one here. Go away, Lass."

"Where can I find one?"

He peered past her. "Soldiers are comin'," he said before slamming the door.

She fought the urge to disappear behind some nearby bushes as two soldiers in red coats walked from the shade of a tree into the moonlight.

"What's all the ruckus about?" one called, his hand on his scabbard.

She ran into the empty street where they could clearly see her. "I need a doctor!" she yelled.

They did not quicken their paces. Instead, they walked cautiously toward her, their eyes scanning the street around them. As they approached, she saw one was very young; he was slightly built with sandy hair, piercing blue eyes and the smooth skin of an adolescent. The other man was burly with dark hair that curled around his tricorn hat and stubble that spoke of days without a shave.

"Did ye come from the Injuns?" the older man said as he studied her hair and attire.

"Yes."

"Then ye need to be returnin' afore we put you in jail."

"I just need a doctor," she pleaded. "Allow me to bring a doctor back to the village with me, please."

"For a human or an Injun?"

"What?" she stuttered. "Both. They are your allies."

"They're the scourge o' the earth, that's what they are." He waved his hand in dismissal. "Git back across the line or you'll wish ye did."

The young man stepped forward. "Jib, let me get a doctor. I'll escort him there and back and vouch for his safety." His accent was flat, neither British nor French, which immediately drew Mary's attention.

The older man hesitated. "If ye're gone longer than ye should, and we have'ta go in lookin' for ye, it won't be a pretty sight. Not a pretty sight at all." He said this last with an unflinching stare into Mary's eyes. "Ye better not be aimin' to spring a trap."

When they reached the camp, White Messenger had managed to get Eagle Feathers back inside his hut and was fighting to keep him prone on his bed. Medicine Woman was clucking and moaning while she wrung her hands in despair. As Mary walked past the others with the young private and an older doctor who had seen better years, she felt pride in her heart. She had managed to bring back a doctor.

The old man covered his face with a handkerchief and stepped into the hut, placing his large black bag on the dirt floor. Then the flap was closed and Mary could see no more.

She stood just outside with the private while they waited. The rest of her Indian family was gathered about, seeming oblivious to the chill that threatened to freeze Mary to the bone.

She spoke quietly, under her breath. "I am a captive here. A slave to these people. Can you help me get away?"

The private glanced about him, his eyes coming to rest on Msipessi, who was staring at him with a dark, solemn face, his hand poised above his sheath knife. "I can't do that," he said.

"All I need is safe passage out of here," she whispered. "I will find my own way back home."

"You are one of thousands," he said. "If I help you, the others will try it also. And we can not have an uprising here. I will not help you."

At that moment, the flap was pushed aside and both the doctor and White Messenger emerged. Mary overheard the doctor saying, "It's swamp fever. There's nothing I can do."

"There is no treatment for it?" White Messenger asked.

The doctor shook his head. "We can't spare any medicines for a—we just don't have it."

The brave's face became clouded with anger.

Mary stepped forward. "What herbs can help?" she asked.

The doctor hesitated as he rubbed his chin. "Wormwood," he said. "Better yet, boil some water and add a pinch of cinnamon, a dash of the liquid of hot pepper, and honey. Force him to drink it as often as he can handle it."

"That will cure him?"

He shrugged. "That's all you can do."

He placed a worn, dusty hat on his head and nodded to the private. As they both turned to go, Mary softly called out, "Thank you!"

The private stopped before slowly turning around. "I'll be back," he said.

38

J im felt the brisk air on his face as soon as he stepped outside the supply building. It was only mid-afternoon but the air was already sending a chill through the fort. He glanced upward as he began making his way back to his office. The warm blue summer sky had given way to a paler one that seemed to foretell a cold, bleak winter ahead.

The leaves had long ago fallen from the trees and the burst of color from summer wildflowers had collapsed into leggy stalks of brown. The fort had taken on a depressing atmosphere, but that, he thought, was as much from circumstance as from nature's changes.

He hesitated before he rounded the corner, soaking in what few rays of sunshine filtered through before he'd have to enter his dark and dreary office.

"Now that savage can't be my brother!"

Jim whirled around at the sound of the familiar voice. "Teddy!" he blurted before striding toward the young man. "Look at you!"

They hugged briefly before Jim stood back and studied his younger brother. "You must be near six feet tall," he mused. "Last time I saw you—"

"—I was seventeen years old and half a foot shorter," he said, beaming from ear to ear.

Jim examined the young man, taking in his sandy hair with a single short tail barely visible beneath the military cap; the trim, hard body well suited to the uniform. His sharp blue eyes peered out from under sandy brows, penetrating Jim with his gaze. "My God," Jim said, "you look like me six years ago."

"Well, you are a sight for sore eyes, I don't mind telling you," Teddy said. "We all thought you'd been run through and scalped. And from the looks of you, we might've been half right!"

Jim glanced at his worn buckskin breeches, tucked into dusty knee-high boots that had long ago faded from dark brown to dappled tan. His shirt had once been white but had yellowed with age and use and a few spots were almost threadbare. "You didn't come all the way out here—?"

"No, but I would have, if we'd gone another month without hearing from you. You forget how to write, Jim?"

Jim nodded toward his office. "Got a letter on my desk, just waiting for somebody to take it to Mother."

"Well, I'll be your messenger," Teddy said. "Looks like I'll be home before you."

"What *are* you doing out here?"

Teddy pointed toward the Captain's house. "I joined the Virginia militia. I'm assigned to Colonel Montgomery now. He's in there talking to Captain Owens."

Jim leaned against the building. "Can you tell me what they're talking about?"

Teddy shook his head. "We're hearing some mighty bad things about this place."

"Fort Jefferson?"

"Yep."

"Like what?"

"Like... families are leaving in droves. You can't keep men here; they're deserting like crazy."

"Well, you heard right. Had a lot of fevers in camp; they've taken their toll. And we've not got enough food to make it through the winter."

"How many families have left?"

"Half. We had forty a couple of months back; about 20 left in mid-September."

"And soldiers?"

"Not many. Colonel Clark left only a few to help defend the fort. About half have come down with the fever in the past few weeks."

Teddy moved in closer to Jim, although no one else was within hearing range. "Colonel Montgomery wants Captain Owens to relinquish his command."

"What?"

"He's brought Captain Williams to replace him."

Jim chewed on this news for a moment. "Does Colonel Clark know?"

Teddy shrugged. "Probably not."

"Then I doubt if Captain Owens will step down. It'll take a direct order from the Colonel, I'm sure."

They were silent for a moment. Then Teddy asked, "How are you doing, Jim?"

"Better than the others. Haven't succumbed to sickness yet and don't intend to." He slapped the dust off his boots as he spoke.

"Are rations as scarce as I hear?"

"I don't know what you're hearing, but like I said, we don't have enough food to carry us through the winter. Unless you've brought us some, that is." He smiled.

"A few things like flour and such. I expect you can make do, though, with meat until spring comes and you can plant a new crop, right?"

"You'd think."

"Am I wrong?"

Jim shrugged. "It's getting mighty dangerous to go outside this fort. Just a couple of weeks ago, we had some men desperate for meat to feed these families. They left for what should have been a short hunting expedition. Indians attacked them."

"Any killed?"

"Four. Four men we couldn't spare. Four families without a provider and now they're looking to us to provide for them."

Teddy shook his head. "And you? You gonna have to stay here?"

"Until I get further orders." He sighed deeply. "I'm not a paper pusher, Teddy. You know that. I need to be out there—in the woods, tracking Indians, scouting the terrain, moving ahead of the army. I don't need to be stuck inside a fort with a bunch of women and children, pushing papers around my desk." He looked away. "I should have left with Danton when he asked me to."

"Danton? Not Augustin de La Balme's Danton?"

Jim peered at his brother. "One and the same."

"He was here?"

"Yep."

"Why?"

"He wanted a detailed route that would take them to Fort Detroit."

"And he came here to get it?"

"It might be hard for you to believe, dear brother, but I've been living in these parts so long that I know the route."

"I'm not surprised."

"Anyway, I turned them down. Told them how to get there with the use of a map, but I declined to join them."

"Good thing you did."

"Oh?"

"He was just about wiped out."

"What are you talking about? They marched on Fort Detroit—and lost?"

"Never got that far. After Le Balme rounded up some Frenchmen from these parts, they went up the Wabash to Kekionga. They took over the town but the Frenchmen went wild, raiding the stores and folks' homes and all… Anyway, the way I heard it, they were expecting reinforcements, from where I don't know, but they never got them."

"Kekionga…" Jim mused. "They were not far from where I directed them to take the portage through the black swamp."

"Well, they didn't follow your advice. They took the Eel River instead."

"That's Chief Michikinikwa's territory," Jim interjected.

"Le Balme found that out."

"What happened?"

"Michikinikwa sent his Miami warriors after them. Le Balme had left a few men at Kekionga. No survivors once the Miami got there…"

"And what of Le Balme himself? And Danton?"

Teddy shook his head. "Michikinikwa caught up with him along the Eel River. It was a massacre."

"They're all dead?"

"I hear there were a few survivors, most of 'em taken by the Indians."

"Le Balme?"

"I've heard different reports. Some say he was killed. Some say he was taken prisoner and might even be at Fort Detroit now, though not as he expected to arrive."

"Well, I'll be," Jim said. "Same for Danton?"

"Danton's dead."

Jim nodded.

"So, you see, big brother, God was looking over your shoulder. If you'd have been there, you'd be dead now or wishin' you were."

The next morning's dawn was barely visible through the gathering storm clouds as Jim bid farewell to his brother. Captain Owens stood stiffly nearby, having refused to relinquish his command unless he received direct orders from Colonel Clark. Colonel Montgomery had accepted that decision, albeit with great reluctance.

"We'll send some provisions from New Orleans," he said now as he gathered the reins in his beefy hands.

"Watch your back," Jim said to his brother as he watched him mount. "There are a lot of Indians between here and New Orleans, and a lot of fever."

"I'll be fine," Teddy said with a grin. "I learned from the best. And what will you do?"

"With any luck, they'll put me back to scouting. It's what I do best."

Teddy patted his jacket pocket. "I have your letter to Mother. It'll be safe in her hands within the month."

"Thank you." Jim hesitated. Teddy had never mentioned Susannah's name. "Do you…?" His voice faded.

"Do I what?"

"Oh, nothing." He straightened and looked his younger brother in the eye. "Nothing at all."

The Colonel gave orders to march, and Teddy fell in ranks, tipping his hat as he swung his horse around.

"You watch *your back*, big brother," he said over his shoulder. "Mother's expecting to see you again."

Jim watched as his younger brother disappeared into the ranks of the other horsemen. He felt the heavy weight of loneliness descend upon him. At a time like this, seeing his brother so, it brought back memories of home and Susannah. And it made him want to wrap his arms around her all the more, to hold her close, and to never again let distance get between them. He wanted to inquire about her, but he couldn't bear to hear that she belonged to another now. If she'd still been his, still waited for his return, Teddy surely would have said something.

The gates to the fort opened. He would have liked for Teddy to have stayed longer, perhaps through the winter. His visit had been too short.

As he reluctantly watched them leave, Tommy entered the fort, his face flushed and cap askew. He rode briskly to Captain Owens on a horse that was frothing at the mouth from apparent overexertion. Tommy began speaking even before he'd finished saluting Owens.

"Ned Boone's been killed."

"Daniel Boone's brother?" Owens asked.

"Yes, sir."

"How?" Jim said, stepping forward and grabbing the reins as he dismounted.

"Indians. Daniel and Ned were out hunting when they attacked. Daniel got away, but Ned was shot and killed."

Jim's jaw tightened.

"And that ain't all. The Indians—Daniel said they were Shawnees—thought they had the great Daniel Boone. So they beheaded poor Ned and now they're on their way up the Ohio, showing his head to everybody."

"Where is Daniel now?" Owens asked.

"Took out after them to get Ned's head back," Tommy answered.

"Let me join Dan," Jim pleaded. "I'd be of more use to you out there killing those Indians than I am here eating up the last of the food."

Owens hesitated. "You're needed here."

"To do what? Sit behind a desk all day? Tommy here can do that—"

"Hey, now," Tommy interrupted.

"I'm not looking to commit suicide," Jim said. "I'm not some young hot-head. I know these parts and I know how to track them. It's not just Ned we're talking about. It's the terror of it all. As this word spreads, you'll have a mass exodus of families who can't wait to get back east. And the fewer families we have here to settle these parts, well, we might as well just hand it over to the Indians and be done with it."

Owens' stare penetrated Jim but he did not back down. At last, he said, "I can't spare anyone to go with you."

"I'm not asking for anyone."

"Then go. Do what you have to do and get back here."

Jim saluted him quickly before turning toward his cabin, his blood beginning to course strongly. He already had the things he would need in a neat list in his head before he reached the doorway. Five minutes, ten at most, and he would be packed and on his way.

39

The young private was as good as his word. His name was Alfred Berwyn and he'd been at Fort Detroit for less than a year, having arrived from Canada to assist the British in fighting the rebels.

When he returned to the Indian camp late the next day, he brought with him a cinnamon stick, two hot peppers, and a jar of honey. Mary held the items in the palms of her hands and stared at them in astonishment. Since her capture, she had subsisted entirely on meat, corn, and what berries, nuts and wild fruits she happened upon. To see something like a cinnamon stick brought tears to her eyes. She held it under her nose, sniffing it and remembering the one time her mother used one—back in Virginia, before they moved to Fort Nashborough.

The peppers were very small and Private Berwyn warned her they were very potent so she should use them sparingly. When she held them to her nose, they made her sneeze. She had never eaten a pepper before and marveled over them.

She held the jar of honey against the fading sunlight, admiring the honeycomb inside and the soft amber fluid. What she wouldn't give for a taste of it!

The other Indians gathered around her, their eyes darting between the private and Mary with growing suspicion. Msipessi's face grew long and dark.

When White Messenger joined them, she explained they were ingredients for Eagle Feather's fever.

"But I can not pay you," she said apologetically to Private Berwyn.

He shrugged. "I know."

"What then do you ask of me?"

His eyes widened. "Why, nothing," he said, clearing his throat self-consciously.

She gave the items to White Messenger. "Will you let Medicine Woman know?" she asked. "I will be there shortly, and I will make the broth."

White Messenger stood silently for a long moment while his eyes traveled slowly from Mary to the young man.

Mary grasped White Messenger's hand. "I will be right behind you."

Reluctantly, he turned in the direction of their huts. They watched him walk away, the others in their small group following. Only Msipessi hung back.

Mary began walking toward Eagle Feather's hut. Private Berwyn fell in beside her.

"Can you help me to escape?" she whispered.

"No," he said after a long pause. "I told you before; I can not."

Her heart fell. "I would be forever indebted to you."

"I can not," he repeated. "There are as many Indians at Fort Detroit as there are whites. If they suspected one of us of helping a captive escape, they would turn on us."

She didn't answer, and after a long moment, he continued, "The army would hang me if they suspected I helped you escape."

She stopped and looked him in the eyes. "Then remember my name," she said. "Mary Neely. Please remember it, in case— in case my family comes searching for me."

He nodded. "That I can do, Mary Neely." He tipped his hat. "You won't see me here again. It's too dangerous. I hope the old man gets well… That's all I can give you."

He turned to go and Mary called out to him, "Thank you!"

He waved briefly and started back toward the town. As Mary watched him leave, she felt that her soul would wither from the pain she felt inside. Just on the other side, there were people who lived in houses and wore cotton clothing, who slept in real beds and ate at real tables, who sat in real chairs. They ate cinnamon and peppers and honey, and she bet they had sugar and canned fruit preserves. They probably canned vegetables, too, from their own gardens—and they had gardens because they were home and their lives were stable.

She watched Private Berwyn until he rounded a corner and disappeared out of sight. With a heavy sigh, she turned toward the huts.

The fever broke a few days later. Whether it was from the strange concoction Mary brewed, she didn't know but her Indian family was convinced she had saved their chieftain and she was not of a mind to correct them.

But as the fever subsided and he became lucid, she realized they were facing a new challenge.

Eagle Feathers rapidly acquired a large audience amongst the Indians, often speaking for hours near a community building. He spoke of lucid visions he had experienced while on the brink of death; of seeing his fathers and their fathers before them. He spoke of a great white buffalo larger than any creature he had ever seen, who could speak eloquently in the Shawnee language.

It was what this creature said to him that caused an instant stir amongst the Indians, causing many to crowd the trading posts for black powder, shot and weapons. Not content with these, they were also buying huge quantities of rum, which they would drink at all hours. The more they consumed, the braver and fiercer they became, until even the Indian women were fleeing into the surrounding areas after dark lest they become a target of the drunken warriors.

Eagle Feathers spoke of a great white warrior who was on his way to Fort Detroit to destroy them all—a warrior known as Sheltowee, a name that caused gasps and further aroused his audience. According to the old man, this warrior's intent was to destroy the Indians who stayed in this village, as well as the British troops garrisoned there. He was gathering a large army as he advanced northward, which would outnumber all the men, women and children in and around the fort.

Mary knew there was much more to the man's ravings but not knowing his language, she could only grasp bits and pieces from other captives as they met at the river. Some were thrilled at the prospect of the Continental Army marching on Fort Detroit, while others were frightened for their own safety. She continued to go dutifully about her business, sewing moccasins and clothing, helping to roast venison and bear until they had the makings of jerky, and making enough hard corn cakes to last for weeks. But as she worked, the thought of an impending battle was never far from her mind; nor was the plan for escape.

Mary lay in her bed in the minutes before the sun rose. The hut was filled with a dampness and chill that caused her to snuggle more deeply into the warmth of the deerskin. It was her job to start the fires around her family's huts that would warm them as they rose to greet the new day. By the time they were awake, she would have ventured down to the river and brought back the water she would need to start the first meal of the day.

The flap parted and White Messenger's voice called softly to her through the waning darkness.

She rose, slipping the deerskin around her for warmth, and joined him just outside the hut.

"We are leaving," he said quietly. "I am taking you where you will be safe, if the white man decides to attack here."

She nodded.

"Awaken the other women and be ready to leave quickly. Do not make a sound."

She quickly made her rounds to Shooting Star, Little Fawn, Buffalo Woman, and Medicine Woman. They packed their possessions and lifted them onto their backs as they had when they'd left the Wabashike River. When White Messenger returned with Eagle Feathers and the braves, they were ready and waiting.

Without another word, they walked silently to the edge of the encampment. The sun was just beginning to rise on their right as they moved along. They reached a small rise and Mary stopped briefly and looked back upon Fort Detroit. The chimneys from the homes were already beginning to fill the air with the reassuring aroma of firewood and the river's edge was already bustling with the activities of tradesmen and fishermen. Indians and their captives were beginning to emerge from the huts below as she turned her back and disappeared into the woods.

40

It had been snowing for hours: a dense snow that saturated the small party and drastically reduced visibility. Mary struggled to see Little Fawn's back, though she sensed she was less than two feet in front of her. She'd already lost one of her moccasins; it was sucked off her foot as she labored to lift it from the thick white stuff. Now she struggled to keep the other one in place by tightening her toes around the thick deerskin until they ached.

They had stopped once to retrieve their blankets from their packs. As they pushed on, she knew the others had their thick new blankets wrapped about their bodies for warmth and protection against the harsh storm, while her threadbare blanket was almost worthless.

She bumped into Little Fawn's back and murmured an apology. Through the thick flurries swirling around her, she barely made out the forms of the others as they gathered in a circle. White Messenger was saying something to them but the wind was howling so fiercely, she could only make out a word here or there.

He came alongside her and shouted in her ear, "We are stopping here."

"Here?" she said, bewildered. "Is there shelter?"

"We shall make our own shelter," he answered. He pulled her to the ground and began digging a trench into the snow.

"Find whatever you can to dig. Make a trench as long as you are tall and three times as wide. Do you understand?"

Mary nodded. She removed her pack from her back and rifled through it, finding a pot she used for cooking. As she began shoveling the snow, she was joined by Shooting Star. During brief intervals in which the swirling snow subsided, she could see the others fanned out around her, each making a trench large enough for two people.

When they had finished their trench, White Messenger returned to demonstrate how to build walls of snow by packing the thick stuff with a pot and utensils.

"Make them thick!" he yelled through the blizzard. He showed them his forearm, gesturing from his wrist to his elbow. "Thick! Leave a doorway here," he pointed to a spot downwind.

Mary and Shooting Star worked feverishly. As cold and damp as it was, she was beginning to feel overheated and wondered if she had succumbed to Eagle Feather's fever. Once the walls of thick snow were in place, they worked on a ceiling. It was painstaking work, as they were forced to pile small bits of snow onto the walls, angling it and using their hands to mold it into place.

Buffalo Woman and her husband attempted to build theirs too quickly; when their roof collapsed, they were forced to shovel out the snow and begin the roof again.

Finally, theirs was done. Mary and Shooting Star crawled inside. Lying prone, they used their hands to finish shaping the walls. Then they both lay down. Shooting Star was trembling and Mary placed her arm around her.

"We'll stay warmer if we hold each other," Mary said, rubbing the young squaw's arms. She doubted if she understood anything she said, but she settled against Mary and closed her eyes.

The air was beginning to warm inside their little snow cave. Mary laid awake, marveling at the roof and wondering why it didn't melt and cave in on them. She could hear the storm raging outside, and a glimpse at the doorway showed a solid wall of swirling snowflakes.

White Messenger appeared and squatted in the doorway. "Are you all right?"

"Yes," she said. Her voice trembled with the cold. "When I was sewing all those moccasins, why didn't you tell me to sew boots?"

His face was dark but she thought she could see his eyes widen. "I am sure it was because we didn't think of it," he said after a long pause.

She pressed on. "But the winter was coming. Surely someone would have thought we'd need them?"

"We did not know it could snow so early here," he said.

"Even if it hadn't snowed, we should have them to keep us warm. We are freezing!"

There was silence and she wondered if she had said too much. She knew Shooting Star was not yet asleep, but she kept her eyes closed.

"We did not know it would be this cold," he said. "We have never been here before."

"What?" she whispered. "Aren't we going to your home?"

"We have no home," he said quietly. "We are searching for a place we can call home."

She fell silent, her astonishment at his words leaving her speechless.

"Hand me your packs," he said.

She pushed the packs down to him.

"Keep them in front of the door here," he said. "It will keep the cold air and snow out. You will be warmer." Before he pulled them in front of the doorway, he said, "Sleep, and when you awaken, the storm will be over." Then he backed away, pulling the packs into the doorway and plunging them into darkness.

Mary lay awake for a long time, digesting his words. They have never been here before, she mused. Perhaps they had never before been through that black swamp. But White Messenger had led them to Fort Detroit, she countered. So surely he had traveled that way before? Or had they been lost and only through the grace of God, they'd found the Myaamia River? And were they lost now, somewhere north of Fort Detroit and only God knew how many miles from the nearest encampment?

Slowly, the air began to warm inside their tiny cave. Shooting Star's breathing was rhythmic.

Mary began to repeat her poem:

Mary Neely is my name,
At the Salt Lick when they came;
North on the Cumberland past the Fort,
Joined at the Red River by additional escort.
North on the Spaylawitheepi,
"Ohio" we call it, white women like me.
Remained for a time at Shawneetown
Until more braves came down.
We fled northeastward on the Wabashike
Crossed to the other shore oh so sneaky.
Wandered in a vast black swamp
Where the ground was too wet to romp...
Found the Myaamia River, big as you please
Reaching Lake Erie with sky blue seas.
North to Fort Detroit where we camped for awhile
Then north through a climate increasingly hostile...

She repeated it several times, though her heart grew heavy with each recital. How many lines would her poem become before she was able to escape? How long had it been since she had been captured? It felt like a lifetime ago when she was laboring over the pot at the salt lick and brushing perspiration from her forehead. Could her family still be searching for her? Or had they given up, presuming her dead?

The poem was worthless, she thought in despair. She could never go back the way she'd come. The great black swamp would have her going in circles until it sucked her into its black depths.

She fell into a fitful sleep, dreaming of the black swamp now covered in snow and ice. Sometime during the night, she vaguely remembered pulling away from the sleeping Shooting Star and scooting to the edge of the snow cave.

41

Mary was dreaming she was floating down the Cumberland River toward her home. The sun was a brilliant yellow and the woods displayed a burst of springtime color. She was mesmerized by the wildflowers and early spring buds on the cherry trees and dogwoods, when she rounded a bend and caught sight of her home through the trees.

She rowed to the bank and quickly climbed out of the canoe. But as she raced toward her home, it began to snow. A single wet snowflake landed on her upturned nose, followed by another and then another, until she was unable to see in front of her.

She turned in circles, searching for the direction of the log cabin with the gently swirling smoke from the chimneys, but she couldn't find it. A growing panic was welling up inside her—

Her eyes flew open.

Her eyelashes scraped the hardened snow. Instinctively, she tried to raise her hand to her eyes but it was blocked. She was unable to move.

She fought to rid herself of the dream in an attempt to remember where she was and what she was doing. Slowly, the events of the trek through the blizzard came back to her until they began to tumble, the minutes of building her snow cave flying through her brain.

Unable to move her head, she could only roll her eyes in a cautious attempt to peer around her. Some time during the night, her cave had collapsed in on her. Now she was wrapped in the snow like a moth in a cocoon.

She took a deep breath. There was still enough air for her to breathe, but she wondered how long it would last. She fought to remain calm as panic threatened to overwhelm her.

She was lying on her side facing the outer wall, one arm twisted underneath her body, the other arm by her side near a bent knee. Her feet were intertwined, her toes able to wiggle.

She moved the fingers on her right hand, slowly at first and then more deliberately. Like tiny shovels, she scraped the snow, pushing it away from her body. She realized the thick outer wall had hardened considerably since she'd lain down and her fingers became no match for the ice. She tried to call for White Messenger and cry out for help, but her words were absorbed by the snow.

She struggled to keep her wits about her. If the others could not hear her, she had no choice but to extricate herself. She would not lie here and die in this frozen wilderness.

She jiggled her toes, first on one foot and then on the other. Gently, she began pushing the snow and ice away from them. It was an excruciatingly slow process. She was afraid to move quickly, lest the walls collapse upon her again. As she increased her movement inch by agonizing inch, she wondered how much it had snowed, whether the blizzard had stopped, and how long she had lain in this frozen condition.

Slowly, the feeling began to return to her ice-covered toes. It was painful at first, like so many needles pricking at her extremities, and she was tempted to stop and allow the feeling to drain from them once again. But something inside her compelled her to continue, to fight against the pain and strain against this frigid coffin.

She was perspiring as she continued to use her feet like shovels, each fresh patch of snow causing another burst of pain that reached across her soles and into her ankles. Then her ankles were free, and she moved them in tiny circles until there was enough space to move her calves and then her knees.

Then her right hand was free, if only within a tiny circumference. Now her breath was melting the snow nearest her, creating a small wind tunnel in front of her.

She didn't know how long she lay there, clearing the snow away from her inch by painstaking inch. It felt like hours.

Eventually, she was able to sit up. Exhausted, she leaned against the ice wall. She drew her knees to her chest and placed her head upon her knees.

Then she was tunneling through the snow at a diagonal, piling the snow and ice into the area where her lower extremities had lain.

When at last a ray of sunlight crept through a tiny pinhole, she felt like it was God Himself beaming down upon her. She thrust her finger into the hole and then two fingers and then three, until her entire hand managed to plunge through.

She shouted again and again but no one answered.

She was standing now in an area no more than five feet in diameter but her head did not reach the top of the tunnel. As the sunlight filtered down to her, she realized her fingers and feet were covered in blood: each effort to push the ice away from her had resulted in razor-thin cuts.

Now she fought to ignore the pain as she created a frozen stairway. Each time she stepped upon it, it sank ever deeper, preventing her from reaching the top. Finally, when her head was barely visible, she realized she couldn't simply step outside, lest the whole thing collapse and tumble her back inside.

So she set to work creating a platform from which she could propel herself out of the hole. When she was ready to try to escape, she thrust herself outward with all her might. But even her best effort only brought her a few inches out of the hole, and much to her despair, the ground began to shift under her. She threw herself outward again, this time grabbing onto a low-lying tree branch as the snow pile beneath her collapsed.

She clung to the branch while she caught her breath and tried to regain her strength.

The clearing was abandoned.

There were footprints everywhere, as if her entire Shawnee family had trampled nearly every inch. There was evidence of at least five snow caves, judging from the mounds of snow and openings. Slowly, she came to her feet and walked the perimeter, peering into each cave as she went and softly calling. They were all empty.

Her own cave had been covered by drifting snow. Now that she was above it looking down, she realized only her section had caved in; where Shooting Star had lain was unaffected.

But where was everybody? She wondered.

She looked around the campsite and discovered a path of footprints tracking northward. She stopped for a moment and assessed her situation. She was upset they left her for dead here, but at the same time, she wondered if this was her chance to escape. Could she make it back to Fort Detroit? Once there, could she find anyone to help her? She didn't know where Private Berwyn lived or worked and hadn't the faintest idea how she would find him. Perhaps she could begin by knocking on doors and asking for help?

She studied the sky. It was clear and the sun was bright. Without a pack, she could make better progress on her journey back. But without a pack, she was without food; and now even her blanket was beneath a sea of snow.

She began to walk through the encampment to the southern side. She took a few steps, her legs sinking with each one. She looked behind her. She would be leaving an unmistakable trail. If they had left only briefly and returned for her, these tracks would easily lead them right to her.

She stopped and looked at the northern end of the clearing. Her curiosity got the best of her, and she returned to the other side and followed their trail. It circled around trees and gullies until, panting, she followed it onto a rise. Once at the top, she shaded her eyes from the sun's strong rays and surveyed the terrain.

She thought she heard a shout but it was so faint, she couldn't be sure. Then movement off in the distance caught her eye and she turned in that direction.

Little Fawn had seen her and was alerting the others. Afraid they would think she had intentionally remained behind Mary began waving with both arms.

Msipessi and White Messenger dropped their packs and began trotting toward her. She figured it took more than an hour for them to reach her while she continued painfully along the path they'd cut through the snow.

She didn't know which one was more concerned about her bleeding feet and fingers. They examined her while she told them of her ordeal; she thought at one point, they would return to view the site of her imprisonment.

Then White Messenger hoisted her onto his back and they began the long trek to rejoin the rest of the group.

42

Jim caught up with Daniel Boone just outside of Boone Station, a small settlement of fifteen families which included Daniel's and Ned's wives and children. As Jim rode up, he nodded to the half-dozen men in the group and then turned to Daniel.

"You joining us?" Daniel asked.

"You bet I am. I figured you might need an extra pair of eyes."

"I can always use extra eyes—and extra hands."

"Where're you headed?"

"Direction of Blue Licks."

"That where it happened?"

Daniel tapped his horse and Jim fell in beside him. "We'd already been to Blue Licks; made some salt for the families here." He waved toward the other men. "We were on our way back home. Stopped at a creek to let the horses drink, and ole Ned found some nuts. So while he sat down and started eating, I decided to do some hunting."

The horses trotted for awhile before Jim asked, "Then what?"

"I had a wild boar in my sights, rifle aimed, just about ready to shoot, when I heard gunfire. I got back to the creek—" he raised his shirtsleeve to expose deep cuts "—and fought with the Indians. Shawnee. But there were more of them than there were of us."

Jim nodded. "That's the way they work. Outnumber and overpower."

"Yep. I was able to get away, but they had my horse. I ran all the way from that creek back to Boone Station on foot… They had a dog with 'em, too, and if that dog didn't follow me for the longest time, just baying and hollering. I had to kill it before the Shawnees followed it right to me."

Jim wandered to Brandy, who had followed him for some time after he left the fort. He'd tried to keep her inside the fort walls, but she was wily and got past him. And the truth was, she'd find more to eat outside the walls than in. "And Ned?"

"Kilt right there."

"So we're going after them."

"I aim to get Ned's body back so I can bury it. And if I happen to kill a few Shawnees in the process, then so be it."

They picked up their pace with Daniel and Jim remaining side by side with the others behind them.

"My wife has taken to calling this place 'Bloody Ground'," Daniel said.

"I imagine she's taking Ned's death particularly hard."

Daniel stole a sideways glance at him.

"I didn't mean nothing by that," Jim said. "Just him being your brother and all."

He nodded and they grew silent. Daniel had come to these parts years before his family settled here, having left them in North Carolina while he helped to survey the area and establish its suitability for settlements. He'd been gone for two years at one stretch, without any word reaching his wife Rebecca as to his whereabouts, when despondent, she determined that he had been killed by Indians. Probably not much different from his own situation with Susannah, Jim thought.

Rebecca Boone turned to his brother, Ned, who had remained in North Carolina as a community leader, serving at different times as a constable, a tax collector, and a surveyor, and even as a deacon in the Baptist Church.

They had a child together, a daughter they named Jemima, when Daniel returned from the wilderness. Hearing their stories, he decided they'd done nothing wrong, seeing as how they thought he was dead, and he raised Jemima as his own daughter. It had been this daughter who had been abducted by Shawnees some years later after their settling at Boonesborough, and whom Daniel pursued for days before overtaking them and rescuing Jemima along with her two friends, daughters of another settler, Colonel Calloway.

They reached the creek when the sun was high overhead. Ned's body lay prone beside the riverbank, the water lapping at his bare feet. The Indians had removed his boots and taken his rifle and other possessions, and had hacked at his body and limbs. Daniel shouted as they approached, frightening away the half-dozen vultures that had come to feast on him.

Don't know when I've seen so much blood, Jim thought as they approached.

A murmur erupted in their small group as they drew near. His head had been removed, leaving only the bloody stub of his vertebrae.

Jim dismounted and peeled off his shirt, throwing it across the bloody stump. He didn't look at the others as he said, "A man ought not to lose his dignity, even in death." He brushed away a stinging tear at the corner of his eye: a tear as much from anger as from sadness.

The others dismounted and Daniel wandered along the riverbank. He stopped at a buckeye tree that stood some fifty feet tall, its stately branches starting low to the ground. It was in the advanced stages of brilliant orange and yellow, heralding the rapid approach of winter.

Jim joined him. "We can't let the womenfolk see Ned like this," he said quietly.

"Last time I saw him, he was sitting right here, eating nuts," Daniel said, as though he hadn't heard him. He reached to the ground and picked up a few broken shells. "This is where we bury him."

They held a ceremony along the side of the river. The men stood respectfully with their hats cupped in front of them, their foreheads heavy with perspiration. The roots from the old buckeye framed Ned's grave, the mound rising at a slope almost as if he could watch the river flow from his last resting place. He was buried with the shirt still around his bloody stump; a detail that Jim was sure was not lost on any of them. There was something particularly barbaric about burying a man without a head, he thought as he listened to Daniel.

"Edward Boone was a good man," he was saying, his voice cracking just a tad, "Born in Pennsylvania on November 30 in 1740. Neddie was known by all as a peaceable man, never meant no harm to nobody. He loved to sing."

He cleared his voice before continuing, "He's survived by his wife, the former Martha Bryan, my Rebecca's own sister; and six young'uns: Charity, Jane, Mary, and Sarah, and two boys, George and Joseph. He'll be sorely missed."

He turned away from the others and toward the river. After a few moments of silence, they retreated to their horses, where they watered them and prepared for the next part of their journey. When Daniel joined them a few minutes later, his eyes were red and swollen. "I'm going home," he announced as he mounted his horse.

Without a word, the others fell in behind him. As Jim stared at Daniel's back, his friend's shoulders slumped. So they wouldn't follow the Shawnees after all, Jim thought. Seeing Ned's disembodied head was a memory he didn't want to carry with him. And apparently, neither did Daniel.

43

Mary had never been so cold in her entire life. As they ventured ever northward, the creeks and streams were often frozen and the ground was covered in snow so solid they no longer sank as they walked but glided along the icy crust.

They often spotted fur traders taking advantage of the cold months to trap beaver now resplendent in their thick winter coats. Sometimes the braves went on ahead to speak with them, leaving the women to shift back and forth from one leg to another in an effort to stay warm. Other times, they simply continued on their way. Mary never came close enough to the trappers to ask for their help in rescuing her, and she grew increasingly curious about this type of folk who sought out the ice and snow and bitter cold.

She was grateful she'd sewn multiple pairs of moccasins at Fort Detroit, especially since she'd lost one already. But they provided precious little protection as the water seeped into the seams and froze. Like the squaws, she wore fringed buckskin breeches and a long-sleeved buckskin dress that fit over her head and reached just below her knees. Medicine Woman promised her through White Messenger that once they reached suitable quarters, she would be allowed to disassemble a few dresses in order to create buckskin boots for each of them. As the days passed by with nothing but the frozen landscape within her sights, she wondered when and where they would find lodging.

The nights were the worst. Once the sun, barely visible during the day, disappeared beyond the horizon, it became so cold that Mary spent each night shaking violently, convinced it would be her last. During those long, miserable hours, she envisioned the Indians awakening only to find her completely frozen to the ground.

Yet each morning the dawn found her still alive, and each morning she spent long, painful minutes blowing her breath onto her fingers in an effort to get them pliable once again. She often had to recruit a brave to hack at the bottom of her pack, as it had been frozen into the ground during the night. More than once, she ripped her thin blanket, a replacement for the one lost in the snow cave, trying to peel it off the ice.

They made slower progress as they traveled, though the land was almost perfectly flat. There were fewer trees here than in the heavily forested region around Fort Nashborough, and the northwest winds ripped through unabated. They took more frequent breaks, softening the hard corn cakes in the snow before chewing them thoroughly, or sucking on frozen jerky to maintain their strength.

Once Mary grew accustomed to this new turn of events, she began to realize they were slowing due to some of the Shawnees' lack of stamina. She had grown accustomed to their stoic behavior, having seen Little Fawn, now heavy with child, carrying packs equal to half her weight without objection. Not once had she heard a murmur she could have attributed to protestations over their current state of affairs.

Now White Messenger was constantly watching each member of their small group and though no one voiced a complaint, he would determine based on some unseen clues of which Mary wasn't privy, when to stop and how long to rest. This resulted in covering far less territory each day.

Now he signaled for everyone to stop. Accustomed to their procedure, Mary dropped her pack and placed it on her north side to break the wind before it reached her shivering body. The others did the same. As she sat with her head down, the flimsy blanket covering her head, she peered at the others.

Shooting Star was nearest. Her forehead was covered with a thick film of perspiration. Mary reached for her forearm and when the young squaw looked up, Mary pointed to her head. Shooting Star made a half-hearted attempt to wipe away the sweat but it reappeared almost instantly.

Mary rose and walked to Little Fawn, placing her finger under her chin and raising her face to hers. She also had broken out in heavy perspiration.

One by one, she walked around the group. In addition to the two squaws, Eagle Feathers and two of the braves exhibited the same symptom.

Medicine Woman appeared at her elbow. She also looked at each of the family, clucking as she did so.

"What is it?" White Messenger asked.

"I don't know," Mary answered. "Does Medicine Woman know?"

He said something to her but Mary knew from her shaking head that she did not know the cause of their fever. Frightened, Mary wondered if Eagle Feather's swamp fever had returned and had infected them. She had used the peppers, cinnamon and honey sparingly and had run out the day before Eagle Feathers' fever broke. With growing apprehension, she realized they had nothing to give them and no one to turn to for help.

Medicine Woman felt the skin of each person, wiping her hands against her buckskin as she went from one to another.

Mary moved alongside her, asking questions which White Messenger interpreted. Half of their group had severe headaches and Little Fawn had a backache.

"We can't continue walking like this," Mary said to White Messenger. "They are sick. They need treatment."

White Messenger conferred with the other braves, of whom only he and Msipessi were unaffected. The two instructed the others to remain at their current site while they canvassed the immediate area. The hours dragged on as the wind grew increasingly more ferocious. Mary began to worry about their fate if they did not return.

At long last, she spotted two lone figures emerging from the horizon at a steady trot. She shaded her eyes against the glare on the pristine snow and watched them approach.

"There is a forest a half day's walk from here," White Messenger said. "We can reach it before the sun sets. It will provide shelter from the wind."

The half day's journey turned into a full day as their small group made increasingly slower progress. Mary was given Little Fawn's pack in addition to her own, which made her feel as though she were carrying a weight equal to her own on her slender frame. She slipped and slid along the ice, hoping and praying God would get them to their destination quickly. But the sun set and they were far from the forest. Perhaps alarmed by his family's condition, White Messenger pressed them on in the moonlight.

When Shooting Star fainted, without a word Msipessi shifted her pack onto his own back and carried her.

It was mid-morning when, exhausted, they reached the tree line and now Mary could not remember why the trees had been so important to them. They collapsed at the edge, each drawing up to one another in a feeble effort to stay warm.

Mary awakened to the sound of tomahawks hacking at slender birch trees. She sat up slowly, her bones aching in the frigid air, her leg muscles cramping from the long walk in the constant cold.

Msipessi and White Messenger were cutting down birch trees and handing them off to the other braves, who quickly stripped them of their branches. In short order, they had more than half a dozen branches.

The squaws were directed to clear the ground within a six foot diameter Msipessi drew with his foot in a small clearing. Using their cooking pots and utensils, they hacked at the ice and snow until they had reached the hard, cold earth.

Curious, Mary watched them secure one end of each branch into the ground. While one man held the branch where it entered the earth, another pulled the other end down to the ground, resulting in an almost perfect circle of branches. Then they busied themselves with fashioning more branches around the first ones. Excited, Mary realized they were building wigwams.

Mary and the squaws were put to work clearing enough space for a total of five wigwams. As the braves continued building the skeleton of each structure, the women were instructed to find bark with which to cover them. Using White Messenger's sheath knife, Mary quickly became adept at stripping the bark from the tree. It was rigid in the cold, but she did the best she could to bend it into the shape needed to cover the wigwam.

When she was finished with her first, she stood back and surveyed her work. It looked like a poorly constructed patchwork, but she was elated. Tonight she would sleep under a roof for the first time since leaving Fort Detroit.

They moved Shooting Star and Little Fawn into the finished hut, where they quickly fell asleep. While Medicine Woman prepared a site for a fire, Mary continued helping the men.

Eagle Feathers was the next to succumb. Mary did not even have the bark in place before he had retreated inside and fallen fast asleep.

They toiled until the sun had gone down and the moon had risen. Then those who were still awake sat around the campfire, the first Mary remembered since leaving the fort, and drank hot water flavored with bear fat and bits of jerky.

Through the light of the red flames, she saw White Messenger's eyes watching her. She thought she detected admiration in them and when he found her returning his gaze, he nodded slightly and said simply, "Good work."

44

The next morning, Mary was up at dawn helping Buffalo Woman start a fire for their breakfast. Medicine Woman was making her rounds, eventually joining them with a grim look on her lined face.

All of the braves joined them at the campfire, but Shooting Star and Little Fawn remained in their wigwam. Mary was directed to take them some of the reheated bear fat and jerky broth from the previous night, as well as some of the corn cakes.

She was startled to find them both unable to sit up by themselves. Working with one at a time, she found that once she brought them to a seated position, they began to waver as though they would drop back to the ground. Afraid they would crash through the wigwam and destroy their tiny shelter, Mary sat behind each one, propping them against her body and hand-feeding them.

She had barely finished feeding Little Fawn when the squaw tried to crawl out of the wigwam. She had only made it into the doorway when she vomited on the ground. This, in turn, caused Shooting Star to begin retching. Mary called frantically for Medicine Woman while she tried to still them, trying valiantly not to become sick herself.

They were both holding their stomachs as though they were experiencing excruciating pain. She helped Medicine Woman as they fed them herbs boiled in water, but they came back up as quickly as they went down.

Mary also discovered it would be her job to clean up after them, which she found to her great chagrin, meant cleaning not just the vomit but the diarrhea that set in as the day wore on. They were completely unable to move from the wigwam into the surrounding forest to take care of business themselves. Mary began wondering what the Shawnees used as diapers for infants, but she could not get Medicine Woman to understand her question and she was too embarrassed to ask White Messenger to interpret.

She finally dragged herself out of their wigwam. The air that had felt so hostile only the day before now felt refreshingly cool and she sat for a time enjoying it after the stale, pungent air of the squaws' confined quarters.

Eagle Feathers was sitting far enough from the campfire to be out of range of its warmth. Mary noticed his forehead still saturated in perspiration, but she said nothing. As she watched, he lifted one arm high and spoke.

The others turned and looked behind them. As Mary followed their gaze, she noticed a lone figure crossing the frozen prairie toward them. As it grew larger, she realized it was a man covered in furs from his head to his ankles.

Eagle Feathers came shakily to his feet, as did all of the other braves. He was the first to speak as the man grew closer. The man immediately answered, and Mary realized they spoke the same language. She tried hard to see his face under the furs, but they stood out from his brow, casting his face in shadows.

He turned toward her. Using his spear, he tapped her moccasins and said something. A murmur went up in the group. They appeared to be asking questions, and the man tapped her moccasins several more times as he answered. Mary remained perfectly still. She searched White Messenger's eyes for an explanation but he did not look at her face, only at her feet and in turn, each of the others' feet.

Then White Messenger and the man walked a short distance from the camp site as the man pointed toward the horizon.

Mary moved closer to the warmth of the campfire, listening to the words but not understanding them. The others appeared to be listening intently as well.

Soon, the man moved on and White Messenger returned to the fire. He spoke for a time to the others. They occasionally interjected to which White Messenger would pause attentively, appear to think through their question or comment, and quietly respond.

Finally, he turned to Mary. "Tomorrow, Eagle Feathers, Strength of an Ox, and I will go to an Indian village two days from here. We will get provisions and return.

"While we are gone, you will make boots. When you sew the seams," he reached across and ran his finger along the seam of Mary's moccasin, "fire-cure it. This will keep the water from your feet."

Fire-cure the seams, Mary thought excitedly. So the lone Indian had noticed their feet in their soggy moccasins.

"Medicine Woman needs swamp tails. Do you understand what that is?"

Mary hesitated. "A plant?"

"Yes. Tall plant with brown flowers. It waves in the wind."

"Yes. We call it cattail."

"Walk that way—" he pointed toward the west "—just over the horizon, you will find a pond. They will be there. Bring back the whole plant. The root, the stalks, everything."

Mary nodded. "How many?"

"As many as you can carry." He rose. "And Songbird," he said, staring into her eyes. "I do not need to worry that you will try to run away. Do I?"

She returned his unblinking gaze. "No. You needn't worry."

Mary lay awake listening to the moans of Shooting Star and Little Fawn. It was unusual for them to emit such noises, as she'd learned the Shawnees did not respect those who complained. She wondered if Medicine Woman would rouse her and send her into the hut to care for them. She hoped she did not, as the only thing worse than caring for them during the daylight hours would be trying to clean up after them in the dark.

She wondered at White Messenger's final words to her. She had not lied. He needn't worry. Even as she began planning her next escape attempt, she knew he would only be wasting his time by worrying.

45

Eagle Feathers, Strength of an Ox and White Messenger had already set out for the Indian village when Medicine Woman roused Mary from her sleep. The sun had begun to rise, casting the terrain into a surreal white wonderland. While Medicine Woman stoked the campfire, Mary was sent into the ailing squaws' hut to care for them.

The stench was overwhelming when she pulled back the bark that hung across the doorway. She removed it so the outside air could penetrate into the hut; though the air was frigid, she thought it would be better than the stale, sickening atmosphere in which they had been living.

Once the bark was away from the entrance, the sunlight penetrated into the tiny quarters. She crawled in between the two women. They were both asleep, though Little Fawn was beginning to stir as the weak sunlight reached her face.

Mary gasped.

Little Fawn's face was completely covered in pustules.

Mary pulled back the blanket and pushed the long sleeve on her buckskin dress to her elbow. Her arm was also covered with the hideous lesions. Shouting for Medicine Woman, Mary raised the blanket and peered at the squaw's legs. They, too, were covered.

As Medicine Woman entered the hut, Mary pointed to Little Fawn's body. The young woman tried to open her eyes, but the lids were covered in the pustules, preventing them from opening.

Mary turned in the cramped quarters and peered at Shooting Star. She, too, was covered in the same lesions.

Medicine Woman backed out of the hut, calling to Mary and speaking words she could not understand. She beckoned to her to follow her, which Mary did. As she exited the hut, she fought the urge to rush to a snow bank and wash every inch of her body, lest she catch whatever gruesome disease the two had contracted.

Medicine Woman pulled her through the campsite, her words arousing the others from their beds. She shouted desperately at Mary, but she could not understand her. Finally, she dragged her to the edge of the camp and pointed.

Finally, Mary understood. She was to go to the pond White Messenger had spoken of and gather the cattails. Now she grasped the full meaning of her assignment: the cattails contained the medicine needed to heal the two women.

She nodded and pointed until Medicine Woman knew she understood. Then she quickly wrapped her thin blanket about her shoulders and head and started on her journey.

She was a short distance from the campsite when she heard something behind her; turning, she saw Msipessi and Buffalo Woman hurrying to catch up with her. So she was to have some help, she thought. She didn't know whether to be thankful for their assistance or wonder if they were accompanying her simply to make sure she didn't escape.

The pond that White Messenger had indicated was just over the horizon turned out to be a marsh a half-day's journey from camp. They alternately trudged through snow or slid on ice until, shivering and tired, they arrived at their destination.

The cattails were frozen in ice that had formed completely over the marsh in a thick crust that easily bore their weight. Mary tried to dislodge the plant with her fingers but realized immediately it was futile. Msipessi pushed her away and used his tomahawk to break the ice around it. While Mary reached into the frigid waters to remove the roots and full stems, he moved on to the next plant.

They worked for a few hours on empty stomachs until Msipessi rose and studied the sky.

"A storm comes," he said in his halting English. "We leave now."

They divided the cattails into three equal parcels and bound each one with switches pulled from neighboring willows. Then the packs were hoisted onto their backs and they set out for camp.

Medicine Woman was wringing her hands in an uncharacteristic display of emotion when they spotted her. The sun had disappeared and a pale moon had arisen in its place when they finally reached the camp and dropped their parcels onto the ground.

While Buffalo Woman and Msipessi ate their first meal of the day, Mary was instructed to remove the roots from all the plants. As she pulled the roots away, a sticky substance leaked onto her hands. Medicine Woman gave her a broad leaf and motioned for her to place the sticky substance on it.

Once she had divided the roots from the leaves, she was put to work pounding the roots with a palm-size rock until she had a large bowl filled with something resembling coarse flour.

Medicine Woman boiled a pot of water and added the leaves. When Buffalo Woman had finished eating, she was tasked with stirring the mixture.

Sometime during the night, the leaves had been properly boiled and the roots pounded to Medicine Woman's satisfaction. Then Mary assisted the old squaw in washing Shooting Star and Little Fawn with the boiled water. It necessitated removing all their clothes, which was not an easy task inside the small hut with women too exhausted to help in removing their own clothing.

Once they were bathed, they applied a thin film of the root substance and held it in place by wrapping the boiled leaves around their extremities and torso.

The women moaned and occasionally cried out in pain, their fever apparent and their shivering heart-wrenching. But the poultice seemed to help eliminate whatever pain the pustules had wrought upon them, and eventually they finished and backed out of the hut.

To Mary's great relief, Medicine Woman dipped her arms in the warm water, gesturing for her to cleanse herself. She didn't have to be asked twice. She was terrified of contracting this strange disease.

She now knew this was not swamp fever. Whatever it was, it was far worse.

Exhausted and aching from the day's exertions, she fell into her own bed. She realized just before she fell asleep that she had not eaten anything at all since the previous day.

A snow storm reached them the following day, dumping another six inches of snow on their camp. Mary spent the next two days caring for the two women; each morning and each evening, the leaves were removed and discarded, the women bathed, and a fresh poultice was applied with new leaves holding them in place. On the third day, Mary, Msipessi and Buffalo Woman were sent to retrieve more cattails from the marsh, their work more difficult than their first trip as they searched ever deeper for more of the plants.

The days dragged on and there was still no sign of White Messenger and the others. When Mary was not caring for the sick, she was busy sewing boots for each of them. She used the moccasins as a guide for their feet and then crafted a longer sleeve that would reach above the knee, and then double back down to stay in place around their calves. She fire-cured the seams as White Messenger had instructed her to do, and even tested the water tightness on one of them.

Another week passed. She was sitting next to the campfire, feeling the warmth while she sewed, when Msipessi shouted from the edge of the camp. Rising, she saw White Messenger walking across the frozen landscape, Strength of an Ox beside him. White Messenger carried Eagle Feathers on his back.

Msipessi rushed out to meet them. Medicine Woman hurriedly gestured to Mary to get the poultice and leaves before also slipping and sliding on the ice to reach them. Eagle Feathers was transferred from White Messenger's back to Msipessi's and carried into camp.

He looked as the two women had; his face was covered in lesions and Mary had no doubt that the rest of his body looked the same. Without Medicine Woman's poultice, he had scratched repeatedly at it, and now the sores were open and festering. They moved him into the hut where Medicine Woman had been staying, removed his clothing, bathed him, and applied the poultice.

Mary sat at the entrance to her hut, watching the braves conferring around the campfire. The squaws had long ago gone to their respective huts, and though Mary could not understand their words, she knew the men were discussing matters of importance. The serious expressions, their downcast eyes, and their slumped shoulders told her something was wrong.

White Messenger spotted her and came to kneel beside her. They sat for a long moment without speaking before he said quietly, "We went to an Ojibwa village."

When he didn't continue, she asked, "Did you find what you were looking for?"

"We brought back provisions… rice, maple sugar. Meat."

"Will we be moving closer to their village?" she asked hopefully. "Perhaps they have better lodging?"

He shook his head. "Eagle Feathers became very ill. When the villagers saw him, they told us we must leave. We are not welcome in their village again. We are not welcome in any villages."

"What do you mean?" Mary found herself whispering hoarsely. "Surely, they don't expect us to remain out here by ourselves?"

He did not look at her, but remained focused on the flames from the campfire. "Yes, that is our fate. They do not know why the Great Spirit has caused this torment—this suffering—among us. But they are afraid. They do not want us in their villages. If we see them in the distance, we are not to approach them."

He sighed heavily.

"Then we will make do," Mary said. "We will build better huts. The men can find us food. And Medicine Woman and I will heal those who are sick."

The next morning, they buried Little Fawn and her unborn baby. And as they stood in a circle around her grave, Medicine Woman shivered violently, her forehead popping out in heavy perspiration.

46

Mary sat quietly at the edge of the pond and watched the sun's rays bouncing off the surface of the water. As quickly as insects landed, they were swallowed by fish which lay in waiting. In a nearby tree, a mother bird fed her hatchlings, their tiny peeps filling the air as they begged for food. The woods were filled with wildflowers in all the colors of the rainbow, and the trees were bursting with spring buds.

She wondered, as she had so many times before, where her brothers and sisters were at this very moment. She wondered whether Ma still yearned for her daughter, and whether the settlers at Fort Nashborough ever mentioned her name. As she looked out over the flat land, she yearned for the hills, to be back at Neely's Salt Lick, to feel the Cumberland River lapping at her ankles, to breathe the fresh, crisp air.

She wondered what month it was. She looked at the sky, at the insects, at the butterflies passing from one flower to the next. She would see these sights in May, she determined, if she were still in the Cumberlands.

It must be June, she thought. Perhaps even later, as far north as they were.

She had made it through the worst winter of her life.

She had been afflicted with the same cursed illness that had befallen Eagle Feathers, Shooting Star, and Little Fawn. The Indians called it mot-chi-te-he-thie, but she came to think of it as simply a Curse or Pox. Her entire body had been covered with the dreadful blisters, except for the palms of her hands and her knees. For four days, she lost her eyesight and during that terrible time, she came to believe that it was gone forever.

If Medicine Woman had been afflicted, it had not prevented her from helping the others. Each morning and each evening, she bathed Mary in the boiled water and packed her boils with a poultice and wrapped her in cattail leaves. There were mornings in which she was awakened before dawn for the ritual and again long after the sun had gone down, and she wondered whether Medicine Woman had gone to the marsh by herself to bring back more of the precious plants.

She was fed broth twice a day and sometimes it even had flecks of jerky in it. Then the flecks became less and less, until she suspected she was drinking water flavored only with bear fat.

When she regained her eyesight, she saw that her pustules were beginning to dry up. As soon as she was able, Medicine Woman pressed her into service, caring for the others as they also went through this terrible hell. It was then that Mary realized Medicine Woman had been caring for their entire family by herself.

Mary learned how to make an ointment from the leaves of the prickly pear and bear's fat, which she suspected was meant to prevent scarring. But poor Shooting Star, though she had recovered, her face and body were covered in scars that would not heal. She thought herself ugly now and went to great lengths to hide her face from the others.

Eagle Feathers, no doubt already weakened from his swamp fever, was unable to fight this new illness. He died one frigid morning. The ground was so frozen they could only wrap him in his blanket and wait until the spring thaw to bury him at the edge of the woods beside Little Fawn. Black Heart died a few weeks later.

Even White Messenger and Msipessi, both strong and fit when they left Fort Detroit, had been infected.

Buffalo Woman and Strength of an Ox had moved away from the rest of the family in an attempt to escape their misfortune. Mary learned during the cold, hard winter months, they had caught what fish they could and killed what animals they could, and had divided the pieces evenly, leaving theirs wrapped in buckskin at a spot some distance from the camp, where Medicine Woman would retrieve it. As the months wore on and game became scarcer, the meat had dwindled. On one occasion, they'd left a single quail, divided into equal pieces, and on another occasion, they'd left a blacksnake.

When the snow began to melt, Msipessi rallied himself from his illness. As the days wore on, they heard no more from Buffalo Woman and Strength of an Ox, and when he was well, he went in search of them. He found them both slaughtered and scalped beside a river's edge. They never knew who had killed them, or why, but their discovery sent terror through the stricken family. Once the dwindling family was well enough to travel, they fled further north and west.

Medicine Woman was stooped now and in failing health and she often shivered violently. She had taken to sleeping close to the campfire and their breaks were frequent and longer.

Now White Messenger called to Mary and she reluctantly rose and joined the others. They were moving eastward now in an attempt to come in contact with traders or Indians along the trail from Fort Detroit to Michilimackinac. Now that winter's snow and ice had melted, game was more bountiful but they had run completely out of corn meal and other food. They still carried a few trinkets White Messenger had obtained at Fort Detroit, and he hoped to trade them for enough corn meal to last through the summer months. He also wanted some seed and to find a small plot of land they could farm; someplace they could call home.

They had plenty of clothing now, having inherited the clothing from those who had passed on. Their blankets were folded and neatly packed away, as were their boots. Mary's breeches had become hot on the long walks, so she now wore only her buckskin dress. Now she bent down to pick up her pack and slung it across her back. Then she picked up Medicine Woman's and added it to her burden. Nodding, the five set off toward the east.

It was dusk two days later when they spotted the small village in the distance. It was filled with a few dozen wooden buildings—not huts, Mary noted. It was also situated along a vast expanse of water so wide she could not see the other side. It was the first time she had seen so much water since she journeyed northward on Lake Erie so long ago. The coastline was dotted with a few vessels and in the distance she saw two more heading for shore.

They stopped along a rise and White Messenger and Msipessi studied the village for a long time.

"We stop here," White Messenger said. "Tomorrow, we go to the village."

Mary lay awake for a long time that night. The windows of the homes were lit by indoor fireplaces and oil lamps, and she realized they were the first real houses she had seen in many months. She couldn't remember the last time she had seen an indoor fireplace; perhaps it was in the community building at Shawneetown, so long ago.

She lay on the ground, her arm serving as a pillow under her head, and wondered how it must feel to be asleep right now in one of those houses on a real bed under real cotton bedding. Eventually, she dozed off to sleep and dreamt of sitting in a real chair by a real fireplace, a blanket about her legs and sewing in her lap, and a kettle of real food cooking over the embers.

She awoke the next morning to find White Messenger and Msipessi in deep conversation as they studied the village below. They appeared to be having a disagreement and Mary noticed Medicine Woman and Shooting Star were listening intently.

Shooting Star began to sob miserably and turned away from the others.

"What did you say to her?" Mary asked, wrapping her arms around the young woman's shoulders.

White Messenger turned to Mary.

"There are no Indians in the village," he answered.

She peered at the village. She could only see a small piece of it, as many of the wooden structures blocked her view, and the people moving about were so small she wondered how they could tell what nationality they were.

Msipessi stepped forward. "You will have to go."

"Me?" Mary asked.

"Msipessi thinks you will have better luck at trading with them, than he or I."

Mary absorbed this information. "Would I go alone?"

White Messenger, normally so calm in the face of adversity, sounded exasperated. "Medicine Woman is not well. Shooting Star—well, her face—we are afraid her face will frighten them."

"So that's why she cries," she said, hugging Shooting Star. The young squaw held a piece of material across her face so Mary could not see it. She suspected she had torn her blanket so she would have material with which to cover her scarred face and neck.

"You will have to go," Msipessi said. "We give you these." He knelt and opened a small deerskin bag filled with trinkets.

"We need corn, vegetables like squash and beans," White Messenger said. "Melons, pears."

Mary sifted through the trinkets. They were cheaply made and some looked to be nothing more than poorly constructed children's toys. How would she ever be able to trade these pathetic things for enough food for five people?

She took a deep breath and returned the trinkets to the pouch. Then she stood and surveyed the village. "I go now," she said simply before beginning the long march down the hill and through the valley.

47

S he reached the village by mid-morning. She knew without looking behind her that her dwindling family was watching her. She also knew that she carried their most valuable possessions in a pouch not twice the size of her palm.

Behind her was a broken old squaw, a once-beautiful young woman with a disfigured face, a white man who believed himself to be an Indian, and a savage warrior who had, for whatever reasons, taken to her. And now it was up to her to find someone who would save them all from certain starvation.

As she entered the village, she sensed the white women murmuring to one another as they crossed the street in an attempt to put distance between them. At Fort Nashborough, she had grown accustomed to men tipping their hats and exchanging polite pleasantries; in contrast, the men here seemed to sneer or gawk at her. She wished she had had the forethought to slip on her breeches, as she began to feel her nakedness under the simple deerskin dress slung over her shoulders. Self-consciously, she wiped her hand over her hair. It was long now and pulled back from her face, and it felt gritty from months of sleeping on the ground.

She made her way to the water, where she found vendors hawking their wares. There were tables filled with fish fresh off the fishermen's boats. There were fruits of every description, vegetables piled high on carts, and even fresh flowers for sale.

There were even merchants selling hand-made jewelry with beautiful turquoise, blue, and green beads.

She wanted to break down and sob right there in the middle of the market, to cry for the days when she had the money for a bouquet of flowers or a bracelet. She wanted to cry for the days when she was a free white woman about whom people did not whisper behind her back or slink away from as she approached.

She thought of Buffalo Woman and Strength of an Ox, slaughtered and scalped, and wondered if those who lived here in the village did not want the Indians near their homes.

She approached a fruit stand and tried to inquire about a trade, but the merchant shooed her away. She went next to a vegetable stand, and then another, but they each turned from her as if she were a dirty dog that had no business in their market.

Dejected, she stopped beneath a tree and leaned wearily against the trunk. The faces of Shooting Star, Medicine Woman, White Messenger and Msipessi haunted her. She could not return empty-handed.

"Tu fais quoi?"

Mary looked up. A middle-aged woman stood a few feet from her. She rested a basket on her wide hip and with her free hand, she pushed a stray wisp of gray hair from her forehead. Her sharp blue eyes pierced Mary with their inquisitiveness, her head cocking as if assessing her.

"Pardon?" Mary asked.

"Tu vas ou?"

Mary shook her head. "I—I don't understand."

"Ah, you are English," the woman said, shifting her basket. "Why are you dressed so?"

"I am a captive," Mary said. "I am far from home, and I need help."

"Come with me," she said, grasping her hand and leading her away.

"She can't simply disappear," the old man said as he took a swig of whiskey. The house was dim but comforting. Mary noticed a dish towel laid across a bowl in the kitchen and wondered when she last laid eyes on such cloth.

"Well, why not?" the woman said, plopping a slice of apple pie in front of her. "She said herself they were afraid to come into our village."

Mary hesitated. Her first instinct was to pick up the pie and eat it with her hands, but the woman had placed a fork across the plate. She raised it now, studying it and marveling at its design, before using it to plunge into the sweet pie.

"If she doesn't return, they will look for her," the old man was saying, his beady eyes fixed on Mary. "They may incite others to join them."

"Well, we can't let her go back. Look at her! She's nothing but skin and bones." She poked at Mary. "She's not half the weight she ought to be."

Mary was torn. She wanted to escape; she wanted to return to her family and leave this place forever. But Medicine Woman's face kept passing in front of her, looking as she did when she washed Mary's body and fed her when she was so ill.

"If you can help me get some food," she interjected. "I have things to trade—" She reached into her pouch and pulled out the trinkets, spreading them across the table. "I need vegetables and fruit and cornmeal."

"Why, child," the woman said in her heavy French accent, "all of these together would not buy you one piece of fruit."

A single tear slipped down Mary's cheek. "It is all we have. And we are starving."

The old man and woman were silent.

The pie was gone and now Mary's stomach was beginning to churn.

When the old man spoke, his voice was soft and raspy. "Laetitia, take that bowl over there," he nodded toward the table in the corner. "Fill it with fruit and vegetables. Send it back with her."

Mary pushed the trinkets toward him. "Take what you want."

"I do not want any of it. But I want the bowl back."

"Of course," Mary said.

"Listen to me, little one. I want the bowl back. This means you must carry the bowl to the Indians and give them the food. Then you must bring back the bowl."

Before Mary could respond, he said, "And when you bring it back tonight, after dark, we will be waiting for you. Bring with you whatever you wish to keep, for you will not be going back to the Indians. We will help you escape."

48

The sun was setting as Mary made her way from the French fishing village to the Indians she knew were waiting anxiously for her return. She carried in her arms a serving bowl filled with leeks, mushrooms, blueberries, dried apples and pears and an assortment of beans. Many of them showed some age and Mary suspected they might have been stored through the winter in Laetitia's root cellar, but it didn't matter. The Indians would be relieved to get it.

She also carried a burlap bag filled with corn meal and even scraps from a wild turkey. She knew every item would be divided evenly among the family, right down to an equal number of blueberries for each.

Her pouch had only a few trinkets left. After careful deliberation, she decided it would arouse suspicion if she returned with so much food and all of the trinkets as well. So she left the best ones inside the pouch and placed the remainder on a table in Laetitia's home; she decided the Shawnees would be better able to trade for valuable foodstuffs if they still had the best of the trinkets available.

Her travel was made more difficult with the heavy items, but her heart was pounding and her head spinning with the possibility of escape. Her legs ached with each step, and she knew she would have only a brief rest before making the return journey, but she would have no choice but to will away the aches and pains in her quest for freedom.

On the long walk back, she experienced a myriad of emotions. It had taken every ounce of courage and determination she could muster to leave the safety of Laetitia's home. Her feet had felt like stone pillars as she departed the village and an overwhelming sense of dread rose within her. What if the Shawnees decided to keep the beautiful bowl and did not allow Mary to return to the village? What if she were walking back into captivity, having let her only real chance of escape slip through her fingers?

Then her dread turned to resignation and a blind faith that she was doing the only thing that was right. In a single day, she would stave off starvation in this tiny band of Shawnees and escape as well.

By the time she was almost to the point where she'd separated from them this morning, her heart was pounding with excitement. She was now worried that she would betray her intentions with a look of the eye or a brief smile or an over-eager movement. She could not act as though she wanted to return, she decided. She must not appear too willing.

She reached the rise where they had surveyed the village early that day, but they were no longer there. She studied the ground and the soft imprints left by their moccasins before descending to the other side. When she was halfway to the shelter of nearby woods, she heard a sudden noise. Startled, she turned and almost bumped right into White Messenger.

His eyes were wide as he studied the bowl, a multitude of questions on his lips.

They were joined by the others, and as Mary set the bowl and the burlap bag on the ground, they gathered around and poked through the contents like children on Christmas morning.

They wanted to know every last detail, and Mary carefully told them the story she had constructed on the long journey back: that she had gone to the market along the river and bartered for everything. She showed them the trinkets she brought back and embellished her story with how she was able to get more goods for some trinkets than others. But she had managed to get so much she had nothing in which to carry them, so a kind farmer had offered his own bowl with the caveat that she return it to him.

"You must bring it back right away," White Messenger said as the others murmured their agreement.

"But I am tired," Mary said. "I have walked all the way there and back. Must I bring it back immediately?"

"You must," White Messenger said. "This was a good man. We must be good in return." He paused. "You may eat something, and then you will bring back the bowl."

Although she had been up before dawn and had walked for miles on rough terrain, she was not hungry. The pie had upset her stomach and she was too excited to eat now. But she nodded and set to work with the others in dividing the food.

As Medicine Woman and Shooting Star began preparing a meal with a fraction of the foodstuff, she feigned tiredness and lay down as though to sleep. She was a bit surprised they did not press her into service, but she reasoned they must be pleased with the items she brought back.

They had a dinner of turkey liver, corn cakes and some of the dried apples.

Msipessi looked across the campfire at her. "You did good work today," he said.

"Wos-sa," Medicine Woman said.

"Wos-sa," they all repeated, nodding their heads.

"Wos-sa," Mary said. "Good."

When they finished eating, she sat for a time and watched the flames leap. The mosquitoes had emerged from their daytime sleep, and she slapped one of them as it fed on her arm. Without a word, Shooting Star retrieved the precious bear fat and began rubbing it onto Mary's neck and arms.

"Keep bug from biting," she said in the broken English Mary had taught her over the long winter months.

"Thank you," Mary said.

Medicine Woman was the first to leave the fire, venturing into the woods for a brief time and then returning to lie on the hard ground, tucking her arm under her head as a pillow. She lay under the stars and the clear sky with no blanket in the coolness of the night, her other hand rested contentedly on her abdomen.

Shooting Star cleaned up the campsite, insisting that Mary remain seated. "You have long walk," she said in her quiet voice. She gathered the bowls and washed them in precious water she'd gathered from a distant stream. In the veil of darkness, she allowed the ragged material she used to hide her face to slip away, and for a moment she was beautiful again. Then when she ventured near the flames, Mary saw the telltale pockmarks of her long illness. Without thinking, Mary reached her hand to her own cheek and stroked the soft, unlined skin. It had only been Medicine Woman's dedicated care that had brought her through her own illness and left her face unmarked, though she didn't know why Shooting Star had been afflicted so…

"You look deep in thought," White Messenger said.

Startled, Mary looked at him. "I am tired," she said.

He nodded and they sat for a few minutes in silence. Msipessi sighed heavily and ventured into the woods, leaving them alone.

"What is the village like?" White Messenger asked.

"The people are French," she said, carefully choosing her words. "They were not friendly, thinking I was… not one of them."

"Yet you traded well."

"God was with me."

He nodded again and they fell silent.

She could not take her Bible with her; it would arouse suspicion. She thought of her meager possessions: her Bible, her comb, her bowl, two pair of moccasins, two sets of clothing that consisted of a buckskin dress and breeches, and a badly worn blanket. She knew they would not be discarded; like the dead family members' possessions, they would be divided amongst the remaining members.

"You must go now."

Mary fought the urge to jump up and eagerly grab the bowl. "I am tired."

"It is not like you to complain."

She shrugged. "I have walked far today. My feet and legs are in need of rest."

"You must not allow your feet and legs to determine your actions," White Messenger said.

She looked across the fire. He was thinner than when they first met, but she could easily see the sinewy strength of his arms against the dancing flames. His warm brown hair was straight and long and cascaded over his shoulders onto his chest. His hazel eyes looked tired and life-worn as they fixed on hers.

"I will go with you," he said. "I will carry the bowl until we reach the village. Then I will wait for you while you return it."

Mary lowered her eyes and was silent. After a moment, she said, "There is no need for both of us to lose sleep." She rose. "I agreed to borrow the bowl. It is my duty to return it."

She stretched in the light of the flames and then picked up the bowl. She turned away from the campfire. The terrain looked dark now and the village was barely visible. She began to realize where she had been able to choose her steps carefully during the daylight areas and thus avoid swampy areas or holes dug by wild animals, now she would be crossing the valley in the darkness, unable to see the ground beneath her feet. She wondered briefly if she should allow White Messenger to accompany her, but abandoned the thought. She could not bear the thought of him waiting alone on the outskirts of the village for her to return.

He did not stand but remained beside the fire watching her. She fought the urge to say good-bye, to look once more at Shooting Star or White Messenger or Msipessi, who was emerging from the woods.

Instead, she picked up the bowl and silently walked away from the camp.

As she ventured into the darkness, she felt White Messenger's eyes on her back. Every muscle in her body wanted to turn around and look back one more time, but she knew she could not. She climbed the rise just beyond their campsite and descended to the other side, knowing as she reached the valley the glow from their fire was no longer visible.

Then she began to hurry, her legs propelling her forward, knowing with each step she was leaving her captivity behind. She was going home.

49

J im closed the leather-bound book after making his last entry from Fort Jefferson. It was June 8, 1781, barely a year and a half after they had cleared the land and built the fort named after Thomas Jefferson that was to secure Virginia territories along the Mississippi.

Now they were abandoning it.

He sighed heavily. It had been a tough winter, the worst most people in these parts could remember. They had experienced unrelenting snowfall that began in early autumn and continued unabated until late spring. The snow and the bitter cold had only served to increase their hardships.

Since the Indians burned their crops and killed most of their livestock, they had been dependent upon outside assistance for food and supplies. Colonel Montgomery had helped as best he could by sending supplies along the Mississippi from New Orleans. Occasionally, they received additional supplies from the Falls on the Ohio, a fort and settlement Colonel Clark had built at a shallow point near the Ohio River, just above a set of steep falls. But the provisions had not been enough to sustain them. And as the weather grew worse and travel became more treacherous, supply shipments became fewer and further between.

One of the remaining men, John Donne, wrote a long letter back in December to Colonel Clark informing him of their desperate straits, but their fortune only became worse as the winter had progressed. Sickness claimed several lives and disabled men whom Jim would have counted on for hunting expeditions and defense. They now had barely a hundred people in the fort and its outposts, and within the hour, they would no longer have those.

Two months ago, they'd received word that Clark was planning another assault on Fort Detroit. It was to occur in the spring after the winter thaw. Jim had been dispatched to the Falls on the Ohio and then northward, deep into Indian and British territories as a scout. But because of the record snowfall, the rivers and streams were overflowing, causing massive flooding. The Army's forces became bogged down in the mud and muck and they were forced to turn back.

Now Jim was back at Fort Jefferson, assisting in the pull-out of their meager forces and the few civilians who had loyally persevered. It was difficult not to consider this a retreat.

He tried not to think what would happen to this fort as he packed his possessions and prepared to leave. The Indians might overtake it and burn it to the ground, or the British might hear of its abandonment and secure it for their own forces. It was a dismal day in this war.

Daniel Boone had left some time earlier en route to Virginia, where he would officially begin his term as a legislator. To Jim's knowledge, they never did find Ned's head.

Jim carried his possessions to his horse, where he saddled up the bone-thin stallion and secured his bags. Brandy ran circles around him. She was never far away, though she was also nothing more than skin and bones. Other than his horse and his dog, he didn't have much. He wouldn't need much. He would stay to make certain the women and children—barely two dozen in all— arrived safely at the Falls on the Ohio. Then he would take the Ohio River to Fort Pitt, where he would receive further orders.

He had a sudden sense of homesickness, and for a brief moment, he wondered whether he might be given some time to visit his family in Virginia. He'd lost touch with Teddy and didn't know if he'd been able to send his letter to his mother eastward.

He checked the wagon trains, accounted for the women and children, and waited for the word to move out. Their trip on land would be short; they would load their possessions onto flatboats for the longer phase of their journey.

As they began their trek, he looked back at the fort he'd called home. The gates were swinging open. It was an odd sight; they had always been diligent about keeping them closed and manned. His heart sank and he turned back around, spurring his horse forward.

50

The knock on the door startled Mary. It was neither loud nor demanding but it caused her heart to begin racing and her face to become instantly flushed. She stood as though her feet were affixed to the floor, the paring knife held in mid-air.

She heard the sound of feet scampering across the floor above her before hastening down the stairs.

"Just a minute!" Laetitia's voice sounded rushed and breathless.

Mary set the knife next to the vegetables she'd been slicing for dinner just as Laetitia hurried into the room. Without a word, she pulled two chairs from under the table and drew back a faded rug that rested neatly underneath the heavy wooden table.

She opened a trap door. "Get in the cellar and don't make a sound!"

Mary fairly flew down the rickety steps and then her feet sank in the soft dirt. Her head had barely cleared the entranceway before the door was shut. She heard the sound of the rug hitting the floor and then the chairs were pushed back in place.

She stood for a moment and tried to adjust to the darkness. She had to stand slightly stooped to avoid hitting her head on the heavy beams that crossed under the main floor and the musty air threatened to overpower her. She swallowed hard in an effort to coat her throat in saliva, lest she cough and reveal her hiding place. As her eyes became adjusted, thin streaks of faded light crossed the dirt floor and she realized several of the wooden boards above her were not flush, allowing the light to filter through the cracks.

She found herself in a storage area that ran the length and width of the house. Against one wall was an assortment of items that included old pottery and cooking utensils, some rusting with the humid air. Mary couldn't help but think how valuable those old items would have been to her just two days before. Against another wall was a table with a broken leg; a pile of scrap wood held it even enough to store dusty jugs on top, but not level enough to keep Mary from worrying about them toppling with just the slightest wind. On the wall nearest her were sacks of potatoes and jars of preserves, pickled pigs feet and boiled eggs.

She heard Laetitia call out again, "Coming!" before she heard the front door open.

Mary made her way toward the front of the house. The earthen floor was uneven and as she grasped a beam with which to steady herself, her fingers plunged into a soft, sticky spider web. Shuddering, she wiped her hand on the cotton dress Laetitia had given her to replace her Indian garb.

When she reached the far wall, she found a warped floorboard, creating a tiny crack in which she could peer upwards into the foyer.

She almost gasped in fear and astonishment. Instinctively, she clamped her hand to her mouth in an effort to stifle any sound from escaping. There on the threshold stood White Messenger.

He was clean and his brown hair had been cut shoulder-length and was pulled back from his face in a single neat tail. His skin was tanned and slightly lined from years living out of doors, but his bright hazel eyes, patrician nose and square jaw were a testament to his European blood, effectively hiding the fact that he lived amongst the Shawnees. He wore the buckskin jacket and breeches Mary had sewn for him, which made him appear like a settler; only the knee-high buckskin boots stood out where there should have been leather.

"I am sorry to disturb you," he said in a smooth, calm voice. "I am searching for my sister Mary."

No! Mary wanted to cry out. She ground her teeth until her jaw began to ache.

Laetitia was silent and Mary could almost feel her bewilderment. "Why would you think I know where your sister is?" she said at last in her heavy French accent.

"She came here two days ago," he said, his head cocked as he tried to look past her into the house. "She might have been dressed as an Indian. She had been captured some time ago, but we rescued her. Sometimes she reverts to dressing as they do and wanders away…"

"Are you going house to house?" she asked.

"Some people told me they saw her with you. You were very kind to give her food and loan her a bowl."

Mary's heart began to pound. Perspiration popped out across her forehead but she was afraid to wipe it lest he sense her movement.

"Yes," Laetitia said. "I helped her." She took a deep breath. "She was hungry and I gave her food."

"Thank you," he said in a voice soft as velvet. "You are a good woman."

Laetitia was silent. Mary could see his eyes through the crack in the flooring; they were fixed seductively on the Frenchwoman. Oh, please, don't fall for his lies! She thought wildly.

"When we saw the bowl, we insisted she return it right away… Did she?"

Laetitia shifted her weight and the floorboard creaked. Mary stifled the impulse to jerk away. "Yes. She brought it back the night I gave it to her."

"Do you know what happened to her? My mother—she is very worried. My whole family is worried about her."

There was a long silence. Then Laetitia stepped outside the house and pulled the door almost to. She stood on the stoop and pointed toward the east. "She said she was tired, and she set out that way, toward Lake Huron."

"Do you know where she was going?" he asked.

"No, I'm afraid I don't… Where are you staying? Perhaps if I see her again, I can contact you?"

"We are searching for her in and around the village."

"Where are you staying?" she pressed.

"I will check back with you, perhaps tomorrow."

Laetitia wandered down the steps and their voices became muffled.

Please, please don't give me away! Mary thought, trying to still her now-violent trembling.

A long moment that felt like an eternity passed before Laetitia returned to the house. She stood for a moment in the doorway, waving politely before closing and bolting the door.

Mary could hear her footsteps above her as she crossed into the parlor; perhaps she was watching White Messenger from the window. Then after another long moment, she could hear her feet scampering across the floor to the back room, where the chairs grazed the wood as she dragged them from the table.

Mary was at the trap door as soon as she opened it. Light flooded into her face and she held one arm above her eyes to shield her from the brightness as she climbed onto the floor beneath the table.

"Child," the woman said as Mary came to her feet. "Have you told me everything?"

"Yes," Mary said, her body still shaking violently. "He is an Indian, I swear to you." She spoke in a hoarse whisper, partly due to her parched throat and partly due from fear that somehow he would hear her through the thick exterior wall. She told Laetitia of White Messenger and his adoption by the Shawnee tribe.

"Please, please don't give me back to them," she pleaded.

Laetitia grabbed her shoulders and looked her in the face with piercing gray-blue eyes. "Did anyone else see you return here?" she asked frantically.

"No," Mary said. "It was late. The market was closed. Most of the houses were dark."

"And no one saw you?"

She shook her head. "I don't think so. I came straight to your house. I didn't speak to anyone."

Laetitia sat in one of the heavy wood chairs. Though her eyes fell on the bowl of vegetables Mary had been preparing for dinner, her thoughtful expression told her that the Frenchwoman's thoughts were miles away.

"He will continue to search for you," she said at last. "And he looks like a white man. He speaks like a white man. If anyone knows you are here, they could betray us. You are not safe. None of us are safe."

White Messenger returned the next day and the day after that. By the end of a week's time, he had reappeared with Msipessi. Laetitia came and went as usual, venturing to the market and running errands. Each time she returned, she was visibly shaken. Her husband Jeannot went to work each morning, returning at lunch time and again in the evening. They often spoke in muffled voices behind the closed door of their bedroom. Mary tried not to let her trepidation and fear get the best of her, but she couldn't help but feel her days here were numbered.

The days were painfully slow and the nights filled with even more apprehension as Mary awakened with each sound. She repaired Laetitia's and Jeannot's clothing, cleaned their home and prepared their meals but she did not dare progress beyond the house. Occasionally, she would venture close to the windows and peer outside. Twice she saw Msipessi and White Messenger conferring at the end of the street, their eyes focused on the house.

They know I am here, she thought, her heart sinking. It is only a matter of time before they come after me.

Two weeks passed in utter torment.

Then one day Jeannot returned from work and sought out Laetitia and Mary. "It happens tonight," he said in a low voice.

"When?"

"After dark. We take Mary to the church. They will meet us there."

51

Mary fought to calm her nerves as she approached the door. Jeannot fidgeted while he waited for her in the hallway, and she tried not to notice the way he shifted from one foot to another with growing anxiety. Laetitia smoothed the back of Mary's dress and as they reached the doorway, she assessed her once more.

She was wearing all of the clothes Laetitia had given her: two pair of undergarments, a soft cotton nightgown, a cotton dress for everyday wear, and a coat. The extra clothing was worn and not carried because Laetitia was almost twice the size of Mary; the extra clothing gave her the bulk she would need to pass through the town as Jeannot's wife. Now the Frenchwoman plopped a bonnet on her head and tied it tight under Mary's chin, tucking her newly shortened hair underneath before pulling the bonnet so low on her forehead that it threatened to block her vision.

"Keep your head down," she said. "Hold onto Jeannot's hand. If anyone approaches, simply begin coughing. Jeannot will do all of the talking." She handed her a large handkerchief. "Keep this over your mouth."

Mary nodded and Laetitia stepped back.

"Take care of yourself, child," she said.

"Hurry," Jeannot said, fumbling for the doorknob. "We mustn't be late."

Mary kissed Laetitia on the cheek. "How can I ever thank you?" she whispered.

"Just remember, child, where you find great evil, you will also find great kindness. Be good to others, and you will repay me."

Jeannot grasped Mary's hand and they disappeared through the doorway into the darkened street. She heard the door close quietly behind her as they scurried down the steps.

The sky was overcast, the clouds painted on a sapphire blue canvas that melted into the night sky. There was a slight chill in the air, but Mary fought to keep from perspiring under the layers of clothing. She kept her head down but her eyes darted continuously as she tried to see from under the bonnet's ruffle. But she knew the visibility was so poor that White Messenger and Msipessi could be upon them both before she even realized it.

She tried not to think of the times when they seemed to appear out of nowhere, when they approached her with the silence of a cat, when she turned and unexpectedly bumped into them. She fought to keep from shaking as they hurried down the street and turned the corner.

Someone called out to them and Jeannot squeezed her hand. Mary complied with a fit of coughing and he answered the person in his native tongue. His feet moved faster as he half-pulled her along.

Two more corners and he whispered hoarsely, "The church is in sight."

It took every ounce of willpower to keep from breaking into a full run, from hiking up the long skirt and dashing to safety as if her life depended upon it—which might very well have been the case. Instead, they continued walking, Jeannot's palm now sweating profusely as he squeezed her hand.

An owl hooted in the distance and she almost froze with fear: was it an owl, she wondered frantically, or Msipessi calling to White Messenger? Another owl answered, and her thoughts turned to the Lord's Prayer.

"Slow down," Jeannot said hoarsely. "You'll arouse suspicion."

She dutifully slowed from her sudden trot to a quick walk, but her mind continued to race. Had she heard the owl yet again, or was it just her imagination?

She could feel someone coming up behind them in the darkness, could feel the breath of a silent Indian bent on whisking her away from the Frenchman and carrying her back to captivity.

Then her foot scraped a stone step and Jeannot was ordering her to hurry inside. She raised her skirt and sprinted up the steps and through an open door into the chapel.

She heard the door slam shut behind her and a heavy bolt was lowered into place. Only then did she raise her head to peer around her.

The church was dark except for a few scattered candles providing weak, dancing lights that cast images across the cold stone walls. The priest was clad in a long white robe; his hair was silver under a white cap and his almond eyes examined her without blinking.

"Come," he said, holding a candle high as he strode briskly through the entryway and down a short flight of steps.

Mary followed him as he led them through a hallway so circuitous that it threatened to disorient her. Then they stopped abruptly at what appeared to be a solid stone wall.

The priest blew out a candle mounted on the side wall, and then lifted the tray upon which molten liquid quickly solidified into lumps of wax. He extricated a heavy skeleton key. Then he placed the key between two stones, almost as if to hide it, when Mary heard a slight click and one of the stones swung out. The priest pulled the stone as if it were a lever. A doorway no wider than three feet across by five feet high became visible in the dim light.

"Se dépêcher! Se dépêcher!" he said, pushing Mary past him.

She bowed her head and squeezed through the tiny opening into the cold and drafty blackness. She was unable to adjust her eyes before he was pushing her further into the tiny hallway, her feet stumbling over uneven ground.

Then the draft dissipated as quickly as it had materialized as the door behind her was shut. She heard someone fumbling behind her, and a candle sprung to light. The priest and Jeannot stood behind her, Jeannot panting heavily as the priest placed the skeleton key in between two stones.

Then the priest slipped past her and hurried down a narrow, musty hallway that wound first to the left and then to the right, up an incline, round a bend, and then back down. Jeannot was huffing behind her, his footsteps falling further to the rear.

But the priest kept going and Mary was so afraid she would get too far from the candlelight that she continued to plunge ahead, offering a quick prayer that Jeannot would not drop dead from exertion behind her.

Then they rounded yet another bend and started up a steep incline. Now she was puffing, the extra layers of clothing cutting into her abdomen as she hiked her skirt around her knees and hurried onward.

One more bend and the tunnel was filled with light. Startled, she looked upward to see the moon shining directly into an open entranceway like an angel lighting the way.

Then she was plunged into the open air, where two sets of hands grabbed her, dragging her across the uneven ground. Behind her a door was slammed shut, the solid noise sounding final and resolute in the darkness of night. She was alone with two strangers who heaved her forward by her elbows.

She could only see the ground rising up beneath her, and now the bonnet shielded the sky and the light of the moon from her face. They scurried over underbrush and piles of brown leaves, and then she was plunged downward beneath a sudden rise, and then downward still.

She smelled the water before she saw it: a vast pool that looked black as tar in the night, the waves crashing against the shoreline with a ferocity that matched the pounding of her heart.

Then she was unceremoniously lifted off her feet and strong, brawny arms plunged under her knees for the briefest of moments as she was hauled over the side of a fishing boat.

Before she could come to a seated position, she was pushed against the wooden flooring and a husky voice whispered, "Stay down!"

Then both men were on board with her and the boat was cast away from the shore and into the mounting waves.

52

Mary found herself in the hull of a canoe-shaped boat about twenty feet in length. But unlike a canoe, this boat had a flat bottom and two masts that allowed it to skim quickly over the surface of the water. As Mary peered over the side, she soon could no longer see the shoreline and the French village as they headed into open water.

One of the men sat near the stern and wrestled with the rear sail to maintain a constant direction as the winds grew increasingly more hostile. The other man was toward the bow; as they shouted over the sound of the waves to each other in French, Mary gathered that the man in the stern was named Francois and the one closer to her was Rene.

She scrambled to come to a seated position as the waves crashed over the bow. The boat was filled with fishing nets and the pungent odor of fish soon filled her nostrils.

Once they were underway, Rene offered her a hand and helped her to a wooden cross beam that was a bit wider than the others, where she could remain seated. In the darkness, she was unable to see his facial features clearly except for his angled jaw and an Adam's apple that bobbed above a cloth tied around his neck. He was wiry and his back was bent like one who was accustomed to hauling heavy loads.

"Stay low," he said in rapid English with only the slightest hint of a French accent.

The waves grew higher, causing the boat to heave. Mary closed her eyes and fought to keep her stomach from churning.

"What was that?" Rene asked.

Mary opened her eyes. Both men were standing and facing outward, their heads tilted as if listening. She could barely see ten feet beyond the boat; the midnight blue sky seemed to be reaching all the way to the surface of the water, engulfing them in the darkness.

"I thought I heard something," Rene said in a hoarse whisper that was barely audible over the waves.

"I heard it, too," said Francois. He was a heftier man; as the moon slid in and out of the clouds, it highlighted a ruddy complexion and dirt-stained hands.

"Indians," he whispered hoarsely.

Mary instinctively dropped further into the hull, seeking to hide her body while still peering over the side of the boat. A thick mist was moving in, almost as if the clouds were battling the sky in their reach to the earth. The boat slowed and Francois sprung into action, steering it toward the north.

"I'm to go south," Mary pleaded with Rene. "South, below Fort Detroit."

He didn't answer immediately, but stole a sideways glance at Francois. "We can't risk being seen," he said.

Francois changed direction again, this time toward the east. The minutes slipped past as they headed further from shore. Mary tried to keep abreast of their direction, but she was becoming disoriented; at times they were surrounded by total blackness and at other times, by a heavy fog. The moon continued to slip in and out of the clouds, appearing only long enough for Mary to see the concern etched across the fishermen's faces.

From somewhere in the darkness, a wolf howled.

Mary felt the hairs on her neck stand up in fear. She tried to see Rene's and Francois' faces but the darkness obscured them. Francois said something in French to Rene.

A moment later, another wolf answered and then another.

Rene and Francois were completely still as their unblinking eyes searched the water in every direction. With each howl, their heads all jerked toward the sound.

"That's no wolf," Rene said, vocalizing what Mary already knew.

Her heart was pounding so strongly she could feel it coursing in her throat. Suddenly, all of the layers of clothes felt as though they were suffocating her and she fought to keep from fainting.

"Mackinaw," Francois said.

"It's our only choice," Rene answered.

"Mackinaw?" Mary said. "Is that south of Detroit?"

"Not south. North," Francois said as he changed course.

"But—"

"We are taking you to an island where you will be safe. No Indians will bother you there."

The hours passed so slowly that Mary felt suspended in time. She didn't understand how they could be navigating toward any particular island; sometimes, they went north and at other times, south; sometimes east and sometimes west. A bird's sudden appearance or a lone wave breaking was enough to change their course. Once an apparition seemed to appear in the mist; they watched with bated breath while a lone Indian in a canoe headed west across their path, his back toward them. Mary's nerves were so strained that her skin felt like pincushions.

Dawn was breaking when Mary caught sight of tall bluffs that rose out of the fog like a stone fortress. Atop the bluffs was a fort under the British flag.

The men steered the boat into a small cove just out of sight of the sentries.

"We leave you here," Rene said, maneuvering the bow so Mary could step off the boat onto a grassy shoreline.

"But—but what do I do?" she said, hesitating.

"We can not risk being seen; the British will arrest us if they think we have helped you. Stay out of sight and we will be back tomorrow night, after dark. Meet us here and we will take you south of Detroit."

"You will be back, won't you?" Mary said imploringly.

Rene avoided her eyes. "We will be back. After dark, tomorrow."

She waddled off the bow in her layers of clothes and they pushed off quickly. She watched them disappear around the eastern edge of the island before she turned toward the island itself.

She had to remain out of sight for two days.

She moved to the edge of the woods and began peeling off her clothes, leaving only the day dress Laetitia had given her. It was bulky and too long, but she felt immensely better once she was out from under all those stifling layers.

She found a shady area where she could lay back upon the ground. She had not eaten since the day before, but she was not hungry. She was bone tired, but she was not sleepy. She curled up, using her extra clothes as a pillow. She would lie here, out of sight, for as long as she could. After dark, she could sneak down to the water's edge and drink some water; perhaps she could wander a short distance in search of berries or wild fruits.

She closed her eyes. Her father's face moved through her mind on ghostly wings and then was replaced with Eagle Feathers' hard, stern features. Then it was White Messenger and his silky voice, "I am looking for my sister…" and then it was Msipessi cackling while he cut off a piece of her father's scalp and tossed it at her feet.

She hadn't realized she had fallen asleep until she heard the sound of a twig cracking. Her eyes flew open but she remained immobile, her entire body alert.

The ground grew shaded until she was engulfed in a dark shadow.

"Well, what have we here?" came a strong British accent.

She turned and looked upward at a hulking man in a British uniform, his beefy face pockmarked and sunburned, peering down at her with narrowed eyes. In horror, she watched as he bent closer to her, his tongue flitting over his parched lips.

53

Jim sat atop his black stallion, his eyes closed as he turned his face upward to the sun, basking in its warmth. It was early summer, too soon for the stifling humidity that would soon overwhelm these parts; it was this season that he loved the most—the stage between the first spring blossoms and the heat of late summer. This was a rare moment, to be able to close his eyes and lean into the sun, an uncommon instant stolen from the time in which his piercing blue eyes were required to roam relentlessly across the horizon, watching and waiting for a sudden movement, the flutter of an Indian brave's feathers or the glint of a tomahawk.

Below him, the sound of children's laughter and Brandy's gleeful barking wafted upwards. It was a comforting sound, one of normalcy in a world that had grown increasingly less predictable and progressively more volatile.

Below his perch atop this cliff was the Ohio River, leisurely snaking its way past green land overpopulated with trees and brush. He had been on this river now for several days, traveling northeastward by flatboat except for the times such as these when the boat was tied alongside the shore and he was able to stretch his legs and that of his stallion. His ultimate destination was the very source of the river, all the way to Fort Pitt. He was accompanied by two families who had had enough of life in the

west and who were seeking safe passage to Pennsylvania from
the Falls of the Ohio and before that, from Fort Jefferson.

He opened his eyes and peered below. Two boys and a girl
were frolicking in the waters, their mirth effectively hiding the
terrible winter of near starvation they had endured. But children
were resilient, he thought as he watched them. With any luck at
all, they would be in Pennsylvania in a few short weeks and their
time in Indian Territory would be only a faint memory.

He couldn't blame them for leaving, though he felt a sudden
pang in his chest when he thought of the exodus of settlers.
They needed those men to stand firm against the Indians and
claim the lands west of the Cumberland Gap as their own;
otherwise, all would be lost. It looked bleak now, with the British
still holding onto Fort Detroit, Colonel Clark vainly attempting
to persuade the Virginia legislature to pay its bills in the west,
and the Indians frightening away so many with their head hunting
and terror tactics.

His eyes narrowed as he expertly searched the terrain below
for signs of movement beyond his small party. Not seeing any,
he spurred his horse onward, stepping sure-footedly along a razor
thin peak that wound its way parallel to the river.

They rounded a corner and he stopped abruptly, one hand
rapidly grasping his telescope while the other remained
instinctively close to his weapon.

A small vessel was moving westward in the center of the
river. He peered through the telescope, noting the gentle wake it
made as it spliced through the water and followed it further to
his party resting along the banks below, oblivious of its presence.
It was less than an hour away, he determined, and possibly even
closer.

He strained to see the occupants of the vessel but could not
at this distance. He retracted the telescope, kicked his heels against
his horse and began the treacherous journey down the navigable
side of the cliff toward the approaching vessel.

Jim watched the boat approach from his new vantage point
along the banks of the river, his figure hidden beneath the

shadowy tendrils cast by the trees that strained over the shoreline. He calculated the vessel's movements with the expertise of one accustomed to navigating the waters in Indian Territory. He knew it would have to slow as it approached the curve to avoid running aground. If the occupants were white, they would begin to nervously peer about, searching the banks for signs of Indian marauders while they tried to maneuver the boat as swiftly yet safely as possible. If they were Indian, they would know who was about without even turning their heads; they were like animals that way, the Indians were, somehow able to sniff the air and catch a stranger's scent.

He watched as the boat came closer. His brow furrowed. There was only one figure, unusual because it dramatically increased the occupant's vulnerability to attack.

Jim held the telescope to his eye and peered at the boat until the occupant's face came into clear view. It was a young white man. And not just any man, but one he once called his neighbor, Sam Neely.

Moving as one body with his horse, they waded quietly into the river, leaving the safety of the shadows. The sun basked down upon them as it had at the top of the cliffs, skipping off the river's currents in a peaceful dance. For a brief moment, he almost felt as though he could shake the reality of the wilderness and its constant life-or-death struggle and lose himself in the gentle cries of the chickadees and kingfishers.

Then Sam raised his head. His hand flew to his longrifle, but Jim remained still. Though he couldn't see Sam's eyes, he knew the young man would be warily watching the shoreline; it was a common custom for the Indians to use their white captives to trick those along the river into letting down their guard long enough to be ambushed. He knew exactly what would now be running through Sam's mind: Was this an ambush? Was Jim alone? What was he doing along the banks of the river?

The boat slowed and Jim called out. "Sam! Sam Neely!"

"Who goes there?" Sam called back.

"Jim Hawkins!"

"Are you alone?"

Jim paused while he listened to the wilderness. Indians could now be laying in wait to ambush them both. After a few seconds, he answered, "No!"

The boat slowed even more as it approached, and Jim allowed his horse to nervously paw at the river bottom while they waited. Sam stopped a short distance away. He was too cautious, Jim thought.

Jim slowly walked his horse parallel to the boat. "Traveling alone, Sam? That's mighty dangerous in these parts."

He followed the movement in Sam's eyes, knowing without turning around that he was surveying the river's edge and the surrounding terrain.

"I wasn't alone until yesterday," Sam said at last. "Ambushed by some Cherokee; killed one and took another."

"Are you wounded?"

Sam shook his head. "No, but mighty tired and hungry," he answered. "I don't mind telling you, it sure is good seeing a familiar face."

The sun's rays had long ago been replaced by the pale white light of a full moon. Jim watched the surface of the river ripple as small fish came to the surface, feeding on the hundreds of mosquitoes that came to life after the sun had disappeared. A dinner of venison, corn and porridge had been devoured.

Four men sat in a semi-circle around the dying embers, their eyes watching the women clean the cooking pots in the river but their minds swirling.

"Can it really be true?" a settler by the name of Richard Pierce mused.

"I'm afraid it is," Sam answered. "I heard it on good authority that Daniel Boone was captured by Banastre Tarleton's men outside of Charlottesville."

"But what was he doing there?"

"Headed for Williamsburg," Jim said, coming to his feet. "He was supposed to take his seat in the Virginia legislature."

"There's talk he'll be tried for treason," Sam said quietly.

The men were silent. The mood in the camp had become melancholy, almost defeatist. And if there was one thing Jim hated more than just about anything, it was defeat.

"The war's not over yet," he said, turning toward the cliffs and skimming them with skillful eyes. "We'll turn the tide."

"Like we did at Fort Jefferson?" Henry Knight asked.

Jim started to retort in anger but caught sight of Henry watching his two young girls assist their mother. It was never a good thing to become embroiled in an argument in front of one's children.

Richard shook his head. "What are we to become out here?" he said in a barely audible voice. "We have no choice but to pick up and leave and head back to the safety of the east. Those left behind are doomed to become bait for the Indians…"

"Speaking of Indians," Jim said, turning to Sam. "Did you ever find Mary?"

Sam sighed deeply. "No. I've been traveling up and down the Wilderness Trail looking for her. This time, I'd gone with two other men to try and find her, but…" his voice faded before he regrouped and continued, "It's like she's just disappeared."

"Are you getting reports? People who have seen her?"

"A Frenchman by the name of Pierre Pierpont said he'd seen her at Shawneetown on the Ohio. She left with a small band of Shawnee, headed north. He suspected they were going to Fort Detroit."

"Ah, yes," Jim said. "Henry Hamilton's idea to pay a bounty to the Indians for capturing our women."

"Hamilton still remains in chains in Williamsburg, a prisoner of war, I presume?"

"Last I heard. The Governor refuses to exchange him. Meanwhile, his replacements at Fort Detroit have continued inciting the Indians against us… Did you follow Mary's trail?"

"It ran cold," Sam sighed. "As it always does."

"The two men who were with you—one wouldn't be Mary's beau, George Spears, would it?"

Sam shook his head. "George went back to Virginia. I hear he's helping Old Man Spears haul supplies for the Army."

"He hasn't given up hope?"

"No. He never will."

Jim hesitated. Most captives were never seen again; in fact, most died shortly after capture. But watching Sam's tortured face, he knew Mary was different. He could feel it in his bones.

"You both will see her again," he said with conviction. "I can feel it."

54

Mary stood in the center of a small room. The only light in the rough-hewn wood structure came from two tall, thin open slits designed for fire ports. She could barely make out the lake swirling past the fort, though she could clearly see ominous clouds forming in the late afternoon sky. The wind had picked up as well sending leaves flying past the open windows and occasionally inside.

Conferring a few feet away from her were two British officers. One, who had been referred to as Ainslie, strategically had his back to her while he whispered; the other, whom the others referred to as Major, nodded and studied Mary from the tips of her borrowed shoes to her bare head.

She looked around her. The man who had found her asleep near the lake had been dismissed soon after he deposited Mary, kicking and screaming, on their doorstep. He'd been a low-ranking guard, while these two were obviously higher in the chain of command. Where her pleas had been ignored by the guard, perhaps these men could be reasoned with.

She tried to make eye contact with the Major, but his light blue-green eyes were busily combing her body like a fresh kill, peering at every inch of her except her face.

She assumed he worked in this makeshift office with its heavy wood table, several straight back chairs, and a small chest. It smelled dank like the inside of a boat that was not quite seaworthy.

Green fingers of moss crept along the corners of the ceiling, their pungent odor adding to the room's claustrophobic feel.

Behind her was a heavy wooden door, now standing open. Just outside, she knew that two guards remained at the ready, one on either side.

"We're going to give you one last chance," the Major said. "Tell us how you escaped the camp and reached the edge of the fort."

"But I told you," Mary said in exasperation. "I didn't escape *from* your camp; I was dropped off here!"

Ainslie chuckled. "And we are to believe that, are we, miss? That you simply took an afternoon sail on the lake and happened on a prisoner of war camp to have a picnic?"

"It wasn't an afternoon sail," she said, jutting out her chin in defiance. "I was escaping from savages. And had I known you were operating a prison camp here, it would have been the last place I'd have gone!" As her own words fell on her ears, she felt her heart sink. Certainly, the Frenchmen knew when they left her here that it was a British-controlled island. And certainly they would have known they were using it to contain prisoners of war. Would they return, as they had promised, only to find her gone? Or would they have assumed when they left her here that the British would soon find her and incarcerate her?

"And I've told you before," she continued, fighting to keep her voice from breaking, "I have no interest in your war. I am not a combatant. I simply want to return home to my family."

"Your family," the major sneered, "who are the very ones fighting us now?"

"That is not true. My father was killed by the savages who captured me. He is of no consequence to you now. And my sisters and mother are not soldiers."

"And you have no brothers?" he taunted.

"None of military age or experience. Besides," she continued, "What fear do you have of me? That if you set me free, I will lead an uprising against you? I don't even know where I am! I could never find my way back here, even if I were so inclined! What you do here should not involve me at all!"

There was a brief moment of silence before the Major answered quietly, "You think you are spinning a good yarn, but we see through you. You have been a prisoner here at Fort Michilimackinac, in the barracks with the others of your age. I don't know how you managed to escape but your entire group will be punished because of your attempt. You should feel very fortunate that you are a woman. If you were a man, you would be flogged in the center of the camp for all to see." He waved his hand as if in dismissal. "But being a woman, you are not worth the effort."

Mary opened her mouth but quickly closed it. Better for her pride to be hurt and to suffer humiliation than to argue in favor of equal treatment.

"Private!" he bellowed.

One of the men standing outside the door marched rapidly inside.

"Take her to a cell. Let her think about her idiotic attempt for a few days. Put all the women in her barracks on half rations and double duty. Let them stew on her actions for a few days. They will mete out their own punishment of her when she returns."

The young man reached for her elbow but she wiggled away from him. "Don't touch me!" she hissed.

"Listen, little lady," Ainslie said, pushing his beefy red face close to hers. "You are a prisoner. We can touch you if we please. Now either cooperate with this man or you will find yourself in ropes and chains, begging for one inch of freedom!"

Mary stared back at his cold gray eyes. But when the private reached for her again, she did not recoil. Instead, she lifted her head and allowed him to lead her out of the room.

The private led her through a hallway that wound its way in a circular fashion past more tiny rooms before they crossed a threshold into an open courtyard. From this vantage point, she could see a wood fence that was so high there was a palisade against it. A number of British troops were walking along it now, their sharp eyes on the lookout for any suspicious movement. Though she could not see beyond the closest buildings, she had the impression this great fence encompassed the entire fort.

They walked along a dusty road wide enough for horse-drawn carriages or cannons, past small buildings surrounded by smaller fences, interspersed here and there with vegetable gardens.

The sound of gunfire rang out, causing her to involuntarily flinch, before she realized soldiers were practicing their marksmanship with smooth bore muskets. As they continued, she kept a wary eye on them, noting how quickly they could reload and fire again.

They passed several land gates where small, open rooms had been erected above them. Occasionally, she spotted a soldier pacing past the open window, his back to the fort and his face to the water. Eventually, they reached a small building.

The private knocked at the door before briskly opening it and shoving Mary inside.

"Prisoner for you," he announced as he stepped in behind her.

A stocky man rose from behind a desk in the outer office where he had obviously been napping. He wiped his eyes with the back of his hand before staring at Mary.

"So take her to the barracks," he said.

"The Major said to bring her here. She attempted to escape. She's to stay in solitary."

The man belched before reaching behind the desk and pulling out a rusty ring of keys. "Follow me," he said.

He unlocked a door and unceremoniously ushered Mary inside. The door was slammed behind her with a dusty thud, and she fought to adjust her eyes to the dim light. Indeed, she noticed as they walked along a narrow hallway, the only light that filtered into the area appeared to be from poorly fitting wood planks that allowed the light from the outside to filter in.

A large black water bug raced across her foot, and she shook it off, instinctively raising her skirt lest it become trapped inside the material. She walked the rest of the way with her skirt hoisted to her ankles, past empty cells with dirt floors containing nothing but single lumpy mattresses of straw.

Only one cell was occupied. She sucked in her breath when she saw its occupant: a rail-thin young man who looked almost like a boy, huddled in the corner, his shirt stuck to his blood-soaked body. His eyes were closed and he did not move at all as they walked past him, and she wondered if he were dead or alive.

Then they were past, turning a corner so she could no longer see him. The jailer stopped and unlocked a corner cell. As the door swung open, he motioned her inside. Once she had stepped across the threshold, the door clanged shut behind her and he deftly locked it, staring at her through the open bars.

Then he was gone, his rumbling cough echoing in the cold darkness of the jail, leaving her alone to contemplate her new set of circumstances.

55

M ary gingerly pulled her clothes out of the wash bucket. It had been four long months since she'd first entered this prison camp. Her undergarments were in shreds and her cotton nightgown had not fared much better. She wrung them out and carried them across the courtyard to the clothesline, where she draped them over the line next to the other yellowed, tattered clothing of her fellow female prisoners.

She could see the lake from here; its blue magnificence stretched as far as the eye could see. The sky had turned a paler shade of blue in recent days, though, and the nights had become cooler, heralding the end of summer.

She'd spent almost two weeks in the jail cell before being released to the barracks where she would spend the remainder of the summer. There were thirty-six women sharing one long room, but much to the Major's disappointment, they did not punish Mary. Instead, they greeted her with open arms, open ears, and the empathy that came from similar experiences.

She learned, in fact, that every woman in the compound had originally been captured by Indians—some by Cherokee, some by Shawnee, and some by other tribes. Some had lived as a British prisoner of war for several years, while others had been captured as recently as this past year. All had either been turned over to the British or captured by them while trying to escape their Indian masters.

Most of them wanted to go home, to find their families and loved ones, and return to the life they had once enjoyed. There were three, though, who wanted to return to the Indian tribes they now considered their families, much to Mary's bewilderment.

There had been advantages to living here. She was no longer frightened of White Messenger and Msipessi finding her and recapturing her. Though Indians sometimes visited the island, they were not permitted near the barracks and no one had ever heard of a white woman being returned to their Indian captors while in British custody here.

There was food. While it wasn't plentiful, it was enough to sustain life and that was all she needed. It was varied—sometimes consisting of berries and fruits, nuts, and different vegetables, though the mainstay of their meals was still cornmeal. Meat was rare and often fatty or full of gristle. And there was always fresh water—plenty of cool, life-sustaining water.

She had a roof over her head each night, though sometimes she preferred to lie on the ground outside and stare at the stars. But when the heavy rains came and the wind blew, there was always refuge inside the barracks.

She learned a lot from the other women, including medicine. When one of their own became ill, they requisitioned the British for herbs; sometimes they received them and sometimes not. But the British almost always allowed them to forage for the herbs they needed, though they were under guard while they did so. And in return, when one of the soldiers became ill, they pitched in to help tend him. Occasionally, she would hear another lament about the lack of medicinal herbs they used in other areas which they did not have here, and Mary remembered each piece of information. She would not be here forever, and when the opportunity presented itself, she intended to take advantage of it; and one never knew what she might be required to do or endure as she made her way home.

For all the advantages of living under British rule and away from the savages who had killed and wounded their loved ones, one distinct disadvantage was always present: they were not free. She could gaze for hours at the beautiful lake, but she could not go there and dip her feet in the cool waters. She could not fish and she could not accompany her brothers on hunting expeditions. She had neither the cloth nor the thread and needle to sew more clothes as hers became increasingly thin. There were a few women amongst them who were literate, but even if they were given supplies with which to write, they would not be permitted to correspond with their loved ones. No one knew they were here.

Her thoughts were filled almost every waking instant with her family. She wondered about Sam, about Ma, and her other siblings. She worried about the Indian raids in the Cumberlands, about the War and how it might affect those she knew and loved. She wept for her father, and knew her life would always be different because of a day and time she wished had never happened.

"It's not wise to think too much."

The voice roused her and she turned to face Arabella, a tall woman who she suspected had once been stout and buxom, but whose skin now lay in folds on her large bones.

"Just looking at the sky," she said, moving away from the clothesline. "It will soon be winter."

"Aye, that it will," the older woman answered.

Mary thought briefly of the coat Laetitia had so generously given her; she hadn't seen it since she'd been captured. It had no doubt found its way to one of the officer's wives. "We're going to need blankets," she said.

Arabella scoffed. "Oh, no, we won't."

Mary turned to her, surprised. "Are you daft? As far north as we are, we'll catch our death of cold without proper blankets."

"Better die from the cold than from a fever!"

"What are you saying?"

"I'm saying," Arabella said, leaning down to place her face even with Mary's, "that everyone knows the British hand out blankets infected with the pox."

Mary gasped. "No!"

"Ask anyone here. They are given blankets from the hospitals and infirmaries that were used by those dying of the pox. And they give them to the Indians and the prisoners. Doesn't take long before the pox spreads right through them. They die or wish they had."

Instantly, the image of Medicine Woman caring for an entire family stricken with this curse rose within her; of Eagle Feathers wrapped in the very blanket that might have killed him and buried in ground they had never seen before and would never see again; of Shooting Star, once so beautiful but now stricken with a pock-marked face that would haunt her forever. And of Medicine Woman, diligently providing Mary with the salve that would prevent her own skin from scarring, and with the herbs that might have saved her life.

Without a word, Mary made her way back to the barracks. She sat in silence on a straw mattress so thin she could feel the ground beneath it. Then she lay prone and stared at the wood beams above her. But nothing she focused on, nothing she believed in, and no amount of prayers she could wordlessly utter, would stop the hatred from boiling inside her.

As nighttime fell and the women returned to their sleeping quarters, the barracks came alive with whispers. They were to be moved. They would leave this island tomorrow afternoon, but none of the women knew their destination.

Mary slept fitfully. She dreamt of the Cumberland River and how the sunrise shone in its clear waters. She dreamt of Indians and raids and her father bleeding alongside the river. She dreamt of long days and longer nights walking in bare feet or moccasins or rowing alongside Msipessi and White Messenger. She dreamt of the night of fear when she escaped her captors, only to be captured again by the British. And as the dawn peaked over the horizon and the barracks began to stir, she came awake with a feeling of dread.

56

The morning sky was the color of flames. As the day crept past, Mary's trepidation increased. They were told to gather all their possessions and place them in a neat pile atop their beds, where they were closely inspected. Mary's pile was scant, consisting only of an extra pair of undergarments and her cotton nightgown, both so thin she could hold her hand beneath the fabric and see it clearly. She wore her only other belongings: another thin pair of undergarments and the dress Laetitia had given her. Four months of wearing the same clothing day in and day out had reduced it to nothing more than a flimsy effort at keeping her appearance halfway decent.

The other women had similar piles, though some had no extra clothing. None of them possessed jewelry or keepsakes, though one woman had a comb that was missing many of its teeth.

They were instructed to cook breakfast. While some of the women eagerly ate their hoe cakes while chatting about their expected change in fortune, Mary found that she could not stomach it.

Clouds gathered as the day wore on, and they were told to cook lunch. Again, Mary toiled over the open flames and the hot kettle as she boiled corn. Though they were given gourds, rare and tasty, she still found she could not tolerate more than a few mouthfuls. There was something wrong. She sensed it.

She searched the others' faces under veiled lashes. Some were laughing while they fantasized about their trip. Others were quiet and appeared introspective. When she caught Arabella peering at her curiously, she turned her attention to her plate and pushed her food around.

The wind increased. By mid-afternoon, the sky was turning midnight blue with roiling, tumbling clouds.

It was late afternoon when some of the women rushed through camp, exclaiming they had seen a vessel approaching their shores. Like the others, Mary stopped what she was doing and rushed to the highest point she was permitted to go to, standing on the tips of her toes so she might see it more clearly.

It was a square-rigged ship with three masts, far larger than any ship she had ever seen. It looked like one designed for ocean voyages, she thought with a sinking heart. Did they intend to take them to England?

As it drew near, she heard shouts from the crew and the ship began to slow, eventually drifting lazily toward the shore. She spotted the British flag, hoisted high and proud above men scampering across the decks in preparation for landing. Then it disappeared from their view beneath the trees and cliff that stood between the vessel and its intended passengers.

Two soldiers who had routinely guarded them strode across the courtyard. "Back to the barracks!" shouted one. "Hurry it up!"

They scurried to the barracks, the long building filled now with the dank air of an impending storm.

"Get your things!" the soldier ordered as they paced the length of the room, eyeing each bed with the tiny pile of belongings on them.

When they were all standing in front of their beds with their possessions in their hands, they were arranged in a single line and then marched through the door into the blustery afternoon. As they walked across the courtyard, Mary glanced back at the building that had been her home through this long summer. Deep in her heart, she knew she would never see it again, and yet she also knew it would remain in her memory forever.

As they descended to the shore, she spotted two more groups of women marched in a similar fashion from opposite sides of the island. For the first time, she realized they were not the only prisoners on the island. From the looks of the lines converging upon them, there were at least three times as many.

"Halt!" the order rang out as they neared the ship.

"Line up! Line up!" the soldiers shouted as they strode between the lines, nudging the women so they stood in a single file.

They remained standing for so long the older women began to teeter and Mary worried they might faint. Then slowly, each woman was ushered aboard the vessel, trudging across a narrow set of planks to the upper deck.

It must have taken the better part of an hour for them to board the ship. Once they were on deck, they were unceremoniously ushered to the far end, where they were directed downward into a dark holding area.

As Mary climbed down the ladder, she was hit first with the overwhelming stench of perspiring women, the pungent odor of stale fish and garbage, and the heavy stillness of the air. When her feet hit the wooden floor, she was not given time for her eyes to adjust to the blackness before the next person was almost stepping down on top of her. She was pushed backward into the holding area, her elbows accidentally slapping into the women even as she was poked and prodded by others attempting to find space.

Her face instinctively tilted toward the open hatch, catching the last thin rays of light before the clouds obscured them, watching as emaciated women joined them, one by one.

"We can't fit any more in here!" one woman cried out in a heavy German accent.

And still they kept coming, and still they kept pushing until they stood so tightly in the confined space they were unable to sit or move. All they could do was stare at the dirty neck in front of them.

"We can't breathe!" shouted another.

The hatch was open now and for the briefest moment, they could see a square of light as the last woman climbed below.

Unable to find an empty spot, she was forced to hold onto the ladder with her feet planted on the bottom step.

Mary was sandwiched midway between the outer hull and the hatch. Her belongings were pushed against her chest and as people jockeyed for position, her feet were unmercifully tread upon. But there was no position better than the one before. They were piled inside, shoulder to shoulder, hip to hip.

As she glanced upward one last time, a solitary soldier lowered the hatch just as the first raindrops fell.

57

There was no way to tell how much time had elapsed. They felt movement but they had no windows by which to gauge their progress. Their legs were cramped and then fatigued, but without light they had no way of knowing whether they'd stood for hours or overnight. The weaker and older women began to faint, and their comrades had no choice but to hold them up; there was no place in the cramped quarters in which they could lie down. The air became thicker and dustier; their faces strained upwards in the darkness to catch more air.

Then as time continued to crawl, they began to lurch and pitch as a storm buffeted the vessel. They had nothing to hold onto but each other, and as they lost their footing time after time, the others close by had no alternative but to keep them bolstered with their own bodies.

Women became sick with the roil and tumble of the vessel, filling the air with the nauseous stench as they slid on the now slippery deck.

Mary fought to focus on something else—anything else. She wanted to scream as some of the others were doing, but she knew their cries would only fall on the other victims' ears. If the soldiers could hear them at all, they would ignore them, as they had been doing for the interminable time they'd stood in this cramped hell. She wanted to cry as she heard others sobbing, but she knew it would only drain her strength. She wanted to pray as others repeated the 23rd Psalm, but she could only utter the words in her head as she gasped and tumbled a few inches this way and a few inches that way.

Then there was a lull in the movement, and the air became perfectly still and silent. As her eyes grew accustomed to the darkness, she could make out only the whites of the others' eyes, round and frightened.

Without thinking, she began to sing. It had comforted the savages; perhaps it would do no less with white women.

She sang the first verse by herself, but when she began the second one, a few others chimed in. By the third, half of the women were singing along. It was a prayer, a collective prayer, she thought as she sang. *Help us, dear Lord!* She thought as her voice rose and fell in cadence. *Save us with your grace and mercy!*

The ship lurched suddenly, and the voices died as they tumbled in the darkness like marionettes. The storm raged again, fiercer than before, pummeling the large vessel as if it were only a tiny branch in strong seas.

With each pitch, they were thrown a few inches forward or a few inches back, until she no longer stood between the same women. The cries began anew, and Mary's heart sank as she realized they might all die here, helpless as newborns.

The ship rolled again, and she frantically reached for something to steady herself. Her hand wrapped around a wooden staff in the pitch blackness. She fought to see what she was holding onto, fought to keep it within her grasp lest she fall backward onto the women behind her. There was an unusually tall woman in front of her, a full foot higher than anyone else. Then she realized she was not holding onto a staff but the ladder, and the poor woman who was lurching to the left and then to the right was trying valiantly to hold onto the ladder as her feet slipped and slid along the bottom rung.

When the ship suddenly lurched, the woman could no longer maintain her hold and she fell backward onto the crowd below. For a brief moment, Mary lost her balance and began to pitch backward, her arms flailing. Then the back of her hand bumped the wooden ladder, causing sharp pains to reverberate through her arm.

She grabbed it, first with one hand and then with the other. As the women tottered behind her, she raised herself onto the bottom rung. She fought to hold on as the ship leaned dangerously in one direction and then rocked to the other.

She reached higher on the ladder, pulling her body upward toward the hatch.

It seemed like forever that she hung there, sometimes able to climb up a rung only to be knocked back down with the next roll of the ship. Sometimes her feet left the rungs altogether and her body sailed outward, held above the crowd only by one hand on the ladder.

The cries surrounded her, rising above the sound of the storm. She slammed back into the ladder. She had to get to the top, she thought frantically. She had to.

She reached the top of the hold, her head butting against the hatch. She was afraid to let go of the ladder, afraid when she reached out to bang on the hatch, another strong lurch would tumble her into the crowd below. Someone was behind her now, trying to climb onto the ladder. A fresh worry rose within her: how strong was the ladder? Would it break apart as the women below scrambled to reach the top?

The ship pitched again, slamming her body into the ladder. As the angle of the vessel pulled her body against it, she realized now was her chance.

She reached upward to bang on the hatch, but to her astonishment, it blew open, pelting her and the women below with a ferocious wind and stinging rain. In seconds, she was soaked through. Without another thought, she scrambled onto the deck above and lay prone.

She heard the sounds of shouting now, but they were not coming from the women: they came from sailors and soldiers clambering across the deck, struggling to stay on their feet. The wind whipped her about, sliding her across the deck with such ferocity that she crashed into the side.

"Mary!" it seemed to scream. *"Mary!"*

The ship lurched again, and she was sent tumbling toward the bow, her body slamming into rain-soaked ropes.

"Mary!"

She gasped. It was not the wind that called her name; it was a soldier a few feet away, hanging onto the forestay.

She fought to see his face, to determine who he was and how he knew her name. The sky was gray with black clouds, effectively cutting off most of the light. His face remained in shadow. He was slightly built, not much larger than an adolescent. Where had she seen him before?

The ship lurched and he was suddenly above her, then tumbling down the deck almost on top of her. As the vessel leveled out, she looked into his eyes. It was Private Alfred Berwyn, the Canadian who had given Eagle Feathers herbs at Fort Detroit.

"Mary!" he cried out. "Hold onto me!"

She reached for his soaked clothing with her bruised and battered fists. Another man only a few feet away was pitched backward, his screams blending with the gale as his body tumbled into the water. With a sinking heart, she knew with the next pitch, there was a chance they would join him in a watery grave.

Vaguely, her mind registered that Alfred was tying their bodies to the mast, frantically wrapping the heavy rope around and around the great pole. Her air was cut off, but she clung tightly to him. After they were secured to the mast, they rocked and tumbled with the pulse of the ship.

58

A frigid chill roused her from a deep sleep. Her muscles were stiff and as she began to stir, she realized she was still tied tightly to the mast, her head resting on Alfred's thin chest.

The storm was gone and as the dawn started to peak over the horizon, the men on deck began to stir. As she unwound the rope that had held them in safety through the night, Alfred opened his eyes and watched her in silence.

His face was smooth and without whiskers; she thought he hardly looked old enough to be away from home. He had a deep gash above one brow, and after she untied them, she whispered, "Let me look at that."

He murmured, "I'm fine." He wobbled a bit as he rose, grasping the mast for support.

"No, you're not fine," she said. "You've injured your head."

As the others began to rouse, she heard a growing chorus of moans. And as more hands came on deck, they began to attend to the injured. Soon, nearly half the soldiers and sailors were bandaged in one form or another—some with wrappings about their heads, others with slings for a broken arm, and others with cotton bandages through which blood continued to seep.

"The women!" Mary cried out, realizing they were all still in the hold.

Alfred and two soldiers rushed to the hatch and threw it open. Alfred attempted to descend the ladder, but stopped. "I can't see," he called back. "Get the captain!"

As they waited for the captain to appear, Mary glanced over the side of the ship. They had run aground in the night. She didn't recognize the terrain, and immediately came to the conclusion that it was not the island from which they'd departed.

The captain appeared in short order. He was a portly man who looked to have had too many muffins in his lifetime. He rubbed his stomach as he spoke, ordering the soldiers to remove the women from the hold and have them line up on shore.

The command was difficult to enforce. The women staggered out of the hold, some weak and sick, and others obviously injured. Most were able to walk—even if others had to help support them—and they were eager to leave the ship, so getting to the shore was a relatively quick matter. But getting them to line up was something entirely different.

They were scattered around the shoreline, on the beach and in nearby woods. The leaves were already blown from the trees by the first shock of winter, and the air was colder; Mary couldn't help but wonder where they were in relation to the island. Had they gone further north, into Canada? How long had they been in the hold?

Of one thing she was sure: they were still on the continent. It would have taken months to reach England, and she had no doubt that none of the women would have survived that voyage.

She wandered from one woman to the next, assessing their injuries and administering any help that was needed. The captain made the bandages and medicines readily available to treat the prisoners, but as Mary made her rounds, she became increasingly angry. What kind of a sailor doesn't pay attention to a red sky at morning? She thought. What kind of a human being would crowd these women into that small, dark hole? It could very well have ended up their coffin!

She glanced back at the ship in time to see the dead bodies of two women being lifted, one by one, out of the hold.

Alfred joined her at the edge of the woods.

"Where are we?" Mary asked.

"Blown a bit off course, from what I hear," he said. He glanced about. "We are in the Territory of Canada, the Province of Quebec on the shores of the Georgian Bay."

"I have no idea what you're talking about," Mary said. "We might as well be on the moon."

He laughed. "You have heard of New York?"

"Why, yes. I have."

He pointed toward the rising sun. "It's that way, about ninety miles."

"Ninety miles," she murmured. "Straight away toward the east?"

"Yep."

She cast her eyes downward. "So is that where we are going?"

He shrugged. "I'm just a private," he said. "They don't tell me much… But the British control Fort Niagara, so I suspect we are headed there."

"And that is in New York?"

"On the border."

Mary watched the women for a long moment: almost a hundred of them in various stages of distress—some dry heaving, others bleeding, and still more crying and moaning.

"And are there Indians between here and there?"

"The Iroquois—wait a minute." He swung her around to face him. "Don't even think about it. You hear me?"

"Think about what?" she asked innocently.

"You know exactly what I'm talking about. It would be suicide, Mary, you hear me? Suicide!"

She wiggled out of his grasp and looked him in the eye. "Don't talk 'suicide' to me. Suicide was putting defenseless women in a hold not fit for animals. Suicide was embarking on a voyage when even I could see the weather wouldn't permit it. Suicide was living every single day in Indian captivity with no one to help me. Suicide was attempting, time after time, to escape, knowing if they caught me, they could torture me or kill me. So don't talk suicide to me, Alfred Berwyn, because suicide and I have gone hand-in-hand for quite some time now!"

His eyes widened and then narrowed. "You've got pluck, I'll say that for you."

She looked beyond him at the woods. If only she could see straight through to New York! If only she knew where to go!

When he spoke again, his voice was lower. "Listen to me, Mary, as I will only tell you this once: head due east until you come to a lake—not one as large as this one, but you'll know it when you come to it. From there, head straight south. There are a handful of families in the region; stay clear of them, as they're Loyalists. Continue heading east and south, and you'll come to a marsh where you can cross into New York. Then head for the south; the further south you go, the safer you'll be. Above all, stay away from people—white or red. You will not be safe until you reach Fort Pitt."

Mary nodded, her mouth suddenly dry. She continued to peer beyond his left shoulder. "How long before I reach Fort Pitt?"

"I have no idea."

"Food?"

"I have none to give you. Your best chance for escape is now, while the soldiers are busy. Soon they will begin lining up the women and then it will be too late."

She nodded.

He reached in his pocket and pulled out a knife. It was small but appeared to be sharp, and he didn't hesitate as he reached for her hand and shoved it into her grasp. Then he took a deep breath and looked at a few women who were recovering in the woods. "Follow me," he said.

She tucked the knife inside her dress pocket as they made their way deeper into the woods. Once there, he knelt and instructed Mary to help him in assessing the women's injuries. She watched him as he worked; his sharp blue eyes glancing up underneath pale lashes, briefly scanning the ship, the soldiers, the sailors, and the women. She knew he was putting together the terrain and assessing the danger like one assembles a puzzle.

She followed his glances and when she noticed the others looking back at her, she busied herself with dressing wounds and caring for the injured. Her heart began thumping wildly and her breathing became labored. The minutes ticked on, and she struggled against making a run for it.

"Now," Alfred whispered hoarsely.

Without a word, she rose and walked deeper into the woods. The trees were bare, and she waited for a soldier to call out for her to halt, but she heard nothing. Her pace quickened, and then she was running, her feet sliding over a ground slippery with the fallen rain.

And then she was slipping and sliding down a small precipice. It wasn't until she'd reached the bottom that she turned to look back. She could no longer see the lake or the ship, the soldiers or the women. And they could no longer see her.

Without hesitation, she turned toward the east. It wasn't until darkness began to descend that her heart rate slowed to normal. She stopped for a brief time after the sun had disappeared, rubbing her feet and her skin to stay warm, until the moon rose to light her way. Then she continued toward the east, toward freedom.

It wasn't until some time during the night that she realized she had never thanked Alfred Berwyn for giving her freedom.

59

The town had mushroomed outside of Fort Pitt; as Jim navigated the seventeen acres that surrounded the fort, he dodged horses and carts, tipped his hat at the ladies he passed, and nodded greetings to the gentlemen. It hadn't been too long ago that a Virginian like himself would have been greeted with suspicion, as both Virginia and Pennsylvania had laid claim to the fort. But all of that had changed with the Revolution: now they banded together in the common goal of breaking the British yoke and claiming America as a free and independent land.

He passed the blockhouse and headed toward the fort itself, a compound encompassing about two-and-a-half acres inside a fortified wall. It was perhaps the most strategic fort in all of the Americas: resting at the Forks of the Ohio, it helped the Americans control the rivers that led to the west and eventually to the south.

It had been that river, he thought as he glanced at its blue waters, that he'd navigated all the way from Fort Jefferson and the Falls of the Ohio. He felt pride in the fact they had not once been attacked by Indians, though his scouting had discovered many in the region, but their numbers had diminished as he headed further east. Every one of the settlers and their families had made it to Fort Pitt without illness or injury, and that was a lot to be said in this dangerous time.

320 p.m.terrell

The streets outside of the fort were bustling with commerce. This had become a crossroads of sorts, filled with people heading west to seek their fortune, purchasing food and supplies for the journey, shoulder to shoulder with others who'd had enough of the western frontier and Indian savagery. The settlers he'd brought here only a few weeks earlier were themselves purchasing supplies and food in preparation for the next leg of their journey as they moved further east. That was a trip he would not be on.

He side-stepped a fur trader as he continued his brisk pace.

"Jim! Jim!"

The voice separated from the rest of the hubbub, and Jim turned around. He spotted a young man weaving in and out of the crowd, waving his hand.

"George!" Jim said as he stepped out to meet him. "George Spears, aren't you a sight for sore eyes!"

As he shook his beefy hand, he asked, "What are you doing here? You're a long ways from Augusta County."

"That I am, that I am. I'm here with Pa; he's been driving wagons for the Patriots."

"Has he now?" Jim's mind flashed back to the last time he'd seen Old Man Spears; he'd been repairing his barn in Virginia on a particularly cold winter day. He could hear his thick German accent like it was yesterday.

"Join us for supper, Jim. You'll have time, won't you?"

"I'll make the time," Jim answered, realizing he had not stopped shaking the young man's hand. "I'll make the time."

The Inn, like everything else in and around Fort Pitt, was just about ready to burst at the seams. It felt odd to see so many people in one place. Jim wasn't sure if he liked it, either; it felt too crowded, too noisy, and too busy.

"I'm heading west again," George was saying excitedly.

"What'ya planning on doing out there?"

"Finding Mary and making my fortune. I hear there's land out there just for the taking."

Jim glanced at Old Man Spears. He said nothing to discourage his son. "What about the farm in Virginia?" he asked.

"Oh, it's fine," Old Man Spears answered.

"Still have the horses? Cattle?"

"And the best tobacco crop we've ever yielded."

Jim's eyes moved slowly from the man to his son. "You're not needed on the farm?"

"Oh, we have plenty of hands," Old Man Spears said before his son could answer. "Though we could use some domestic help for the Missus, that's for certain."

"They're too busy running the farms," George said with a cackle.

"That they are," Old Man Spears bellowed. "That they are!"

Jim took a bite of his stew. It tasted of too many spices and competing flavors. Or perhaps he'd just become too accustomed to a slab of meat and a side of cornmeal. "So what do you plan to do out west, George?"

"Jim, you know better'n anybody how much there is out there. I saw it with my own eyes; there's so much game you can stand on your front porch and shoot 'em. So many fish they near 'bout jump up in your lap when you come close to the water. And land—land there just for the taking."

Old Man Spears interjected. "I've been working for the Patriots, Jim. And part of my pay will be in land."

"Do you know where abouts?"

"I'm not quite certain, but it's in the general area of Daniel Boone's."

"Speaking of which—what's happened to him? Last I heard, the British had captured him."

"Oh, they couldn't hold him," Old Man Spears laughed. "Had to parole him a few days after his capture. Maybe he signed something that said he'd lay down his arms, I don't know. But he's headed back west, if he's not there already, and I'd bet my last bull he's fighting 'em again."

Jim grinned. "That'd be Daniel, all right." He took a swig of his drink. "So are you headed out west from here?"

George shook his head and pushed his food around on his plate. "I wish I was, but we got to take some supplies back to Virginia first. We're leaving tomorrow morning."

"Are you heading west, Jim?" Old Man Spears said. "Can't you come home to see your mother first?"

"I'm hoping to. Tell her that for me, please? I'll get my orders in the next few days, and I'm hoping to take some time off and go see her before I head to my next assignment."

Old Man Spears nodded as a fiddle player struck up a song in the corner of the room. The three men sat there listening, their eyes wistful with thoughts of the war ending, the expansion of the west, and of times gone by.

60

Mary could barely put one foot in front of the other. Ninety miles, her brain kept chanting. Ninety miles. How far had she come already? She wondered. She'd walked a full day and then all night, and now the sun was rising high overhead. Had she come thirty miles already? Twenty? Forty?

She'd long ago forgotten the blisters on her feet and the aches in her calves. She had to ignore the pain, if she were to reach New York. She had no choice but to keep trudging.

But as the minutes passed into hours, she knew her pace had grown sluggish. She couldn't cover ninety miles without a rest or without food or water. Where was the lake that Alfred told her about? Had she walked too far south or too far north of it? How would she know if she were still on the right course? How would she know when she reached New York? There wouldn't exactly be a sign waiting for her there.

She must stop. Yet even as her brain began the refrain, her feet still moved forward, one raw step in front of the other, as though they had a numbed mind of their own. She didn't know how far she had come before she noticed a thin trickle of blood oozing from one foot. Exhausted, she sat down on the bare ground. She struggled to remove her shoe, biting her lip to keep from crying out as dried blood stuck to the leather. She inspected the swollen member, taking it into the palm of her hand and caressing it in an effort to stop the agony.

Then her weary fingers ripped a piece of material from the hem on her cotton dress and wrapped it around her foot as best she could. The shoes Laetitia had given her were clearly not meant for a journey such as this, she thought as she crammed her foot back into the shoe.

She drew her knees up to her chest and hugged them, eventually running her hands down to her calves and massaging the sore muscles. She was in desperate need of rest. But where? Where could she possibly hide long enough to steal some sleep, without the possibility she'd be recaptured?

She wished she'd asked Alfred if the soldiers would walk overland along the same route he'd directed her to take, but it had all happened so quickly.

As she stared in front of her, the terrain became blurred, the trees merging together into one solid mass. She didn't know how long she'd sat there, asleep with her eyes wide open, but eventually the trees began to separate, their branches once more taking shape. She soon realized that two trees in the distance sat higher than the others, where the ground formed a knoll. She shielded her eyes from the sun and peered at the branches—tall and hefty, an easy climb. She would set her sights on those two trees. Once there, she would climb to the highest point and see if she could spot the lake. She needed water more than sleep.

She didn't know how long it took for her to reach the trees. What appeared to be in close proximity turned out to be further than she had bargained for on the uneven terrain. She had to make a detour more than once, as the ground was too inhospitable to cross, but she kept her eyes trained on those two trees. She hoped it would be worth it in the end.

When she finally came close enough, she reached out to the trunks, her arms and legs shaking with exertion. But to her dismay, she discovered the tree she had depended upon was dead. It was in such a state of rot she knew the branches would not support her weight. It had apparently been dead for quite some time as the trunk, though at least three feet in diameter, was hollowed out, the large knotty hole staring at her like a gaping wound.

But the second tree, while not as tall or mature, was alive. It would be a tougher climb, but she had no alternative.

She rested for awhile on the ground between them. She wanted nothing more than to fall into a deep sleep that would last the rest of this day and into the night, and even to sleep into the morrow. But she knew she did not have that luxury. She had to bring her aching body to a seated position; she had to compel herself to stand once more on legs that wobbled like a newborn colt's. Even her arms throbbed as though they had supported her all these miles; but she had no choice but to force them to pull her weight upward into the branches.

Slowly, torturously, she climbed up the trunk to the first set of branches, her teeth grinding against the pain. The branches were wide and firm and easily supported her fragile weight. In an awkward movement that felt agonizingly slow, she forced herself to climb higher. Each time she reached a loftier position, she stopped to catch her breath and ease her aches and to peer about.

She had climbed more than halfway up the tree when she spotted the lake. It beckoned to her with its life-sustaining liquid, though it was much smaller than the bodies of water near Fort Detroit. It was perhaps another half day's journey from where she sat.

But as she stared across the terrain at her goal, her heart sank as she fought an almost overwhelming sense of despair. For surrounding the water she needed so desperately were British soldiers—perhaps a hundred or more. They were camped along one side of the lake, their tents lined up in neat rows, their horses drinking freely of the water. At least a dozen campfires wafted smoke into the air. She could almost smell the meat cooking over the open flames. Her swollen tongue could almost taste it.

She turned to face the south. Her only hope would be to bypass the lake altogether and move to the south of the Army. It was forested, the ground gently sloping, but she could not detect water as far as the eye could see.

At last, she reluctantly climbed down and sat again upon the hard ground. She could not give up. She couldn't.

Continuing her original path was no longer an option. She could not risk capture, and the last thing on earth she planned to do was walk right into the camp and give herself up. At every step of the way, every moment of her captivity, she had been brought farther north and farther from her home. Now that she was finally free, she had to avoid capture at all costs. She had to get home.

She leaned back, intending for the trunk to support her weight, but her head wobbled into the open trunk of the dead tree. Please, God, she prayed. Please have mercy.

She moved her head a bit to the right and curled up beside the tree. She closed her eyes and searched her brain for any possibility. Nothing came to her; nothing but a want of water and sleep. She opened one eye and unenthusiastically pondered her predicament.

A small spider climbed out of the tree trunk and sat for a long moment on the wood, as though it were surveying a yard from a comfortable front porch. Oh, to be a spider, Mary thought tiredly. To be able to crawl inside that trunk and sleep forever...

She bolted upright, startling the spider into dashing down the trunk and onto the ground. The hole in the tree's trunk was at least a foot wide, maybe more. She could get inside.

Her energy renewed, she picked up a few pebbles and tossed them inside. No squirrels or other animals hissed or ventured forth. She placed her hand inside and then her whole arm, feeling around the base of the tree and nature's walls. It was empty. And it was large enough for her.

Deliberately, cautiously, she crawled inside, ready to bolt if a snake or other critter were to protest her entry. One leg and one arm, and then her torso and head; another arm and finally her other leg. She was in.

It wasn't as dark as she suspected it would be; the sunlight filtered between the trees and cast a slim trail of light. She leaned against the trunk, delicately at first, but when she became confident it would sustain her weight, she leaned back with as much resignation as placing her tired body on a feather bed.

Before she knew it, she was asleep.

61

The beads of water dripped onto Mary's forehead and cascaded along her cheekbones and nose. Eventually some of the liquid teased her mouth, and she parted them to allow the soft, steady stream to moisten her parched lips. Her tongue was swollen from dehydration and her lips were chapped from the sun and wind. But as she dreamed of a vast waterfall, those ailments slipped away from her. She turned away from the water and allowed it to drench her clothing and back. Then she faced the waterfall and permitted the beautiful, clear water to douse her face and quench her thirst.

The liquid flowed down her open throat and she coughed. It was gurgling inside her, and she tried to turn but her body was caught in a coughing spell as it tried to dislodge the water.

She heard moaning and realized she had been asleep, but as she roused herself, she discovered she was covered in water.

It was raining, the strong droplets flying sideways in the wind, pelting her face. She opened her mouth again but this time, she welcomed the water. It was sweeter than the sweetest pie Ma had ever baked, and it filled her far more than Christmas dinner ever had.

She leaned back in the tree, her muscles aching from the cramped position. How long had she slept here? She wondered. She gazed out of the hole and tried to see the sky but it was obscured by the heavy rainstorm. Was it nightfall?

She was wide awake now. She twisted in the cramped quarters. She would rouse herself and step outside, she determined, spread her arms wide and allow the rain to wash her and feed her.

She stirred, placing her hand on the edge of the hole, when she heard something. She froze. After a long moment, she began to think it had only been her imagination. Then as she moved forward, she heard it again: a horse neighing.

No, not one horse but several.

She twisted inside the tree and looked through knotholes until she spied a column of soldiers marching past her, the horses trudging in the downpour while the men hunched forward in their saddles to counter the water's onslaught.

She held her breath, afraid they would hear her. But amidst the rattling of long knives and spurs, the clatter of hooves on an occasional boulder, and the chatter amongst the men, she knew they did not know she sat only a few yards away.

Some of the men were walking, by turns cajoling and threatening livestock that appeared to want nothing more than to lie down and wait for sunnier skies. A pack mule wandered too far to the north or a horse, too far to the south, and with a crack of a whip or a shout almost lost in the storm, the animal was brought back into line.

As she remained there, leaning forward while she stared out a small knothole, something pressed against her back. It was wet and it nuzzled her, pushing against the thin, soaked cotton dress.

She closed her eyes, breathing a tiny prayer, afraid to turn around but just as terrified to ignore it. As it continued, she knew whatever was behind her was not going away.

She cautiously turned her head. The nuzzling moved up the side of her face, leaving her sticky and smelling like a sweaty horse.

It jolted her and she turned almost completely around in the cramped quarters, coming face to face with a dappled gray horse.

Its entire mane was poking inside the tree, its black pupil larger than any eye Mary had ever seen. It seemed to be studying her, watching her movements, even as it continued nuzzling.

"Shoo!" Mary hissed, trying vainly to push it back. "Shoo!"

She couldn't see beyond its mane, but it was not wearing a bridle. Was there someone on its back, riding bareback, perhaps?

She pushed herself as far from the horse as she could get, though it wasn't far enough in the cramped space. She waited for someone to climb down and push their head inside the tree and discover her there, cowering amidst the rotted wood. She thought of forcefully pushing the horse away, of climbing outside the tree and shouting, "Here I am!" instead of being found in such a cowardly pose. But the horse would not budge and she found herself stuck inside the tree trunk, unable to move unless the entire tree was to move with her.

She glanced out the knothole. The men and the horses continued to file past her, only a few yards away. Surely someone would see this horse and come after it, she thought, and wonder what it had found inside a dead tree to raise its curiosity so.

But they continue to move past her, and eventually the horse backed away. She turned awkwardly, watching it through the larger hole in which she'd entered the tree. It moved around the two trees and stood on the far side. Then she realized the men on the other side probably could not see the dappled gray mare in the rain, standing amid the thick trees.

But why didn't it join them? She wondered. It didn't make sense.

Please go away, she thought frantically. Please go away before someone comes after you and spots me here!

She closed her eyes and prayed fervently. When she opened them some time later, the horse was gone. And as she continued to sit there, curled up in the tree with her knees to her chest, she realized there was nothing for her to do except capture as much water in her palms as possible, to drink her fill while she could, and to try to get back to sleep.

When she awakened again, the sun was shining. She cautiously leaned out of the tree and spotted the raindrops overhead, clinging to the tree branches. The ground beneath was moist and slippery. But the sky was a pale blue and somewhere the sun was lighting her way.

Her bones ached with the hours of her contorted position, and she eased herself out of the tree. A few yards away were the muddy remnants of an army past – hoof prints that ran deeper and messier with every animal that had passed her by.

She slowly stretched. She could not dare to venture from the tree without checking their position. She climbed back into the adjacent tree, hiding amidst the branches and the brown leaves that hung on stubbornly even as winter approached. She climbed higher than she had before, but there was no sign of the Army that had so recently pitched their tents beside the lake. Some time during the day or previous night, they had all marched westward toward Alfred and the ship.

As she turned and twisted, eyeing every angle, every direction, a movement caught her eye: it was the gray mare. She was standing between Mary and the lake, calmly eating the tall grass.

Mary remained in the tree for a few minutes, watching and waiting. Was the Army really gone? She wondered. Could she dare consider herself safe now to continue her travels?

Her eyes kept returning to the mare. It was as if Pa was right there beside her in the branches of that tree, and he was saying, "Don't look a gift horse in the mouth, Mary."

Her energy redoubled, she slid down the tree. Then with a quickstep she hadn't felt since the moment she first escaped, she trudged down the knoll and made her way to the horse.

It did not whinny or back away from her but stared at her calmly as if to say, "What took you so long?"

She spent a few moments running her hands through its mane and cooing softly to it. It was not a wild horse, of that she was sure. When she felt as though the horse would not bolt, she eased it to a fallen trunk, which she used to climb upon its broad back.

She didn't know when she had felt so much happiness. She was rested; she'd had her fill of water. And now she had a ride.

They remained close to the woods, though as they traveled toward the lake, Mary began to spot signs of a trail. She eyed it suspiciously; she had no idea whether there were Indians or more soldiers in this area, but she knew she couldn't take a chance of finding out. She would have to treat each and every step as though she could be spotted. The mare weaved through the trees, and when they came within view of the lake, Mary stopped to survey it before venturing forth.

It was larger than it had appeared from the knoll. She realized now the area she'd spotted from the tree was perhaps the smallest part of the lake as it jutted southward. A short distance to the north, it spread out as though the water nearest her was a finger and the remainder of the lake was a great fist.

The soldiers had apparently been there for some time judging from the scattered debris and the campfires that no longer smoldered.

She planned her movements carefully: a piece of charred meat hung over blackened chards of wood, long since doused; something shone in the sunlight a few yards away; and so many items littered the ground she felt as though she stood in the doorway of a general store.

Slowly, she dismounted. She spoke quietly to it, hoping it would remain near. She had nothing with which to secure it.

Carefully, cautiously, she made her way to the spit. Then despite herself, she ferociously tore the meat from the wooden stake, stuffing it into her mouth, hardly chewing it before stuffing more inside. She had no idea what it was: it might have been a piece of venison or bear; it was so burnt that it was no longer recognizable by her eyes or her tongue. But it was food. She stripped it bare, leaving only a bone licked clean and the wooden stake upon which it had cooked.

As she ate, she eyed the camp. A piece of cloth grabbed her attention; a piece of heavy wool, possibly part of an outer garment at one time, but now only a scrap of torn cloth. She held onto it as she continued to browse through the debris.

She was thrilled to find a stubby knife almost buried in the dirt. Its blade was dull but she knew how to sharpen it; she dusted it off and used the cloth as a makeshift pouch.

When she was finished a few minutes later, the knife had been joined by a piece of hemp rope, two short poles, a battered tin that would serve her well as both a bowl and a cup, and enough scraps of food to keep her alive for several days. She even located a weather-beaten canteen, which she promptly filled with lake water. She had so many newly found possessions she searched for additional pieces of abandoned cloth in which to store them. Then with the pride of one with newfound wealth, she packed the food inside one of the cloths and then tied it to a pole, while she packed the remaining possessions in the other cloth. Then she looped the rope around both poles so they swung about four feet apart.

The mare was still standing along the edge of the woods, and she walked back to it with a bounce in her step. She slung the rope across the horse's back so a bag hung on either side of her neck; then, as she did before, she walked the gentle creature to a fallen trunk, where she managed to mount it.

She nudged the mare around so she could take another look at the area. Perhaps she had missed something that would serve her on her journey.

Something moved in the corner of her eye, and she almost jumped. Purposefully keeping her head and body as still as possible, she followed the movement, squinting in the sunlight.

It was an Indian child.

She did not see Mary; her head was down as she bent to inspect something in the dirt—the same way, Mary noted, as she herself had done just a moment earlier.

Mary's eyes combed the shoreline. More Indian children were rounding the area where the lake widened substantially—so many that she realized there must be a village nearby.

And where there were children, there would be squaws. And where there were squaws, there would be braves.

She backed the horse into the woods and warily turned her around. Then with a quick kick of her heels, she spurred south to freedom.

62

The mood at Fort Pitt was ecstatic: the British were retreating from Yorktown, Virginia. British Rear-Admiral Sir Thomas Graves had been soundly thrashed by a French fleet that had rushed to the Chesapeake under the command of Admiral Count François Joseph Paul de Grasse. The French had far outnumbered the British, and now they had successfully blockaded the waters off the coast of Virginia, cutting off any hopes General Lord Charles Cornwallis had of a retreat by sea. Further, additional French troops stationed at Newport, Virginia were on their way to provide reinforcements in and around Yorktown.

With France's assistance, the tide had turned and success was imminent.

Now word spread like wildfire: the British fleet that had managed to escape before the blockade was retreating to New York, where they maintained a stronghold. Canadians and Loyalists who were serving in the King's Army were amassing just north and west of New York, ready to surge by sea or land with a desperate push. But while the troops were preparing to rush southward, civilians who had been loyal to the Crown were fleeing to Canada.

"New York is the last place I'd want to be right now," Jim said to no one in particular as he lifted his whiskey and toasted the other militia.

Colonel Daniel Brodhead raised his cup only partway. "I don't know if I can drink to that."

Jim laughed and patted him on the back. "You were only born there," he joked, "Pennsylvania is where you call home." Then he became somber. "New York has to be in an uproar, though. I bet you can't walk a mile without bumping into the Brits and Tories, going every which way. It's not a place for the faint of heart these days."

"So are you saying you're faint of heart?" the Colonel said with a sly grin.

"Now, you know me better'n that! I should be in Virginia now, though," he added.

"You're referring to de Grasse, sending his ships up the coast to collect Washington's and Rochambeau's armies, I presume?"

"Indeed I am. I should be there for the final assault on Yorktown. You know I'm a Virginian—"

"—and if I ever forget, you'll be the first to remind me." He downed his drink and ordered another one. "Now, Jim, you know you can't reach the coast before de Grasse arrives."

"Who said anything about going by sea? I can travel by land—"

"Oh, no, you won't. We need some to stay here and defend Fort Pitt."

"You have plenty of men," Jim said, waving his arm to encompass the roomful of soldiers. "There are plenty of Pennsylvanians here. You have to understand, Virginia is my home."

Colonel Brodhead leaned forward and lowered his voice. "I need your Indian expertise."

Jim guffawed. "Right. You need *my* expertise!" It was well known that Colonel Brodhead had been fighting the Indians since 1778, ranging from New York to the Muskingum River in the Ohio River Valley and throughout Pennsylvania—and as far west as a failed attempt to capture Fort Detroit. He'd fought the Shawnee, the Wyandot, the Mingo, Seneca, Oneida, and even the Lenape-Delaware tribes. "You're a belly full of laughs tonight, old friend!"

Colonel Brodhead did not return his laughter. "We can fight the British in battle," he said, "but we have to subdue the Indians. The King's Army will retreat across the ocean, but the Indians—they aren't going anywhere."

Jim grew serious. "What do you need?"

"You know the west like the back of your hand. You've traveled the length of the Ohio River. You know the Indians—especially the Cherokee and Shawnee. We might be pushing the British back in the east, but I need you to return to the west, to fight the Indians."

"You know I've been serving under Colonel Clark—without a furlough and for many months without pay."

"And you'll continue to serve him well and be justly rewarded. Clark is at the Falls of the Ohio now. He hasn't given up on Fort Detroit, and he's going to need you."

Jim set his empty glass on the table and waved off another shot. "So am I to turn around, just having come from there, and head back straightaways?" he asked incredulously.

"I'll know soon—perhaps by the end of this week. Keep it to yourself, man, we don't need word getting out."

"So it's a secret expedition, then?"

The Colonel glanced over his shoulder but didn't answer.

Jim followed his gaze and fell silent with his thoughts. To be so close to Virginia and not be able to see his family—and Susannah! It wasn't fair—but nothing in this blasted war was fair. He pushed his chair back and rose. "I'll go where I'm needed," he said with resignation. "If I could see my family, just once—once in four years, mind you—I'd be grateful."

"I'll see what I can do," the Colonel answered.

Jim nodded. He didn't expect his request to be granted. He was a soldier and that was that. As he tossed some coins on the table to pay for his drinks, he thought wryly, *At least I'm not going to New York.*

63

ary had lost track of the days; perhaps four had passed, or possibly five. The one thing she knew for certain was Alfred had greatly underestimated the distance to New York. Or had she somehow missed New York altogether?

There was a body of water to the east that she saw every now and again. She'd kept her eyes on the sunrises and sunsets and knew her course had been steadfast toward the southeast. Of that she was confident.

She could have traveled due east and followed the water's edge but she'd thought better of that plan when she spotted ships heading northward. She'd watched them from a distance. They appeared to be filled with British soldiers, one right after another, and she wondered if they would come ashore and head across the same area she'd just come through.

She stayed in the woods, finding foot paths as she rode, but staying clear of the wider Indian trails. Twice she'd seen Indians, though they were far enough away not to alarm her. Still, it quickened her heart and made her breathing shallower.

The mare appeared to know this terrain well, often leaving the safety of the trees for grassy areas but returning back to the woods when her stomach was full. To Mary's relief, she knew how to stand perfectly still, without even the swish of her tail, when Mary pulled her to a stop to watch the Indians or the

British. Once, she had even stopped on her own; when Mary tried to persuade her to move forward, she refused with the stubbornness of a mule, until Mary realized she had eyed an Indian moving along the trail nearer the water.

The horse was a God-send. Though Mary's thighs were chafed from the long hours riding bare back, it was far more preferable than walking in those uncomfortable, ill-fitting shoes. And there was no doubt they had covered more terrain than she could have accomplished on foot.

The steady plodding of the horse's hooves upon the ground lulled her into a soft sleep. She was only faintly aware that she'd slumped forward, her fingers entwined in the horse's mane.

She had become so accustomed to the movement and the gentle sound of the mare's solid footing that when she stopped, Mary instantly recognized the change, though it took her several seconds to groggily open her eyes.

The sun was high overhead and appeared directly in her eyes, blurring her vision. As she attempted to steady herself, a dark brown spot came into view. It grew legs and a long neck but stood perfectly still. As her focus returned, she realized a body grew out of the creature. She blinked then squinted into the path before her.

The mare had left the woods and ventured into a stream of clear, rushing water. A mist rose from it, which encircled the ground before her. Rising out of the mist like a mystical creature was a tall brown stallion, his head held high and proud. And atop the horse sat a muscled, bronzed Indian.

Mary felt the blood draining out of her face, leaving her cold and clammy. She remained like a statue on the dappled gray mare, her eyes now locked on the Indian.

His face was immobile, his black eyes penetrating hers. His hair was long and straight. Three feathers rose high above his crown. Her eyes took in his chest, bare although it was cold, his long buckskin breeches, and his moccasined feet held securely in worn stirrups.

The horses stood not twenty feet apart.

"You are Songbird," he said in a firm, confident voice.

At the mention of the name, she wanted to plunge her heels into the mare's sides and bolt away from him, but she was frozen in position. In the fraction of a second, her mind played out her horse racing out of the stream and into the woods, the Indian fast on her heels, perhaps joined by others waiting in ambush.

She could never outrun an Indian, no matter how sure-footed or fleet her mare could be; even if he lost visual contact, an Indian could track her down by scent alone.

The Indian lifted his chin. "You brought medicine to Eagle Feathers."

When she spoke, her voice sounded detached and not hers at all. "Yes. At Fort Detroit."

"And how is Eagle Feathers?"

Her eyes did not waver from his. "He died. Not from the fever, but from the pox, north of the fort."

There was a long silence. "Yes. So I heard."

Her heart quickened.

The Indian continued, "I warned Eagle Feathers not to take the blankets, but he did not believe me."

She felt her breath grow shallow and her fingers instinctively grasped the horse's mane tighter.

"And what of Strength of an Ox?"

"Dead also. We found him with Buffalo Woman."

"Yes." His horse pawed the ground once. "I know."

Mary felt a chill wind whip through her body and she shuddered.

"And White Messenger. What has happened to him?"

She could not lie. This Indian, whoever he was, wherever he had been, already knew too much.

"I don't know," she answered. "I was captured by the British and separated from him."

The Indian did not respond. His eyes continued to stare into hers like black pools. His face was immobile, neither threatening nor friendly. After a moment that felt entirely too long and too awkward, his horse began to move forward. The mare remained perfectly still as the stallion circled her from a few feet away.

The Indian was behind her when he spoke again. "The horse belongs to Wait-in-the-Bush."

She started to turn but he was moving up beside her.

"I did not steal it," she said, her voice steadier than she felt.

He stopped when the horses were neck-and-neck. "It doesn't matter. He stole it from a white woman."

She was so close to him that she could detect a musky odor emanating from him; perhaps it was bear fat or it might have been from the furs that were slung across the horse's mane in front of him.

"Where are you going?" he said. "You are a long way from where the British captured you."

"I am going to New York," she said with defiance.

For the first time, she saw emotion cross his eyes, though it was fleeting: it was simply an instant of surprise before they became unreadable again.

His horse pawed the ground again. This time, the mare nuzzled the stallion. The horses stared at each other as if they were conducting an inaudible conversation.

"If you continue the way you were heading, you will only get to New York by crashing over the great falls."

She shivered again.

His horse shifted and he pointed toward the northeast. "There is a portage to the north. It provides safe passage."

Her eyes followed the direction he pointed. There was nothing there except marshy land and more trees.

"I will take you there," he declared.

She hesitated. She realized quickly she had no choice; he could kill her and scalp her right there and she was defenseless to stop him. She remembered the knife hidden in her bundle, but she could never reach it without observation and besides, it would prove to be less of a weapon than she needed.

It could also be a trap. He might lead her to other Indians, who would enslave her yet again.

He turned in his saddle and headed upstream.

Her eyes skimmed the southern horizon. Head south and east, Alfred had told her. South and east.

She looked again to the north. The Indian was moving steadily away without so much as a glance behind him.

She could simply continue moving south. If the Indian wanted to capture her, he would have to turn around and follow her. Then she would have no choice but to go with him.

Or… She looked again at the Indian's back. Then she kicked her heels and turned the mare toward the north.

They reached a thin strip of land surrounded by marshland near sunset. They had not spoken again during the hours they moved steadily northward and then due east. They had encountered a handful of Indians moving to the west along the same trail, and each time Mary had held her breath and offered swift prayers. Each time, the Indian had raised his hand in greeting and passed by them, with Mary following closely behind. And each time, though she felt the others' eyes upon her, she was allowed to pass freely.

They stopped at a spot where white men and Indians alike had gathered—perhaps a dozen in all, Mary noted.

"Eagle Feathers' daughter wishes to cross the portage," the Indian said.

The others looked at him with respect, she thought, and she wondered who this person was who seemed to know so much about her and who appeared so well known.

"What do you have in payment?" one of the white men asked.

Mary looked at the hemp rope, still slung across the mare's back. Two packages still hung, one on either side, but they had diminished greatly in size as she had eaten the scraps along the way. Now they contained a few pieces of rotting food and the small items she had taken from the campsite.

The Indian pulled a beaver pelt that had lain across the stallion and handed it to the white man.

The man inspected it briefly and then nodded.

The Indian turned his horse so he was facing Mary. He reached behind him and pulled a blanket from a tied parcel and offered it to her.

She hesitated, and then shook her head.

"It is an Indian blanket," he said in a voice so low that she doubted the others could hear him. She thought she detected a slight smile. "It did not come from the British."

Cautiously, she reached for it. It was stiffer than the British blankets and was decorated in red dye. She nodded and wrapped it around her shoulders before she realized she was still shivering. "I have nothing to repay you," she said, "except my horse."

"Your horse is worth more than the blanket," he said. "And you will need it." He moved so close to the mare that the horses were touching. "Do not trust these men. They will get you to New York; that is their business. But when you reach the other side, do not take their directions."

He pulled his reins and the horse stepped away.

"Wait," she said. "What is your name?"

"I am Karhakon:ha of the Mohawk nation."

With that, he was gone, his horse plodding calmly away with an occasional swish of his tail.

64

Jim was growing increasingly more frustrated. It had been more than two weeks since George and Old Man Spears had left Fort Pitt to return to Virginia with supply wagons for the Continental Army. Yet here he still sat, waiting for definitive orders to return to the Falls of the Ohio. He knew by this time, his friend and neighbor was almost home—if he hadn't reached there already—and if he'd known he would still be stuck at Fort Pitt, he might have pled his case more strongly. As the days crawled by ever more slowly, he was fast coming to the conclusion that he could have taken his furlough and been back in the time he still waited here, cooling his heels.

His disenchantment certainly wasn't a secret. He'd been at Colonel Brodhead's door almost every day. He'd stopped asking his question; all it took now was for the Colonel to see his face, and the answer was the same: "I am still waiting on a dispatch."

Jim half-heartedly shuffled the papers on his desk and looked through a window streaked with dirt. He was a soldier, meant to be in the field and on the battle lines. He was at his best scouting or planning retaliatory raids against the Indians—or the British. It was nothing but a waste for him to be stuck at Fort Pitt pushing papers.

Meanwhile, General Washington's troops were massing for a siege of Yorktown. The French were there as well with ships just off the coast, ready to lend support as the Continental Army needed.

I should be there, Jim thought for the millionth time, his lips pursed and his brows furrowed. It would be days, if not weeks, before he would know the outcome. He wondered what his family might be experiencing, though they were some two hundred and fifty miles from Yorktown. It felt strange, all of a sudden: he'd been in the west for so many years, going for months without thinking of his parents and siblings, but now—now that he was back east, he was eager to see them. And Susannah—oh, Susannah! What I wouldn't do to see you now!

He didn't even remember the last time he'd received pay for his duties in the Virginia militia. But dangling in front of him like a carrot in front of a horse was the promise of land. Once this war was over, he would be given land in the west in payment for all these months.

His mind wandered. Privates were expected to get at least a hundred acres; as a lieutenant, he might get as much as two thousand. He thought of a pasture filled with horses and cows; of chickens getting fat and happy until they landed on his dinner table; and tobacco. After the war was over, he would return to the west, claim his land, and plant some tobacco.

A shadow crossed his desk and he turned from the window.

"Tommy!" he said, coming to his feet so quickly that he threatened to topple the papers onto the floor.

"Jim! How are you, my good friend?" Tommy said, crossing the room in two long strides. "I see you still have Brandy. You both look none the worse for wear!" He scratched the dog behind her ears.

"Where have you been?"

"Here, there, everywhere, it seems. Stayed at the Falls of the Ohio a mite longer than you. Then they sent me northward to do a little scouting just outside Fort Detroit. Don't mind telling you, Jim, I'm glad to be back in the east. I don't know if I want to go back out there."

"Why's that?"

"The British, they got a real stronghold. I don't know how Clark is planning on toppling 'em. And the Indians! They are in their back pocket, yes siree, they are. Still attacking the settlers, left and right. Lots of 'em headed back east; they've had enough—"

Jim listened to the younger man. He knew they'd had a tough time, what with the hard, cold winters, no pay, and little food, but the defeat in Tommy's voice was almost more than he could bear.

"Anyway's," Tommy was saying, perking up, "got a dispatch for you."

Jim almost tore the paper out of Tommy's hand. As he broke the seal, Colonel Brodhead appeared in the doorway and Tommy edged into the small room to allow him entry.

Jim read through the orders and then read them again. "What the devil—?"

"Family by the name of Riddle," the Colonel said, "left yesterday from Philadelphia. They're to meet up with you along the *Susquehanna River*. You're to escort them south."

Jim did not attempt to mask his annoyance. "All due respect, Sir, I'm a soldier; not a guard. The trails are well marked and well traveled; they don't need me to take them south."

Colonel Brodhead smiled. "This family has close ties to the Governor of Virginia—"

"Thomas Jefferson."

"They'll require an escort."

"But there are privates," Jim almost spat. "Sir—"

"They're going to Virginia, Lieutenant. Think about it."

He stopped short.

"Once there, you'll have earned a furlough."

Jim could feel his pulse quickening. "When do I leave, Sir?"

"As soon as you can pack. In thirty days, you'll be leading some Virginia militia to the Falls of the Ohio."

"Yes, sir." Jim began straightening the papers on the desk.

"Leave it," Colonel Brodhead said. "Lieutenant Buckingham—" he waved toward Tommy "—will take it from here." He stepped out of the path to the doorway. "Now, go," he said.

Jim didn't need to be told twice. He was halfway out the door when Colonel Brodhead added, "Oh, and your friend

George Spears will be returning to the west with you. Godspeed, the both of you."

65

The sound of church bells awakened Mary. She nearly leapt off the straw in the decrepit barn. *Ma will be upset if we're late!* She thought before she stopped herself. When she eased back onto the makeshift bed, she marveled at the thought. *It's Sunday, the first time I've known the day of the week since—well, since I don't know when.*

With daylight streaming in through the cracks in the boards, she eventually eased herself out of her bed and wrapped the Indian blanket around her for warmth. She'd nestled deep within the straw and slept well and long, and hardly noticed the mice that scampered around her all night long.

The mare appeared content as it nuzzled its way around the barn, finding bits and pieces of long ago treats and foodstuffs.

Mary had first noticed this barn from a distance as she passed along a high ridge some miles away. The house appeared to have burned down some time ago and from the looks of the barn, it had been abandoned. There were multiple holes in the roof, but it hadn't rained, so the night had been spent high and dry, as Ma used to say. Now Mary made her way to the doorway and stood just to the side of it and stared wistfully toward the sound of the bells.

She was acutely aware of her tattered and filthy cotton dress and her dusty, ill-fitting shoes. She tried to run her fingers through her hair but they became snagged almost immediately. She hadn't seen herself in a mirror in so long. She wondered what she looked like, whether she had bags under her eyes or gaunt, high cheekbones. She wondered if her once sea-green, mischievous eyes were sunken and dark, and whether her hair, now grown back from the insane ritual she'd been forced to endure, was streaked with gray.

A brook babbled a short distance from the barn, and she made her way down an overgrown path to the water. After drinking her fill, she impulsively dropped the blanket and plunged into the water, gasping at its iciness. Once she was immersed, her body adjusted and she rubbed every inch of her skin with her bare hands.

Her nails were broken and jagged with layers of dirt encrusted under them. She dipped her whole head under water and rubbed her hair between her hands, watching the dirt and dust of hundreds of miles drifting downstream.

She was free.

She had made it to America. She'd continued moving southeastward in an area that grew steadily more populated and well-traveled. And yet, she still did not feel safe. So many wore the red uniforms of the British soldiers, and so many of the civilians were friendly toward them, that she was frightened to make herself known. They had captured her once and held her prisoner; might not the British capture her again? The mere thought of being transported under guard back to the island was more than she could bear.

So she set her course when she reached high terrain, knowing or feeling her way just out of sight of trails that would be populated, just out of earshot by those who might hear her.

Her horse was like a gray ghost who instinctively stayed by the trees with bark the color of her coat and who froze at the sound of a human voice or foot upon the path.

Food was plentiful. There were cornfields with scattered ears of corn that had been overlooked when the fields were harvested. There were pumpkins and gourds. There were nuts of every description; she had only to look beneath the right trees.

She'd managed to start a fire, but she'd been careful about the location and the materials she placed on it. She remembered how the Indians had been able to keep fires going without more than the faintest trace of smoke. So she'd only started one fire in the early morning hours, under a bridge during a rainstorm. She'd caught several frogs with a makeshift trap made from twigs and a wooden poker and cooked them whole as they lay skewered over the fire. The flames had been snuffed out after only a brief time, the moisture having gotten to it, but the frogs were so small they had cooked quickly. They tasted so good that she knew, had she not been able to start the fire, she would have devoured them raw.

She had learned how to survive, and now that knowledge would continue to keep her alive.

She wondered what month it was. September, possibly October. She didn't think it was November; there had been no snow. Still, there had been plenty of flocks migrating south for the winter, and as she raised her head and watched them fly over her, they served as a reminder that she also must reach the south before the harsh winter months set in.

The church bells stopped.

She wondered how far she would have to travel before she felt safe enough to ask for help. Where was she in relation to Fort Pitt? She would know when she spotted the Continental Army that her ordeal was over. And she might know when she detected settlers she had possibly reached Colonist sympathizers. But she would not know for certain if a civilian was a friend or foe, while on the other hand, a member of the Continental Army...

At long last, she stopped her internal debate and climbed out of the water, shivering in the cold morning air. She wrapped the blanket around her shoulders and dashed back to the barn. The mare had followed her outside and was now grazing in a nearby field.

She dried herself off as best she could and made her way to the horse. The mare was thinner than she had been when Mary had first encountered her; her ribs were beginning to show. Mary ran her open palm along her bones. "I promise you'll have as much food as you could possibly want," she said. Then she marveled at the sound of conviction in her own voice. How could she possibly make such a promise when she did not know what fate had in store for her?

The morning sun was moving higher in the sky when she climbed atop the mare and set off once again toward the south.

66

Jim raised his face upward and took a deep breath of the morning air, still heavy with the dew. He loved the great outdoors. There was nothing better than to ride along on the black stallion that had been with him all these years, during Indian battles and scouting expeditions, through fighting the British, and even in the abandonment of Fort Jefferson. As he patted his side, he noted it hadn't taken long for the horse to put on weight. And as he watched Brandy chasing a rabbit, he noted her ribs were no longer visible. All three had made it through a mighty lean winter.

A day's ride behind him laid Fort Pitt and less than three hundred miles to the east stood Philadelphia. He admired the huge red sun that rose to greet him along the horizon, heralding the start of a new day.

He didn't know much about the Riddle family. He imagined they'd been promised land in Virginia, fertile soil on which to raise their crops or tall green grasses in which to let their livestock graze. Perhaps they had a deed in their possession now, or they might wait until they reached Virginia soil before settling on a spot. They might be a young couple with their whole lives ahead of them, or a family with many grown children. He didn't know, and he didn't much care.

He was going home.

His years in the west trained him to hear every noise as he made his way along roads and trails. At the sound of every bird crying as it cleared the trees, he tilted his head and listened for horses' hooves. At the wail of every animal, he listened for an answering call. There were Indians here, too, though not the problems they had in the west. The problems here were different, fueled by British officers who promised the Indians whatever they wanted to hear to raise up arms against the Colonists.

There were also problems with thieves along the road to Philadelphia; low-lifes they were, to be sure, men who hid along the road waiting for the wealthy to leave the safety of the city. Sometimes they stole the jewelry right off the women's necks and fingers; and sometimes men were left penniless. A man could be hung for such thievery, if one could catch him, but often it was too late to prevent a life from being ruined.

He crested a hill and pulled on the reins of the stallion. The dutiful horse came to a stop and immediately began feeding on the grass beside the road. Jim reached into a leather pouch and pulled out a piece of jerky. He ripped a piece off with his side teeth and chewed the tough stuff while he studied the land below. He would reach the Riddle family in a matter of days, perhaps a week, as the roads here were passable and easy to navigate. He would spend the nights outside, looking at the moon through bare tree branches, as he lay huddled inside his fur overcoat. He would cook over open flames again and breathe in the fresh air.

It felt so good to be on the move again.

His eyes traveled the length of the road before him. He knew once he descended this hill, he would be flanked by tall trees that would block his view on either side. The road would wind gently, creating curves in which travelers could be hidden until they each rounded that last bend and came face to face.

Perhaps he was overreacting from his years in the west but old habits died hard. As he chewed the jerky, his eagle eyes scanned the road looking for movement.

Some distance from him, he spotted figures progressing toward the west. They weren't in the middle, where travelers tended to stay, but appeared to be hugging the side of the road where the woods sheltered them. He could feel the hair along

his arms bristling. It was too cool on this autumn morn for anyone
to seek the shadows; any sane person would be searching for
what little bit of warmth could be had from the rising sun.

Without removing his eyes from them, he reached into the
buckskin pouch strapped to his thigh and pulled out his telescope.
Before he had the scope to his eye, he knew there was but one
horse and no rider; now as he peered through it, three men came
into focus.

They were dirty as men were who spent their time in the
outdoors. Even from this distance, he could tell their long hair
had not been combed or washed in some time. Their clothes
were covered in grime; it was more than the dust of the road, he
determined, but the kind of heavy stains one gets from layers of
perspiration and filth.

They appeared to be arguing, their hands waving wildly as
they spoke. One man pulled a reluctant, gaunt horse along by its
reins while simultaneously batting the others away.

Jim half-smirked. Three men and one horse. Not a good
combination.

The man in the front stopped abruptly and lifted his arm up
as if to halt the others. They all came to a standstill, the men
simultaneously tilting their heads as though listening. Then with
the stealth of cats, the two without the horse appeared to tiptoe
into the woods, slipping and sliding until they came to a natural
trough some yards away, where they ducked into the shadows.
The third man led the horse to the opposite side of the road,
where he tied the reins to a tree. Then he also stooped low, his
body almost hidden by the gloom of the trees.

Jim followed the road with his telescope, moving it
methodically away from the men and toward the west. At first
he didn't see anything, but as he continued scanning the area in
which the men faced, he saw an almost imperceptible movement.

A lone figure atop a horse moved slowly through the trees,
a short distance from the road. The horse was gray and blended
almost seamlessly with the shadows. The slight figure was
hunched forward as if cold or tired.

They crossed into a small open area and the rising sun struck
them for an all-too-brief moment.

Jim sucked in his breath. It appeared to be a squaw. Slender, bare legs rode the horse bareback. The willowy torso was wrapped in an Indian blanket, one hand holding it together just under the neck while the other grasped the horse's mane.

Then they were back in the shadows of the woods, moving steadily southeastward. His brain calculated their movement; if they stayed their course, they would encounter the road in the curve where the men lay waiting.

Instinctively, his spurs hit the stallion's sides. The horse immediately sprang into a full gallop, careening down the hill at breakneck speed. As they reached the road below, he spurred it onward ever faster. He hoped he would reach them in time.

67

Mary bent forward as she rode atop the mare, her slight shoulders trembling with the early morning chill. It had been an unusually cold night, one in which she had despaired she might freeze. The cotton dress was worn so thin she could easily see right through sections of it, and she dared not wash it again for fear it would fall apart in her hands. The blanket was a God-send; repeatedly she found herself asking God to bless the old Indian who had given it to her so freely.

Even with the blanket, she had been forced to use her bare hands to dig through decaying leaves along the forest floor into which she could lower herself before pulling the leaves back onto her for warmth. She hoped and prayed through a fitful night that the horse would not leave her. But before the dawn, she had been awakened by the faithful mare nuzzling her, perhaps checking to see if she were still alive.

She knew her time alone must come to an end. She had traveled too many days to count and too many miles to know exactly where she was. She had tried to keep the horse on a southward course, but each time she fell asleep on its broad back, she could sense the mare turning back to the east as though on a path of its own.

They had come close to encountering both Indians and white men, but her instinct had kept her from venturing near enough to be detected by them. But now she was exhausted and famished.

Winter was fast approaching and she was frightened that another cold night like the one before would do her in. As she rode along, her brain sank into a weightless chasm in which she felt she was no longer able to think or even to pray.

The mare stopped abruptly and Mary groggily opened her eyes. She had learned to trust her loyal companion, and she did not spur her onward. She felt as if her mind was enveloped in a thick fog as she struggled to keep her eyes open and peer around her. Her hands seemed frozen in place, one grasping the the blanket around her throat and the other entwined in the horse's mane.

A bird broke through the tops of the trees, its cry sounding an alarm.

Her eyes opened and her pulse quickened, her blood coursing hotly through her veins.

The horse stood perfectly still as if it were just another of the majestic trees that surrounded them.

Then hurried feet pounded the ground beneath them and men seemed to rush them from all sides at once. Panicked, the mare rose up on its hind legs as Mary struggled to hold on to her. She could not see in front of her as the horse's long neck thrashed first to the right and then to the left, and she was barely aware of its front legs battering the air. Her fingers slipped through the silky mane and she grasped desperately for a piece of horseflesh to hold onto. Then the mare bolted through the woods, slinging Mary into a tree. She grappled for something to break her fall, but she hit the forest floor with a thud that sucked the breath right out of her body.

"Git the horse! Git the horse!"

The man's voice rang out beside her so close it made her ears ring. Then there was shouting as they rushed through the woods after the mare. It seemed as though there was an entire army of them; they were in front of her, then behind her, then on either side of her.

She was yanked rudely to her feet and the blanket was ripped from her body.

"Well, well, what have we 'ere," a man breathed into her face.

If Mary lived to be a hundred, she knew she would never forget the man's features. His skin was ruddy and leathered with a thick crop of coarse black hairs erupting from his chin and cheeks. One small, dark eye focused on her while a lazy eye dropped downward toward her feet.

She jerked her arm from his grasp. "Let go of me," she hissed.

"We got 'er," another man said breathlessly as he led the mare back to them.

Mary could see the panic in the horse's moist brown eyes, and she struggled to keep her own fear from rising.

They stopped just short of her. A stocky man with dirt-encrusted hair and clothes cinched the hemp rope that had hung loosely across the mare's neck tight—too tight, Mary thought—and led the horse toward the road.

"Looks like ye got yerself a woman," the third man said. His hair might have been blond were it not for the grime, but his eyes were the sharpest blue Mary had ever seen. The whites of his eyes were threaded with pink veins, causing him to look almost pop-eyed at her.

"She's mine first," the man who had grabbed her off the forest floor warned in a guttural voice.

"I'm not yours," Mary shouted. Her strong voice was in contrast to the vulnerable picture she knew she must have portrayed, standing there helpless in her thin dress as the men eyed her from her neck to her legs.

One of the men chortled and Mary instinctively balled her fists. "I will kill anyone who touches me."

"Is that so?" said the first man, grabbing a fistful of hair and dragging her through the woods to the side of the road. "Just how you figurin' on doing that?" he said as he threw her against the nearest tree.

Mary heard a crack thunder through her head as her skull hit the broad, solid trunk and she sank to the ground. Her hand moved instinctively to her head and came away soaked in bright red blood.

Then she was being pulled backward by a fist entwined in her hair. She cried out. Her arms flailed above her, trying to free her hair from this monster that pulled her through the underbrush.

He slammed his fist against her chin and she felt the earth swim beneath her. Somewhere she heard the mare whinnying and a dog barking and then the sounds melted into her ringing ears.

The man had her pinned to the ground as he struggled to sit atop of her. Through the blood, she could see his cracked, dry lips parting in a sadistic grimace.

Then her entire body jumped with the sound of a shot that rang out just as a bloody hole erupted in the center of his forehead. As he fell atop of her, she thrashed about to keep from being trapped under him.

There was barking and shouts all about her and suddenly there were horses everywhere. She wrestled free of the dead man and came to her feet, her legs wobbling in terror.

Then she was running, scrambling back to the road. She was racing away from the carnage, the gray mare's tail some distance in front of her; and then it was gone as it rounded a curve at breakneck speed.

She stopped and held onto a tree while her lungs cried out for air. Though she felt as if she'd run a mile, she was only a short distance away from the two remaining assailants. Instead of an army of horses, there was only one: a black stallion that seemed to be everywhere at once. And darting around the horse's hooves was a yellow dog, its teeth bared as vicious guttural sounds slipped past its lips.

Shots rang out and the horse threw its head unnaturally to the side as the rider leapt to the ground, tackling one of the men as he landed. Then both of the men were upon him.

She looked to the east but could no longer see the gray mare. She knew she should continue running as fast as her legs could carry her, into the woods and away from these men—but even as her body turned, her eyes could not. She watched with mounting horror as the two men pummeled the fallen rider even as he shouted for her to run to safety. He was grappling for something and as she watched, he pulled a sheath knife from a pouch on his buckskin breeches and plunged it into one of the men. The man shouted but continued to fight as blood spurted over them. The dog tried valiantly to pull the men off, alternately rushing, biting, and retreating, but in the mayhem she heard it yelping in pain as it continued to fight.

The stallion had stopped a few yards away and she leapt to it, pulling a longrifle from its saddle. In three quick steps, she was near enough to aim.

The rider of the horse was flat against the ground, his fist trying to make contact with the quickly moving men. She now saw that both her assailants had knives and were jabbing at both the man and the dog. Then the stocky man raised his knife high in the air above the man's chest, grasping the handle with both hands.

Mary pulled the trigger, hoping against hope that it was loaded and primed.

As he began to plunge the knife downward, the shot rang out and found its mark on the back of his head, exploding it like a pumpkin thrown against a wall.

In a split second, she was beside the two remaining men with the rifle turned around, its barrel still smoking as she swung the stock against the last assailant's head. A loud whack resounded through the woods as he fell over.

She thought for a moment the rider was dead. An eerie silence enveloped her; the birds that had chirped their greetings to the rising sun were gone now. All that was left was the stillness of the forest. Not even a single leaf blew in the motionless air.

Then a moan escaped the rider's lips and he raised his forearm to his head. As he wiped the blood from his face, he exclaimed, "Mary! Is it you?"

Mary rushed forward and knelt beside him. "Jim! Jim Hawkins!"

He was covered in blood. He groaned as he struggled to sit. "Are you alright?" he asked.

"I'm fine, thanks to you," she answered. "It's a joy to see you!"

She threw her arms around him, grasping his shirt with her fists, holding the material so tightly, she thought she could never release her grip. She rested her head against his chest and felt his strong arms curling around her body, holding her safe within his arms. It was over. It was all over—her capture, her captivity, the Indians, the British. She was back amongst her own kind.

She felt him loosen his grasp on her as he exclaimed, "Brandy!"

She pulled back and stared into his face. It was as though the blood had drained out of it. She followed his wide eyes to the yellow dog lying a few feet away, her crumpled body covered in blood, a barely audible whimper escaping from her lips.

They moved to her; Jim reached her first and slumped over her, pulling her head onto his lap. Mary knelt beside him and together they inspected her. She was covered in lacerations; some of them had barely grazed the surface while other knives had plunged deep within her.

"I can help her," Mary said, coming to her feet. She raced into the woods, quickly and deftly assessing the plants and grabbing handfuls of leaves.

Within a matter of minutes, she had made a crude poultice, mixing crushed leaves and plant stems with water from Jim's flask. Jim held the dog still while Mary cleaned the wounds and applied the poultice, using broader leaves to push the mixture into the dog. She winced and tried to get up, but Jim gently but firmly pushed her back to the ground, his voice soft and soothing.

"Where did you learn this?" he asked.

"From the Indians," she said. "If we can keep the wounds from flaring up, if we can suck the poison out with the poultice, she has a chance." She stood. "Do you have extra clothing?"

"Why, yes, but—"

"Then tell me where it is. My dress is thin and I can easily rip it. I'll tear it into strips and we'll wrap her body, but I'll need something else to wear—"

"In my haversack."

She raced to the stallion, tore through the haversack until she found a pair of breeches and a cotton shirt, and quickly changed. Then she used her teeth to rip the cotton dress into strips. With each tear, she felt as if she were shredding the last two years' events, as if the memories were now just that—

memories, ones that would hopefully fade fast. She was going home.

68

Mary walked alongside Jim while she held the reins to the black stallion. She could see the concern etched on his face as she watched his constant glances to the bundle he carried in his arms. Brandy was almost as still as death, her body wrapped securely in the thin cotton. And as they marched closer to a nearby stream, it wasn't lost on her that two wounds had begun to bleed again.

Jim was covered in blood, partly from his dog and also from his own wounds. He had been stabbed and sliced, but he was focused more on the safety of his dog than on his own injuries.

Three men lay dead behind them, propped up against the trees. She wondered about leaving them thus, without proper burials and graveside prayers. But Jim had been in no mood to dig their graves and frankly, she hadn't been, either. Better to leave them as a warning to other thieves, at least until they reached the next town and proper authorities.

They'd cleaned their pockets of jewelry, trinkets, and a small number of coins, which Jim put into a small pouch. Most likely, everything they possessed had been stolen and they had readily reached a consensus to turn over the items in town.

They'd found the men's horse a few paces away, skittish and half-starved. It looked as though it could barely hold itself upright. Mary had gently taken its reins and now it walked haltingly beside them.

They reached the water's edge and stopped, allowing the horses to drink of the cool water while Jim gently laid Brandy in the soft grass. They inspected her, tying the cotton tighter around her middle to keep the worst of the wounds from bleeding too profusely. Jim gave her water and tried to feed her, but although she eagerly drank, she turned her head away from the food.

They had been at the water's edge only a few minutes when Jim cocked his head and signaled for Mary. Without a word, he reached for his longrifle and reloaded. He lay prone amidst the grasses, looking upward at the road above.

The horse's hooves were rushed but slowed as it reached a curve in the road, almost as if it sensed them on the other side. Then haltingly it moved forward and came into view.

It was the dappled gray mare.

The setting sun found them still along the water's edge. They had talked well into the afternoon, pausing only to start a fire and prepare a meal.

She spoke for the first time about her father's death and her capture and of her travels with her little Shawnee tribe. He listened intently, interrupting only to suck in his breath or offer a curse to those who had taken her. He was wide-eyed as she recounted her time at Fort Detroit, her escape and her capture by the British, interrupting her to ask questions about the enemy and then cursing them.

After eating, they rested along the banks, watching as the horses got their fill of water and grazed. Jim offered some grain and corn to the half-starved horse and inspected her, declaring her to be an old horse, long in the tooth. They would turn her in at the next town for undoubtedly, she had been stolen from her rightful master.

They discussed transporting Brandy, as the dog was too severely injured to walk on her own and it wouldn't be practical to carry her for miles on end. Under Mary's guidance, they fashioned something akin to a papoose from Jim's blanket and some carefully selected tree branches. They would spend the night here; in the morning, they would secure Brandy within the papoose and hoist her onto Jim's back for the journey atop his black stallion. Mary would be alongside them on the gray mare while she would lead the third horse.

Now they lay on the grass and watched the stars emerge in the dark sky. "I am meeting a family at the Susquehanna," Jim said. "I am taking them to Virginia."

"I must get home," Mary said. "—to Fort Nashborough and Mansker's Station."

Jim nodded. "I know. Sam has traveled the Wilderness Trail these past months searching for you. He has never given up hope of finding you."

Jim leaned on his elbow, his sharp blue eyes locking onto hers. "Come with me to Virginia. Once I have delivered the Riddle family, I will take you to the Spears' home. Then I will return to the west and get word to Sam."

"The Spears..." Mary's voice faded.

"George is there," Jim said softly. "He is joining the militia and plans to move west."

"Has he—?"

"No."

Mary nodded and picked out the North Star in the clear black sky as they fell silent.

They reached the Susquehanna in a few days' time. The Riddle family was waiting with their covered wagons and more cattle than Mary could count. It reminded her of a time long ago when her own family had gathered some 300 cattle and headed west from Virginia to Fort Nashborough. As they had waved good-bye to their friends and neighbors, she could never have imagined a homecoming such as this.

They followed the birds as they migrated south, reaching Augusta County before winter set in. After depositing the Riddles at their intended destination, their pace quickened. Brandy now ran alongside them, frequently leaving the road to chase a myriad of critters; under Mary's care, her wounds had healed though some scars remained. Both the mare and the stallion had flourished on the trip, as food had been plentiful and towns more frequent. The old horse and the bag of possessions they'd taken from the men had been turned in to the local authorities at the first town they'd come to. A reward had been posted for the return of the horse, enough for Mary to purchase two real dresses at the general store.

They could smell the change in the air as they neared home. Families rushed to their fences and called their hellos, many of them recognizing Jim and Mary. The years melted away as she became reacquainted with old neighbors and friends.

By the time they reached the Spears' homestead, they had gathered a following behind them. They pulled their horses to the fence line and stopped. Hounds they had both known since childhood rushed from the front porch as well as several new generations of dogs that moved out ahead of the old-timers.

They had begun to dismount when the front door opened and Old Man Spears stepped into the doorway. At first he appeared puzzled but then a wave of recognition washed over his face. He shouted something over his shoulder in his thick German accent as he rushed across the porch and down the steps.

Mary opened the gate as the dogs swarmed around her. Old Man Spears was halfway across the front yard, his arms wide, his eyes locked on hers. But as she started toward him, she stopped short. Behind him, leaping off the front porch and clearing the steps, was George.

He passed his father in a race to reach her, his strong arms enveloping her thin frame, one beefy hand grabbing the back of her head and pressing her to him. He held her so tightly she thought she would faint from the lack of air, and reluctantly she pulled back. His face was streaked with tears, his gray-green eyes staring at her in a mixture of disbelief and unbridled love.

Somewhere her brain registered there were people around them, people crowding in to welcome them home, people urging them into the house for rest and food, but she didn't want this moment in George's arms to end.

When they finally pulled apart, her small hand found his larger one.

She turned back to Jim, but he was no longer watching them. His eyes were fixed on the Spears' front door. As she followed his gaze, she caught sight of Susannah's golden hair as it caught the sun's rays, the curls bouncing as she rushed toward the gathering crowd. As she approached, the crowd hushed. "I've been waiting for you, Jim," she said.

Mary caught sight of Jim's face as he grabbed Susannah and pulled her to him, his expression a mixture of relief and happiness, his shoulders beginning to shake as he buried his face in her hair.

Then they were moving as one from the lawn to the house, walking up the steps Mary had left so long ago. By the time she crossed the porch and strolled through the doorway, it was as if only a single day had passed since she'd last been there.

They had both come home.

Epilogue

I t was springtime. The daffodils had long since bloomed and only their tall green leaves remained. The dogwoods were turning from white and pink to a pale, soft green. And as Mary walked along the dirt road with George Spears' two sisters, she could smell the earth from the recent spring rains.

Church had been especially pleasant this morning. Through the winter, she'd lived in the Spears household, helping to clean, cook, and sew. She practiced the medicine the Indians had taught her and was called upon to help with birthing babies and tending to the sick.

Jim had long ago returned to the west with militia reinforcements but this time, he had taken Susannah with him. They'd seen them off after a wedding ceremony at the local Presbyterian Church. Before they departed, Mary had given a letter to Susannah in the event they could find her family. Mary wasn't quite sure what to say except that she was well and wanted to come home.

George had not gone with Jim but had followed some time later. Mary would never again think of winter as a cold, inhospitable time; she would forevermore remember it as the season in which she fell in love with George all over again.

Now she walked home from church, her nose in the air taking in the scents of springtime. They rounded the curve and came into view of the Spears' home. Old Man Spears sat on the front porch in the straight-back chair he loved so much. Though she wasn't near enough to see it, she knew the area around his feet would be covered in curls of wood from his whittling.

As they approached, a man rose from a chair beside Old Man Spears. Slowly, he drew near the rail and appeared to be watching them.

Mary recognized the way his head cocked to one side. She knew his posture, his bearing as he left the railing and almost cleared the steps from the porch. By the time his feet hit the ground, she was running, her arms outstretched, tears streaming down her cheeks.

Before she reached him, she could see the tears running down his face.

"Sam!" she cried. "Sam!"

In the time that elapsed since Mary was taken, Ma and her ten-year-old brother John had been killed in a separate Indian ambush. Between the Indian raids and the British, Neely's Bend had become increasingly unsafe.

Mary returned with Sam to Carpenter's Station in Lincoln County, Kentucky, where she was reunited with George. At the end of the war, most of her family returned to the area around Fort Nashborough. Sam became known for his success in fighting the Indians; he also killed the Indian who had killed his mother. He settled down at the age of thirty-one, marrying Mary "Polly" Watkins. He died in 1845 at Neely's Bend and is buried near his homestead. His log home, which he built himself, was dismantled and moved to Clarksville, Tennessee around 1968. As of this writing, the home is located at Hachland.

Mary remained in Kentucky with George. They married on February 24, 1785 in Lincoln County. They raised a family and lived in Greene County until 1824 when they moved to Sangamon County, Illinois. Throughout her life, she continued to encounter Cherokee and Shawnee Indians, who were sometimes friendly and sometimes not.

She learned enough medicine from the Indians to establish a reputation as a healer and legend has it that people came from miles around to be tended by her—some journeying from as far away as Missouri, Iowa, and throughout Illinois.

George and Mary remained husband and wife until George's death on April 16, 1836 at the age of 72.

Mary returned to Neely's Bend in 1843 at the age of 82 to visit her brother Sam. She remained in his home for a month before returning to Illinois; it was the last time they would ever see each other. She died in Illinois on January 26, 1852 at the age of 90.

Fort Nashborough gave birth to Nashville, Tennessee and Neely's Bend is now a populated suburb. Neely's Salt Lick became known as Larkin's Sulfur Spring. The six hundred and forty acres William Neely had chosen for his homestead remained in his family for generations. And to this day on Gallatin Pike is an historical marker that tells the tale of the first settler killed at Fort Nashborough by the Indians and of the capture of his brave young daughter, Mary Neely.

A Note from the Author

Two hundred and twenty-five years after Mary Neely was captured by Shawnees, my father, John William Neelley, Sr., was continuing the family tradition of researching and recording the family's history and genealogy when he came across her story. Finding where she fit into our family tree was a daunting task, as generations continued using the same names— William, John and Mary among them. The spelling of the last name often changed, partly due to the way the census takers wrote it, sometimes due to family members changing it, or due to the misinterpretation of handwritten information. We have come to the conclusion if Mary were alive today, she would be my cousin.

The first details of her capture and captivity were sketchy at best, and we truly didn't know if we had enough to fill a book. However, as we continued our painstaking research, we discovered a treasure trove of information. Still, there were periods in which we knew very little—such as the summer in which she was a prisoner of war at an island in Lake Huron. Once she escaped, accounts varied as to her exact route, as she didn't always know exactly where she was. Piecing together a logical route involved meticulous research based on where we knew her to be at different times in her captivity and flight to freedom. There will no doubt be those who claim different facts than those stated in this book, but with regard to Mary's journey and experiences, this book is as true to fact, except where noted here, as we were able to reconstruct.

The first written accounts of Mary's capture were recorded by her grandchildren and passed down through the generations. In all of these records, her captors were referred to only as "Indians" and not a specific tribe. My father and I researched the Cherokees, Shawnees, Chickasaws, Chickamaugans, and other tribes in the vicinity. Because of her captors' actions, migration, and destinations coupled with the role of the Shawnee Indians during the Revolutionary War, we determined her captors had to be from a Shawnee Indian tribe. During the same period in which Mary was captured, literally thousands of others were captured or killed by the Shawnees as well.

Through old records, we know there were nine braves and five squaws in Mary's Indian "family" but we have not located any documentation that lists names. I decided to give each of the Indians a name to avoid confusing the reader with "person #1", "person #2", and so on. It is impossible to know what was actually said, since the people privy to those conversations have long ago departed, so the dialogue is fictional but I attempted to stay as close to historical facts as possible. In all of the conversations, I tried to remain faithful to Mary's courageous spirit.

If you were to follow Mary's trail in the present-day landscape, you would begin just south of Nashville, Tennessee, along the Cumberland River and Neely's Bend, which is now a bedroom community of Nashville. Two miles west of Neely's Salt Lick (now known as Larkin's Sulfur Spring), a sign has been erected on Gallatin Pike commemorating the location of that fateful day.

Mary's canoe trip would have taken her northward on the Cumberland past the original site of Fort Nashborough and present-day Clarksville, Tennessee, before heading northwest into Kentucky.

At the time Mary was captured, the area now known as Nashville, Tennessee was considered to be North Carolina Territory. In what is now Kentucky, the area was considered to be Virginia Territory.

The bison, elk, and bald eagles mentioned in Chapter 6 are in present-day Land Between the Lakes, an area between the

Tennessee and Cumberland Rivers. It is now under the management of the USDA Forest Service. It consists of 170,000 acres and 300 miles of undeveloped shoreline. Since Mary's time, dams have been built which created two lakes, from which this land now gets its name.

Traveling northward, Mary would then have reached the Ohio River, known as the Spaylawitheepi by the Shawnees. The location at which they changed to larger boats for the trip on the wider Ohio River was once known as Savannah Old Settlement. It was briefly occupied by the Shawnees around 1720 before being abandoned after numerous battles with the Cherokees. It fell into disrepair and was used by various Indian tribes in the latter part of the 18th century only as a stopover.

As the Shawnees approached Savannah Old Settlement and other places along their route, the howl Mary described was one in which the Indians would add a syllable for each captive they had in their possession, a way of announcing the number of captives before they were visible.

Mary could not have known the events unfurling around her as a result of the Revolutionary War. I added Lieutenant James J. Hawkins to provide the reader with a more complete picture of these events and how Mary's capture fit like a piece of a puzzle into a much broader picture. The information concerning George Rogers Clark and the battles he and his men participated in, including Chillicothe and Piqua, are historically accurate, as well as the reference to John Morrison loading thirteen times during the heat of battle. However, Jim Hawkins is a fictionalized character, a composite of many men who served with Colonel Clark.

Also true is the Indian raid on Fort Jefferson, John Donne's letter to Colonel Clark begging for supplies and reinforcements, the fall and abandonment of the fort and the movements of Augustin de La Balme as he sought to march on Fort Detroit. Today, there are no physical remains of Fort Jefferson; it is rumored that a factory is built on the original site but sadly, there remains no evidence the fort ever existed.

The information concerning Daniel Boone, his brother Ned, and their families is also historically accurate, including Daniel's capture by Shawnee Indian Chief Blackfish, his involvement in the battles at Chillicothe and Piqua, Ned's murder, and Daniel's capture by the British as he traveled to Virginia to take his seat in the legislature. The water beside Ned's original burial site was named Boone Creek (in Bourbon County, Kentucky) and today a buckeye tree grows in the very spot where Ned was cracking nuts when he was attacked. As the decades passed, the burial site became eroded by the encroaching water and he was reburied about a mile from the original site.

The information concerning Jemima Boone has been handed down through Daniel's and Ned's descendants. Jemima's and her friends' capture by Indians was the inspiration for James Fenimore Cooper's book, *The Last of the Mohicans*, originally published around 1826.

The information regarding George Rogers Clark's cousin, Joseph Rogers, is historically accurate, though we do not know his words as he lay dying.

Simon Girty was a white man loathed by settlers: by most accounts, he was ruthless, cunning, a murderer and thief—and a friend and ally to the British and the Indians. He had been captured by the Seneca Indians when just a boy and was reunited with his family seven years later, but he had been so indoctrinated in their culture that he preferred it to the company of white men. It is rumored that he taught the Indians many of the methods they used to capture additional settlers, including the method described in Chapter 20. Although many in the Continental Army wanted to capture and hang him, he was never caught. After the Revolutionary War, he moved to Amherstburg, Ontario in Canada, where many Loyalists migrated. He died there in 1818 at the age of 77, completely blind and crippled with arthritis. There is no evidence to support that Mary had ever actually met him.

Mary traveled by a larger canoe up the Ohio River to Shawneetown in present-day Illinois. During her captivity, this Indian village had approximately 2,200 inhabitants. In contrast, the 2000 census showed a population of less than 100 households and 278 people; 99.64% were white and 0.36% were Native

American. It is now known as "Old Shawneetown"; three miles inland is a slightly larger town also called Shawneetown.

Mary's Shawnee "family" took the Ohio River to the Wabash River (known as the Wabashike River to the Shawnees). This took them further northward into Indian Territory and toward Fort Detroit. They left the Wabash near present-day Harrisonburg, Indiana and traveled overland through the Great Black Swamp in northeast Indiana and northwest Ohio, a wetland that existed until the late 19th century. The area was known for its endemic malaria, which is the disease that afflicted Eagle Feathers. Today, the wetlands are gone, replaced by developments.

Some accounts have Mary living in Illinois or Indiana during the first winter. I have shortened Mary's captivity in this book because so little was known about the months in between the time she resurfaced elsewhere. She eventually came to the Maumee River, on which they traveled northward to Lake Erie and Fort Detroit.

It is well documented the British under Henry Hamilton's orders encouraged the Indians to capture and kill the settlers, their women and children. The British at Fort Detroit routinely paid the Indians for their captives and scalps. Hamilton was captured by George Rogers Clark's men at Vincennes in February 1779 and sent to Virginia, where he remained in a Williamsburg prison until he was part of a prisoner exchange in March 1781. However, the policy he began of paying for scalps and captives continued well into the 1790's. He later became the Deputy Governor of Quebec before becoming the Governor of Bermuda and then the Governor of Dominica. He died in 1796 on the island of Antigua.

Ironically, it was that same year—July 11, 1796—when the British surrendered Fort Detroit to the Americans, a full thirteen years after the signing of the Treaty of Paris.

Once the Shawnees with Mary were paid for the scalps and their sole captive, they migrated into northern Michigan.

Sadly, it is well documented that both the French and the English had provided the Indians with blankets from the beds of small pox victims. It was small pox that swept through Mary's Shawnee "family", including Mary herself. And at one time, as detailed in this book, only the eldest squaw was not afflicted and cared for the others by herself. She also cared for Mary, going as far as dressing her wounds so her skin would not be scarred.

It was in the vicinity of a village on Saginaw Bay where Mary was helped by a French couple in escaping the Shawnees. We were unable to find the name of this couple in all of the records we searched. The fishermen who were to assist in her escape brought her instead to an island in Lake Huron, where the British kept prisoners of war that included women. It is doubtful Mary ever knew the name of the island or the fort in which she was held; in our research of islands in Lake Huron, only Fort Michilimackinac was mentioned as possibly having a prisoner of war camp.

After spending a summer in the camp, she was loaded onto a ship that was to take her to another British stronghold to the east. A strong gale almost wrecked the ship. When she reached dry land, she managed to escape, setting off on foot. The soldier who allowed her to escape has never been named, so we don't know if Mary herself ever knew his identity.

In Chapter 58, Private Alfred Berwyn described their location as the "Province of Quebec"; The Quebec Act of 1774 included what is now known as Ontario in the Province of Quebec. It wasn't until 1867 that the Dominion of Canada was formed and Quebec divided into the French-speaking Quebec and English-speaking Ontario that we know today.

George Rogers Clark operated in the west under the direction of the Virginia Legislature, who agreed to reimburse him for all the expenses necessary in fighting the Indians and British and erecting forts and settlements. However, the government never made good on their promises. Though he was granted more than 8,000 acres eight miles from present-day Louisville, Kentucky, most of that property was seized by creditors because he had personally guaranteed payment for his militia's debts. Clark died almost penniless only five days before Simon Girty died, on February 13, 1818 at the age of 66.

Mary Neely acquired so much medical knowledge from the Shawnees that when she returned to Kentucky, she began studying medicine in earnest. Though she never became a medical doctor, she practiced homeopathic medicine for more than fifty years, and it is said the sick traveled hundreds of miles to see her.

William Neely's family was given 640 acres of land in the Nashville area by the State of North Carolina. Many of his descendents and his sibling's descendents continue to live in the Nashville area, including my sister Nancy, who lives in Nashville, and my brother John, who lives in nearby Columbia. Readers familiar with two of my earlier books, *Kickback* and *Ricochet*, might recall the description of Sheila Carpenter's homestead; that house and land is based on Neely Valley, Sunnyside, and Neely's Bend. As of this writing, my aunt, Florene Neelley Lambert, lives at Sunnyside and my aunt and uncle, Ewing and Juanita Neelley, live in Columbia.

For more information on Mary Neely, visit www.maryneely.com or www.pmterrell.com.

About the Author

p.m.terrell is the pen name for Patricia McClelland Terrell, shown above with her father, John William Neelley, Sr. at Fort Nashborough. She is the internationally acclaimed author of the suspense/thrillers *Ricochet*, *The China Conspiracy*, and *Kickback*, all published by Drake Valley Press. She is also the author of *Take the Mystery out of Promoting Your Book* (published by Palari Publishing) and several nonfiction computer books, including *Creating the Perfect Database* (Scott-Foresman), *The Dynamics of WordPerfect* and *The Dynamics of Reflex* (Dow Jones-Irwin), and *Mememto WordPerfect* (Edimicro, Paris.)

Ms. Terrell is the co-founder, along with Officer Mark Kearney of the Waynesboro, Virginia Police Department, of the Book 'Em Foundation, a partnership between authors and law enforcement agencies dedicated to raising public awareness of the correlation that exists between high crime rates and high illiteracy rates, increasing literacy, and reducing crime. Their web site is www.bookemfoundation.org.

Ms. Terrell is also proud to serve on the Robeson County Friends of the Library Board of Directors (www.robesoncountylibrary.com) and on the Board of the Robeson County Arts Council (www.robesonarts.org). Both organizations are committed to supporting the arts, science, history and heritage of Robeson County, North Carolina.

Ms. Terrell is the founder of McClelland Enterprises, Inc., one of the first companies in the Washington, DC area devoted to PC training in the workforce, and Continental Software Development Corporation, which provides applications development, website design, and computer consulting services throughout the United States and its territories. Her clients have included the U.S. Secret Service, CIA and Department of Defense, as well as various local law enforcement agencies.

She is also a staunch supporter of Crime Stoppers, Crime Solvers, and Crime Lines, which offer rewards and anonymity to individuals reporting information on criminal activity. She is proud to have served as the first female President of the Chesterfield County/ Colonial Heights (Virginia) Crime Solvers Board of Directors (2003-2004) and as the Treasurer for the Virginia Crime Stoppers Association.

Visit her website at www.pmterrell.com for more information.